2019

A Colonial Woman's Bookshelf

A Colonial
Woman's Bookshelf

Kevin J. Hayes

The University of Tennessee Press
Knoxville

Library of Congress Cataloging-in-Publication Data

Hayes, Kevin J.
    A colonial woman's bookshelf / Kevin J. Hayes. — 1st ed.
        p. cm.
    Includes bibliographical references and index.
    ISBN 0-87049-937-8 (cloth: alk. paper)
  1. Women—United States—Books and reading—History—
17th century. 2. Women—United States—Books and reading—
History—18th century. I. Title.
    Z1039.W65H38 1996
        028'.9'082—dc20   95-41824
                                                          CIP

For my sister

Contents

Preface

The intellectual life of early American women continues to be neglected. Despite significant advances in women's history, literary history, and the history of the book, the bookish interests of women in colonial America have received little attention. Recent efforts in early American women's history generally have taken one of two directions. Sharply focused studies based on archival research and concentrated on limited geographical regions have provided intimate glimpses of the colonial woman's workaday life and have reconstructed early American social and family relationships. The work of Nancy Cott for Massachusetts, Laurel Thatcher Ulrich for northern New England, Alan Watson for North Carolina, and Lois Green Carr and Lorena S. Walsh for the Chesapeake region deserve special mention. Other studies, such as Carolyn Johnston's *Sexual Power: Feminism and the Family in America,* Maxine Margolis's *Mothers and Such: Views of American Women and Why They Changed,* Mary Beth Norton's *Liberty's Daughters,* and Nancy Woloch's *Women and the American Experience*, more sweeping in scope, have surveyed the history of the American woman, starting with colonial times and extending into the nineteenth or twentieth centuries, to examine her changing position in American society.

Neither focus has given the colonial woman's intellectual life the attention it deserves. Though most of these studies mention the idea, now widely accepted, that many more early American women could read than previously has been supposed, none specifically has asked what books women read in colonial America. Nor has any asked: In what contexts and for what reasons did early American women read? Such questions lie at the core of the present study.

Some literary historians have meticulously scrutinized the canonical writers—Anne Bradstreet, Sarah Kemble Knight, Mary Rowlandson, Phillis Wheatley—and provided increasingly sophisticated interpretations of their works. Other scholars—notably Pattie Cowell, Susan M. Harris, Carla Mulford, and Susan Stabile—have helped to broaden the canon of early American women's writing by recovering the works of lesser known writers. None has devoted significant attention to the books women owned and read. While my study makes use of these early American women's writings, I am much more interested in looking at what women read than in looking at how what they read affected what they wrote. I am interested in those women who read avidly but left no documents behind to record their existence, those women whose only written legacy may be an autograph in a surviving book, or even those women who read but could not write.

Exciting work has been taking place among the intellectual historians and historians of the book, but these scholars, too, have failed to give women the attention they deserve. Neither Richard Beale Davis's *Intellectual Life in the Colonial South, 1585–1763,* nor his subsequent *A Colonial Southern Bookshelf* has much to say about intellectual life or reading among colonial southern women. To be sure, I have great respect for Davis's work; it is not coincidence that the title of the present study echoes Davis's title (or that both his title and mine echo Lawrence Wroth's classic *An American Bookshelf, 1755*). More recently, excellent studies by David D. Hall and Richard Brown have devoted some attention to women's reading in early America, but, as Pattie Cowell has observed in "Knowledge and Power: Cultural Scripts in Early America," both marginalize colonial women by treating them as just another occupational group. One work which has integrated women's reading tastes within the overall historical context is Edwin Wolf II's *The Book Culture of a Colonial American City.* I am indebted to Wolf's numerous treatments of reading in early America, especially his invaluable but little known *Annual Reports of the Library Company of Philadelphia,* as well as to the *Annual Reports* of Wolf's successor at the Library Company, John Van Horne.

Important studies have been made of early American women's reading—most notably Cathy Davidson's *Revolution and the Word* and the eighth chapter of Linda Kerber's *Women of the Republic*—but these works treat the period after American independence. The present work focuses specifically on the colonial period, a time which differed from the federal period, not only politically, but also socially and intellectually. As recent studies in women's history have noted, women's roles and American attitudes toward women changed significantly during and after the Revolutionary War.

My title, *A Colonial Woman's Bookshelf,* implies continuity throughout the colonial period, as if colonial women formed, to use Stanley Fish's term, a unique "interpretive community." This implication deserves to be explained. In her authoritative essay, "The Evolution of White Women's Experiences in Early America," Mary Beth Norton defines three chronological divisions within the early American woman's experience: (1) the initial period of settlement, from the early seventeenth century to about 1660, during which important patterns of family and community were established; (2) a transitional period extending to the mid-eighteenth century; and (3) the period of the American Revolution, extending two decades before and after the Revolution itself. Nancy Cott, in *Bonds of Womanhood,* focuses on the 1780–1835 period, a time of wide-ranging transformation, she argues, in which the "cult of domesticity" emerged.

In terms of early American women's intellectual history, I distinguish three periods which correspond roughly to the subdivisions outlined by Norton. The first encompasses the years from 1608 (when the first English woman arrived at Jamestown) to approximately 1680. The second period, 1680 to about 1760, saw a significant increase in women's literacy. Here I follow J. Paul Hunter, who convincingly argues that literacy among English women greatly increased during this time; there is no reason to believe that American women lagged behind their English counterparts. The third period is 1760–80; during this time, learning opportunities for women began to be challenged by the emerging notion of a separate domestic sphere.

My title implies continuity among the different geographical regions in America. After all, most women from Maine to Georgia shared a common European cultural heritage. When women from different cultural backgrounds—Native American or African—were taught to read, they were acculturated within the dominant (i.e., British) culture. Women in the thirteen colonies read the same conduct books, the same cookery books, and the same novels. The most significant intellectual differences among the European populations of various geographical areas concern religion. The most widely-read religious texts, however, were also similar—in format, if not in denominational slant. In the seventeenth century, as N. H. Keeble has noticed, nonconformist publications were read widely among Anglicans. In the eighteenth century, as Norman Fiering has noticed, an American trend toward a unified Protestantism allowed enlightened Anglican writers to be read widely throughout Puritan New England.

Part of the reason why the colonial woman's intellectual life has been neglected is that the surviving evidence frequently is elusive. Here, I make use of wills and estate inventories, surviving volumes inscribed by women, public and private library catalogs, sales ledgers, surviving subscription library borrowing records, literary references, and contemporary biographical sketches of notable colonial women. Many of the sources of evidence, as I explain in the introductory chapter, are problematical. To compensate partially for the sometimes sketchy evidence, recent advances in bibliography—most notably the completion of the *National Union Catalog* and the ongoing conversion of much bibliographical data to electronic formats have made it easier to identify the frustratingly brief book titles mentioned in letters or listed in estate inventories. It is important to note that many books listed in surviving documents are identified here for the first time. Where I discuss inscribed surviving volumes, I give the place and date of publication in parentheses within the text. Elsewhere, places and dates of publication are given parenthetically only when they seem necessary for clarification. In those instances where a date of publication is given without a place, London can be assumed.

My introductory chapter outlines the nature of the evidence upon which this work is based and discusses the methodological problems involved with such evidence. It also deals with the availability of books and the opportunities women had for reading. The remainder of the work is organized according to the different types of books owned and read by women in colonial America. Chapter 2 discusses the various religious tracts available to colonial women and the ways they used books to enhance their piety. The chapter also discusses the earliest books women read as children, which usually but not always were devotional in nature. Chapter 3 treats conduct books—those works which attempted to prescribe or, perhaps more accurately, to circumscribe a woman's behavior. Furthermore, the chapter touches upon the periodicals women read which were also largely prescriptive. Chapter 4 concerns cookery books, medical works, and midwifery books. In Chapter 5, I discuss novels and travel narratives. Chapter 6 looks at science books and their relation to domesticity during the late colonial period.

Rather than using more traditional literary categories, I have made my subdivisions according to how the colonial woman read the books. For example, originally I had planned a *belles lettres* chapter to deal with poetry and novels, but it simply would not hold together. I found little connection between novel reading and poetry reading. An overwhelming percentage of the poetry read by women in early America was devotional or at least contemplative. Thus I broke up my *belles lettres* chapter, placing poetry with devotional books. Of course, not all poetry women read was devotional, but I have sought to identify general reading patterns among colonial women as a group. Later I realized that the novels fit well with travel books, because both were forms of narrative discourse. For those colonial readers who remained reluctant to read novels, travel books provided alternative stories of adventure. Fictional narratives and factual narratives, in other words, similarly allowed readers to escape into another world.

Admittedly, my choice of subject categories is, in part, arbitrary. Of course the categories overlap. The devotional works told the woman how to conduct her life based on Christian principles, and the conduct books recommended piety as the most important feminine virtue. Some cookery books contained advice reminiscent of the conduct books, while others deserve to be treated as scientific works.

Chapters 2, 3, 5, and 6 (and the individual subsections of chapter 4) are each organized in a roughly chronological fashion. In other words, I generally begin discussing a particular genre with the books women read in the earliest part of the colonial period (though evidence of specific books is especially scant for the seventeenth century) and progress to those books read during the late years of the colonies. The organization of the book as a whole also follows a chronological pattern. For example, the novels, travel literature, and science books discussed in the last two chapters of this book were read during the last part of the colonial period. While women had opportunities to read a greater variety of material at the end of the colonial period, by no means did they stop reading devotional literature and conduct books.

The nature of the surviving evidence has given this book an unevenness which cannot be remedied. The extended discussions of how one colonial woman (Elizabeth Ashbridge) read religious books, presented in chapter 2, and of Samuel Richardson's *Pamela,* contained in chapter 5, may seem disproportionate to the treatments of other individual readers and works elsewhere in the book. I treat these two subject in such detail for one simple reason: because I can. I discuss Ashbridge's reading at length because no other colonial woman left as detailed an account of her reading process. I discuss *Pamela* in detail because no other novel elicited such lengthy comments from colonial women.

A portion of chapter 2, entitled "Reading and Identity: The Example of Elizabeth Ashbridge," was presented at the 1994 Conference on American Autobiography at Cabo San Lucas, Mexico. A portion of chapter 5, entitled "Reading *Pamela* in Early America," was presented at the American Literature Association's 1994 meeting in San Diego. The rest of this work appears before the public for the first time.

The reader may notice an extraordinary number of names in this book. I hope the names do not overwhelm. I have attempted to identify many hitherto unknown women who played vital roles in early American intellectual life. I have not been able, nor have I even tried, to identify every woman whose name appears in this book. In a way, I have designed my work as a reference guide, a starting point for further research. Other scholars may recognize names I mention but have not identified and be able to advance the study of early American intellectual life.

I must acknowledge thanks to those who helped along the way. First I would like to thank Meredith Morris-Babb and Kimberly Scarbrough at the University of Tennessee Press for their careful attention. Pattie Cowell read my manuscript for the press and had many good ideas for enhancing my work. Catherine Carr Lee, J. A. Leo Lemay, David Shields, and Regenia Woodberry each read the manuscript and provided helpful suggestions. Wayne Craven taught me the importance of early American women's portraiture. The conference on the history of the book in early America, held at the American Antiquarian Society in September 1992, gave me an excellent opportunity to work out many of my ideas. Among the conference participants, I especially would like to thank Hugh Amory, Jerome E. Anderson, Susan Berg, Alan Degutis, James Green, David D. Hall, Elizabeth Reilly, David Shields, and Thomas Siegel for their input. Finally, I would like to thank the various libraries which have provided important resources. The Library Company of Philadelphia, with its pleasant ambiance and helpful staff, was immensely useful. I am also grateful to the American Antiquarian Society. Its new on-line cata-

Preface

log made it possible easily to locate information on those books in its collection which formerly were owned by colonial women. The excellent collection of early American books at the Clements Library, University of Michigan, Ann Arbor, provided much additional information on provenance. I also thank the always helpful reference staff of the Max Chambers Library at the University of Central Oklahoma. Finally, I would like to thank Richard and Carole Hayes for their encouragement and support from the beginning.

Kevin J. Hayes
Oklahoma City

CHAPTER 1

Reading Women

When Philip Vickers Fithian came to Nomony Hall in Virginia as tutor for Robert and Frances Carter's children, he found their daughters especially eager to learn. Priscilla, the oldest daughter, had recently turned fifteen, and the new teacher soon had her reading the *Spectator*. The inventory Fithian made of her father's library—which included several works specifically for young women—suggests that Priscilla read a wide variety of secular and religious books. One day, the family had a dinner conversation about women's souls. When Frances Carter jokingly suggested that women hadn't any souls, Priscilla quickly replied, "If I thought so I would not have spent all this morning in Reading."[1] Embedded within Priscilla Carter's comment are the contradictory attitudes toward women and books which had been circulating throughout colonial America for the preceding century and a half.

By the middle of the eighteenth century, the idea that women were without souls had become a facetious commonplace. In the *History of the Tuesday Club,* Dr. Alexander Hamilton joked that the club president conversed with women "as rational Creatures, which showed, that he was too much of a Christian to believe with some Philosophers, that women had no Souls."[2] As Dr. Hamilton's remark implies, suggesting that women were without souls was downright un-Christian. Anyone caught admitting that women did have souls, however, was putting men and women on an equal basis—at least as far as spiritual matters were concerned—and was coming dangerously close to acknowledging equality when it came to earthly matters. If men's and women's souls were equal, then, arguably, both men and women deserved equal chances to improve them. Women should have just as much opportunity to edify their souls as men. Besides prayer, the most important pathway to heaven, as Priscilla Carter's remark implied, was reading. To suggest that a woman should not read was tantamount to suggesting that she had no soul.

In the preface to his widely read conduct book, *The Ladies Calling* (1673), Richard Allestree wrote that women's souls were "as divine an Original, as endless a Duration, and as capable of infinit Beatitude" as men's souls: "That spiritual Essence, that ray of Divinity owns no distinction of Sexes." While Allestree granted the equality of souls, his comments concerning women's education remained ambivalent. He suggested that women, like men, could "have their parts cultivated and improved by Education, refined and subtilized by Learning and Arts"; yet he wrote: "But not to oppose a received opinion, let it be admitted, that in respect of their intellects they are below men."[3] Instead of boldly asserting women's intellectual equality, he evasively relied on "received opinion." The remainder of the book, however, reveals Allestree's stance. Reading is not listed among the duties of a woman.

Mary Astell recognized the hypocrisy of conceding the equality of souls while denying women opportunities for study. In *A Serious Proposal to the Ladies for the Advancement of Their True and Greatest Interest* (1694–97), a book which could be found in the Virginia libraries of the Byrd and Custis families but was much more likely to appear on the colonial woman's bookshelf as excerpted in *The Ladies' Library,* Astell argued:

> For since GOD has given Women as well as Men intelligent Souls, why should they be forbidden to improve them? Since he has not denied us the faculty of Thinking, why shou'd we not . . . employ our Thoughts on himself their noblest Object, and not unworthily bestow them on Trifles and Gaities and secular Affairs? Being the Soul was created for the contemplation of Truth as well as for the fruition of Good, is it not as cruel and unjust to exclude Women from the knowledge of the one as from the enjoyment of the other?[4]

With the phrase "intelligent Souls," Astell combined the two faculties Allestree tried to keep separate. If reading edifies the soul, Astell's argument goes, the two cannot be detached.

The inextricable link between reading and salvation made it virtually impossible for any colonial American to suggest seriously that women should not read; on the other hand, the equality of souls hardly created educational equality. Women, it was generally believed, did not need to read as much or as widely as men. Every good schoolboy's education included Latin, Greek, and sometimes Hebrew, but the girls could get by with English. Fithian's duties as tutor, for example, required him to teach Carter's daughters English while teaching the boys English, Latin, and Greek.[5] Still, evidence exists to suggest that some women—usually daughters of clergymen—learned Latin and other ancient languages.[6] For example, the American Antiquarian Society's copy of Nathan Bailey's *English and Latine Exercises for School-Boys* (Boston, 1720) was owned by Elizabeth Ballard in 1726 and also by Mary Prince. Hannah Mather's copy of Erasmus's *Epitome Adagiorum* (1593) suggests that, like most of the family's women, she could read Latin. Some of Jonathan Edwards's sisters were taught Greek, and all learned Latin.[7]

Eliza Haywood's *Female Spectator* took the equality of souls argument one step further. Women should be allowed to read not only devotional works, but every other subject men were privileged to read. Haywood wrote: "There is, undoubtedly, no sex in souls, and we are as able to receive and practise the impressions, not only of virtue and religion, but also of those sciences which the men engross to themselves, as they can be. Surely our bodies were not formed by the great Creator out of the finest Mould that our souls might be neglected like the coarsest of the clay!"[8] In other words, any woman who did not read was neglecting her God-given capacity for learning.

Recent studies of women's reading tastes in early America have focused on the last quarter of the eighteenth and the first quarter of the nineteenth century—the historical period when American women emerged as writers of novels.[9] While the proliferation of women novelists during the early federal period is a sure sign of the lively interest women had in books, American women were reading long before they were writing and publishing novels. Within the marketplace, in other words, American women emerged as consumers well before they emerged as significant literary producers. Of course, this does not mean that women were not actively writing throughout the colonial period. Rather, their chosen literary genres, by and large, were more appropriate for circulation in manuscript among small groups of friends and neighbors. Cotton Mather suggests the kinds of reading and writing which took place among seventeenth-century New England women in *Awakening Thoughts on the Sleep of Death* (Boston, 1712), one copy of which survives with the inscription, "Mary Williams her book." Mather wrote that these early New England women "replenish'd and accomplish'd their Minds with Reading the Word of God, and Books of the best Composition. Yea, they have *wrote* such Things as have been very Valuable; Especially relating to their own Experiences. Many Volumes of the Works which have been wrought and wrote, by those *Dorcas's,* are to be seen in the Private Hands of their Surviving Posterity."[10] Manuscript works as lofty as spiritual diaries and autobiographies to those as earthy as cookery books were written by colonial women, circulated among their friends, and passed down to their daughters throughout the colonial period. Even after women began actively publishing, a lively manuscript culture persisted.[11]

Many more colonial American women could read than is generally known. The long-standing test to determine literacy has been to select a geographical jurisdiction, count the number of wills signed and the number of wills marked with an "X," add the two figures, and divide the number of wills signed by the total. Results concerning colonial women's literacy so derived have varied widely, from around 30 percent during the mid-seventeenth century to between 46 and 90 percent by the last decade of the eighteenth. As Jennifer Monaghan and others have demonstrated, reading in colonial America almost always was taught before writing. Consequently, literacy percentages based on writing ability inaccurately reflect reading ability.[12] Monaghan's findings hint that many more colonial women could read than the literacy figures reveal, but they effectively discredit the only available, broad-based, quantitative way to measure literacy. Such percentages remain useful, but only as starting points. If 30 percent of women signed wills in 1650, then it can be inferred that more than 30 percent could read. How many more remains impossible to pinpoint. For colonial New England, David D. Hall estimates that literacy, defined as the skill of reading English, "was almost universal. . . . Women were especially lacking in the skill of writing, though it is likely they were readers as much as the men they lived and worked with."[13] The diverse and largely qualitative evidence which forms the basis of the present study supports the notion that literacy percentages based on writing ability inaccurately reflect—indeed, greatly underestimate—the extent of colonial women's reading.

As a side note, it is important to mention that books also could function in ways which had nothing to do with literacy. They could be used in ceremonies and as totems. When William Byrd returned to Virginia in

1720, for example, he let it be known that he was looking for a new Mrs. Byrd to replace his wife Lucy, who had died of smallpox a few years before. One evening, Hannah Ludwell and another young woman suggested a way to improve Byrd's marriage prospects. As he described the incident in his diary, they "put a drawn sword and common prayer book open at the matrimony on my head and made me dream of my mistress Annie Carter." The religious significance of the *Book of Common Prayer,* Byrd's anecdote shows, could be experienced in ways other than reading its text.[14]

Wills and estate inventories provide much information concerning what books women may have owned and read, but many are frustratingly brief. Inventories of women's estates further obscure the evidence. When husbands predeceased their wives, women inherited property when there was no male issue.[15] Some women undoubtedly inherited some books they could not read. Elizabeth Tatham of Burlington, New Jersey, for example, owned 552 books at the time of her death in 1700. Mrs. Tatham's library quite possibly was the largest then extant in New Jersey, but it seems unlikely that she had much to do with assembling the collection. Her husband John had died just three months before her, and his will named her sole heir.[16]

One published list of inventories from several colonial Virginia counties further suggests the problems involved. Among the hundreds of inventories provided, only fourteen are women's. Two of these simply list a "parcel of books"; five list a "parcel of old books." At her death in 1717, Katherine Benam of Westmoreland County owned "a large old Bible" and "a parcel of old books." In 1720, Elizabeth Banks of Northumberland County owned twenty-eight books. Mary Swan of Lancaster County owned thirty-two "old books." In 1726, Barbara Tayloe owned three Bibles and a parcel of old books. Mailana Drayton of Middlesex County died in 1760 leaving eleven volumes of French books, "a parcel of novels," six "picture books," and a "parcel of Latin books." In 1770, Rachel Blair of Amherst County owned "1 Bible & Prayer Book." In 1774, Elizabeth Cox, also of Amherst County, owned "1 Bible."[17] Could Rachel Blair, Elizabeth Cox, Katherine Benam, and Barbara Tayloe read their Bibles? Almost certainly. What were the titles of the thirty-two books Mary Swan owned? Of the twenty-eight books Elizabeth Banks owned? There is no way to know. Could Mailana

Drayton read the novels listed in the inventory? Almost surely. The French books? Quite likely. The Latin? Perhaps, but there is simply no way to know.

The most revealing wills and estate inventories are those listing book titles and stipulating who would inherit which volumes. At his death in 1669, Virginia Col. John Carter specifically left his wife three devotional books; in addition, Carter's will mentions that she had "her own books." It is a poignant comment on the legal status of early American women to read that Carter specifically had to will his wife "her own books." During the last third of the seventeenth century, Virginian John Sampson willed Sarah Suggett a Bible and three additional religious books. In 1693, John Wallop willed his daughter the family Bible, a woman's advice book, and a cookery book.[18] The inventory of Rev. Thomas Teackle designates which books went to his children. His daughter Elizabeth inherited many theological works; a Greek and Latin dictionary; and Latin works by Lucian, Cicero, Horace, and Sallust. Catharine Teackle inherited many Latin works and several biblical commentaries. She may have had a greater interest in natural philosophy than her sister, because she received books on astronomy and geography. The fact that each daughter inherited Greek and Latin lexicons hints that their father had given them some training in languages.[19]

Similar bequests took place throughout the colonies. In 1735, David Howell of Southampton, New York, willed his daughter "my Great Bible." In 1742, New York merchant Cornelius Santford willed his daughter Helena "my Large Family Dutch Bible." The following year, William Burling willed his wife a "Quarto Bible" and his copy of Willem Sewel's *History of the Rise, Increase, and Progress, of the . . . Quakers.* Mary Smith of Burlington County, New Jersey, also owned a copy of Sewel's *History* at the time of her death. Sometimes these references to books, brief as they are, provide clues to women's reading tastes and education. Bequeathing his daughter Judith a "French Psalm Book," New Yorker Frederick De Voorse revealed his desire for her to learn French. Many young women knew the psalms by heart; reading a familiar text in a foreign language was the easiest way to learn that language. Mary Gouverneur, widow of New York merchant Abraham Gouverneur, bequeathed her grandson Abraham Gouverneur "my Large Book of Martyrs, with silver hooks, and all other printed books that did belong to my deceased husband." Mary had inherited her husband's books upon his death, but she apparently never considered them hers. The will specifically distinguishes his books from her book, a copy of John Fox's *Acts and Monuments; or Book of Martyrs*. Her physical description of the book shows its value. The "silver hooks" or clasps, a type of adornment often reserved for Bibles, indicates that a precious text was contained inside the book's covers.[20] At her death in 1725, Samuel Sewall's friend Bridget Usher had an impressive, largely devotional book collection. It can be safely assumed that this was her own library—she had left her cantankerous husband Hezekiah Usher, Jr., over thirty years before, and he had cut her off from his estate.[21]

Extant volumes inscribed by colonial women provide the surest indication of book ownership, but the evidence these volumes supply can be problematical. Few women dated their inscriptions. If a book survives with an undated woman's autograph, and the woman cannot be identified, it is difficult to pinpoint when she lived or when she acquired the book. This study uses such evidence with caution, restricting examples from undated, unidentified women's autographs to those which occur in American imprints before 1776. Of course, such constraints provide only a partial indication of women's reading tastes, since so many of the books read most widely, especially in the southern colonies, were imported from London. Though inscribed copies of books printed in London survive in American libraries today, in most cases no evidence survives to identify their owners or to show that they lived in colonial America.

Most surviving volumes inscribed by women are religious books. For example: Deodat Lawson's *Duty and Property of a Religious Householder Opened* (Boston, 1693; inscribed "Eliza Freeman"); Robert Russel's *Seven Sermons* (Boston, 1705; inscribed "Hannah Lovejoy her book, 1705"); Nehemiah Walter's *Body of Death Anatomized* (Boston, 1707; inscribed "Elizabeth Kidder"); Richard Baxter, *A Call to the Unconverted* (Boston, 1717; inscribed "Thankful Briggs her book" and "Abigail Basset"); Benjamin Colman's sermon on the accession of King George II to the throne, *Fidelity to Christ and to the Protestant Succession* (Boston, 1727; inscribed "Margaret Bliss"); William Cooper's *Early Piety Joyful to Beholders* (Boston, 1728; inscribed "Eunice Evans"); Thomas Foxcroft's *Pleas of Gospel-Impenitents* (Boston, 1730; inscribed "Sally Frothingham"); Jonathan Edwards's *Treatise Concerning Religious Affections* (Boston 1746; inscribed "Elizabeth Hazard"); the Quaker Thomas Chalkley's posthumous *Collection of the Works* (Philadelphia, 1749; inscribed "Rebecca Hutchin"); and Solomon Stoddard's *Appeal to the Learned* (Boston, 1709; inscribed "Hannah Foster,

1773").[22] The precise identities of the women who inscribed these books remain unclear. Women who owned books but were not members of prominent families sometimes are impossible to identify. Often, a woman's autograph in a surviving book remains her only written legacy.

More detailed inscriptions, however, help reconstruct the matrix of book giving and book receiving which took place throughout the colonies. The American Antiquarian Society's copy of Israel Loring's *Nature and Necessity of the New-Birth* (Boston, 1728) is inscribed "The gift of the Honourable Judge Sewall to Abigail Williams 1728" and therefore is one of the many books Sewall presented to his friends.[23] The Clements copy of Joseph Bellamy's *Essay on the Nature and Glory of Gospel* (Boston, 1762) is inscribed "Rachel Kneeland." Since the work was printed by Samuel Kneeland, the inscription suggests that Rachel received the book from her kinsman. Susanna Steere received a similar gift, Samuel Fuller's *Some Principles and Precepts of the Christian Religion* (Newport, 1769), which she inscribed "Susanna Steere her book given to her by her honoured grandfather T. Steere."[24] In Virginia in the 1770s, Landon Carter ordered several books for his grandchildren, including six copies of *Poetical Description of the Beasts, With Moral Reflections for the Amusement of Children,* "Mother Bunche's Fairy tales," many of John Newbery's "little books for young children," the second volume of *The Young Gentleman and Lady's Philosophy,* and Thomas Marryat's *Sentimental Fables. Designed chiefly for the Use of Ladies,* a collection of didactic verse.[25] Clearly, these examples suggest that the old colonial patriarchs wished their granddaughters to become well read.

Often books were shared among a family's women, sometimes between a mother and her daughter and other times among sisters. Surviving copies of such books include: Robert Dodsley's *Oeconomy of Human Life* (Philadelphia, 1766; inscribed "Rebeckah Harper, Sarah Harper"), a work which the New Yorker Jane Colden recommended to her sister Elizabeth Delancey; Robert Russel's *Seven Sermons* (Philadelphia, 1766; inscribed "Margret Louder" and "Hannah Louder"); Oliver Goldsmith's *Vicar of Wakefield* (Philadelphia, 1772; inscribed: "Sarah Horner"; "Mary Amy & Sarah Horner"); and the tenth edition of Edward Fisher's *Marrow of Modern Divinity* (Boston, 1743; inscribed: "Hannah Soule" and "Rebeckah Soule, 1775"), a work popular among Boston booksellers, according to Dr. Alexander Hamilton. Women also sold books to one another. A surviving copy of Mary Collyer's translation of Salomon Gessner's *The Death of Abel* (Boston, 1762), the German work most widely read in early America, survives with the inscription: "Ruth Russells books bought of Mrs. [Abigail] Brandeges."[26]

A delightful inscription occurs in the American Antiquarian Society's copy of the *Husband-Man's Guide* (New York, 1712), the second edition of the earliest known agricultural treatise printed in America. The end paper is inscribed "Joseph Walker his Book 1726/7" and "Sarah Walker her Book 1726/7." The joint autographs, obviously inscribed at the same time, suggest that their marriage was an equal venture. The work itself was a kind of home and garden *vade mecum* which both man and wife could have used. The Walker copy of the *Husband-Man's Guide* confirms the idea that men and women in agricultural communities shared many responsibilities and supports Maxine Margolis's assertion that early American domestic guides frequently assumed that both men and women worked together in the household.[27] The work described how to care for the orchard, the kitchen, and flower gardens, and it included a brief discourse on mathematics. It also contained remedies for consumption, gout, ague, scurvy, piles, and toothache, as well as directions for making a glister, stopping a nosebleed, and letting blood. The *Husband-Man's Guide* may have been the only book the Walkers owned. They filled blank leaves at the front with their children's birth records from 1724 through 1738, details that most parents conventionally recorded in the family Bible.[28] Such information must have enhanced the volume's worth to the family and helped assure its permanence.

Inscribed copies of books whose owners can be identified help shed light on colonial women's reading tastes and dispel long-standing rumors about attitudes towards women's reading. A copy of *The Emperor Marcus Antoninus: His Conversation with Himself* survives from William Byrd's splendid Westover library with the autograph "Lucy Byrd."[29] This one book challenges the general assumption that Byrd refused to let his wife in the library. On 30 December 1711, Byrd wrote that he had a little quarrel with Lucy, "because I was not willing to let her have a book out of the library."[30] Just because Byrd refused to let Lucy have a book that day does not mean he always discouraged her from reading. Lucy had a fiery temper, and when she disagreed with her husband, she let him know it. Byrd resented her attempts to undermine his control, and ordinarily their arguments ended only when Lucy acquiesced. Denying her a book, Byrd made the library walls his palisade. He liked her to read, but he did not want her challenging his power. When they were not arguing, he had no qualms about letting her in the library. Her belligerent nature makes her copy of Antoninus, a warrior's spiritual meditations, especially appropriate. Significantly, the catalog of the Byrd library lists none of the popular women's conduct books. Lucy Byrd would own no work which recommended a wife's unquestioning obedience to her husband.

Byrd's relationship with his second wife, Maria Taylor, confirms his appreciation of women's learning. While courting Maria, Byrd discovered that she knew Greek. He wrote her: "When indeed I learned that you also spoke Greek, the tongue of the Muses, I went completely crazy about you. In beauty you surpassed Helen, in culture of mind and ready wit Sappho: It is not meet therefore to be astonished I was smitten by such grandeur of body and soul when I admitted the poison of Love both through my eyes and my ears."[31] In the one diary which survives from the period of his second marriage, Byrd never records refusing Maria a book from the library. Some of the books were hers, such as a copy of the ninth edition of Abraham Cowley's *Works,* which survives with her autograph. After her husband's death, Maria knew the library well enough to recognize that it contained two copies of Cowley. She kept her copy and gave Landon Carter her husband's copy, the eighth edition.[32]

Byrd's daughters also were well educated. His library catalog lists multiple copies of such schoolbooks as John Clarke's introductory Latin texts, John Ward's *Young Mathematician's Guide,* and, most importantly, Elizabeth Carter's translation of Francesco Algarotti's *Sir Isaac Newton's Philosophy Explain'd for the Use of the Ladies . . . Six Dialogues on Light and Colours.*[33] Since William Byrd had only one son who survived beyond infancy, the multiple copies suggest that his daughters learned Latin, mathematics, and the sciences.

Three books in James Logan's Philadelphia library bear inscriptions concerning his oldest daughter Sarah (or Sally, as the family called her). In 1729, Logan bought her a copy of Hyacinthe Thabaud de La Touche's *L'art de bien parler francois* (Amsterdam, 1696). The Logan copy of Fénelon's *Avantures de Telemaque* (Amsterdam, 1719) also survives with her autograph. James Foster's *Sermons* (1736) contains the inscription, "The Gift of the honble John Penn Esq to Sarah Logan Sent from London 1737." Other books survive outside the Loganian library with evidence of Sarah's ownership, such as John Langhorne's *Correspondence of Theodocius and Constantia.* Logan actively encouraged the education of both Sarah and her sister. He began teaching Sarah French when she was nine, and he also taught her some Hebrew.[34] Instead of teaching the girls how to read Latin so that they could read Cato's distichs in the original, Logan translated the work himself as *Cato's Moral Distichs* (Philadelphia, 1735). He explained in his preface: "For however common the Book is in Latin, many of the Precepts are Excellently Good and useful and well worth young peoples remembring." Benjamin Franklin, who believed "such excellent Precepts of Morality, contain'd in such short and easily-remember'd Sentences, may to Youth particularly be very serviceable in the Conduct of Life," printed the work and sent copies to his sister-in-law Ann Franklin to sell at her Newport, Rhode Island, bookstore.[35] I suspect that many young women unable to read Latin did read Logan's *Cato.* Similar collections of pithy maxims frequently were found on the colonial woman's bookshelf.[36]

Book ownership is only one indication of women's reading. Books were expensive, and few people could afford everything they wanted to read. Subscription and circulating libraries helped solve the problem. Beginning in 1731 with the Library Company of Philadelphia—the "Mother of all the North American Subscription Libraries," as Benjamin Franklin called it—subscription or "social" libraries flourished, although initially no women were members. The subscription library was, after all, a gentlemanly undertaking, the product of a group of men with shared intellectual concerns. Among the 375 titles listed in the 1741 Library Company catalog, only two works specifically concerning female education are listed: Fénelon's *Instructions for the Education of a Daughter* and *The Ladies Library.* Both are works a father might acquire for his daughter. Two other Library Company titles might be considered women's books. Lord Halifax's *Miscellanies* contained his "Advice to a Daughter" and *The Complete Family-Piece* provided a "valuable Collection of above 1000 practical Family-Receipts, in Physick, Surgery, Cookery, &c."; neither book was designed specifically for women, however.[37] Besides recipes, the *Complete Family-Piece* contained hunting and fishing advice. Since subscribers to the Library Company could help decide what it acquired, the library's contents reflect the fact that, as of 1741, there were no women subscribers.

In 1769, the Library Company admitted Sarah Wistar, its first woman member;[38] and the 1770 catalog listed, among its more than two thousand titles, many additional works which often were read by contemporary female readers: Oriental tales such as *Almoran and Hamet,* Edward Moore's *Fables for the Female Sex,* the *Memoirs of Mlle de St. Eugene,* Charlotte Lennox's *Henrietta,* George Ballard's *Memoirs of Several Ladies of Great Britain,* and E. Smith's *Compleat Housewife,* to name a few. In 1773, the charter of the New York Society Library named Anne Waddell among its members. Her husband had helped establish the library, and, after his death in 1762, she continued his business and perpetuated his cultural interests.[39] The New York Society Library contained such works as James Fordyce's *Sermons,* Eliza Haywood's *Female Spectator,* and Halifax's *Advice to a Daughter.*[40] Although these two libraries each had only one woman subscriber during the colonial period, their contents suggest that male subscribers were bringing books home for wives and daughters.

The borrowing records of the Union Library of Hatboro, Pennsylvania, from 1762 to 1774, suggest that men indeed were bringing books home for women to read. In 1763, for example, Joseph Delworth borrowed Eliza Haywood's *History of Miss Betsy Thoughtless.* In 1768, Isaac Hough borrowed Elizabeth Rowe's *Letters,* and Jacob Cadwalader borrowed Eliza Haywood's *Fruitless Enquiry: Being a Collection of Several Entertaining Histories and Occurrences, Which Fell Under the Observation of a Lady in Her Search after Happiness.* In 1769, William Folwell borrowed Eliza Haywood's *The Wife,* and Amos Watson borrowed the *Female Worthies: or Memoirs of the Most Illustrious Ladies of All Ages and Nations.* In 1772, James Young borrowed Fordyce's *Sermons to Young Women.*[41] I do not mean to imply that the colonial woman read only books written by or about women. Rather, these few titles selected as examples suggest the likelihood that the patrons of the Hatboro Union Library and, by inference, of other subscription libraries were bringing books home for other family members to read.

Happily, the Hatboro Union Library borrowing record lists a woman among its colonial patrons. After the death in 1762 of David Rees, one of the library's original shareholders, his wife Margaret held the share until her death five years later.[42] Margaret Rees's literary tastes were wide-ranging. She read epic poetry, history, biblical commentary, devotional works, letters, and novels. In August 1764, she borrowed Milton's *Paradise Lost.* When she returned the book two weeks later, she borrowed one volume of Tobias Smollett's *Compleat History of England.* She spent that October reading the *Spectator.* In November, she borrowed Milton's *Paradise Regained, Cato's Letters,* and two volumes of Matthew Poole's *Annotations upon the Holy Bible.* After keeping Poole's *Annotations* for over a month, she exchanged it for Alexander Pope's *Works.* In 1765, she borrowed such diverse works as a four-volume dictionary of arts and sciences; Henry Fielding's *Tom Jones*; Elizabeth Rowe's *Letters*; and the first volumes of the *Guardian,* the *Spectator,* and the *Female Spectator.* In 1766, she borrowed James Hervey's *Meditations,* Lady Montagu's *Letters . . . Written, During Her Travels in Europe, Asia and Africa,* and the seventh volume of Lewis Theobald's edition of Shakespeare.[43] However broad, Margaret Rees's tastes were not unusual. Many American women of the 1760s read similar books. Rowe and Hervey were the two devotional writers most popular among women during the last three decades of the colonial period. The popularity of Eliza Haywood and Lady Mary Wortley Montagu reflect a renewed desire among colonial women to read female authors.[44]

While obtaining reading material from subscription libraries was less expensive than buying books, shares in the early libraries sometimes were too expensive for the average reader. Colonial entrepreneurs recognized what the people wanted and rose to meet the demand. During the 1760s, they established circulating libraries in major cities throughout colonial America. While the library companies in Philadelphia, Charleston, Newport, and New York were social undertakings, circulating libraries were commercial ventures. Profitability was linked to the number of patrons, and circulating libraries welcomed all readers, men and women. In Annapolis, William Rind established the earliest known colonial circulating library. Rind announced his purpose in the *Maryland Gazette* of 2 September 1762: "To open and extend the Fountains of Knowledge, which are at present shut against all but Men of affluent Fortunes." He planned to make his books available throughout Maryland, but his scheme was too ambitious and his books too few. In 1763, he restricted his readership to the Annapolis area and reduced the subscription price, but he soon went out of business.[45] Rind may have failed because Annapolis did not have the population to support a circulating library or because he did not have the capital to stock enough books to make the venture worthwhile; but he had a good idea. Many soon followed his lead.

Within the next few years, circulating libraries were established in Charleston, New York, and Boston. All welcomed women. Charleston bookbinder and stationer George Wood announced in the *South Carolina Gazette* of 26 February 1763, that he had "A Collection of curious

Books, consisting of histories, voyages, travels, lives, memoirs, novels, plays, &c." and "intended to set on foot A Circulating LIBRARY; Gentlemen and Ladies that approve this plan, and are willing to encourage so useful an undertaking, are desired to give in their name."[46] Later that year, Garret Noel began a circulating library in New York for "those who delight in Reading, And would spend their Leisure Hours, and Winter Evenings, with Profit and Entertainment." He advertised that it contained "several Thousand Volumes of Choice Books, in History, Divinity, Travels, Voyages, Novels, &c."[47] When John Mein opened his Boston circulating library in 1765, he announced the hope that his venture would "insinuate knowledge and instruction, under the veil of entertainment to the FAIR SEX."[48] Surviving information about the circulating library Lewis Nicola established in 1767 at Philadelphia further suggests that women formed a large portion of his clientele. Nicola shared the premises with milliner Ellenor Fitzgerald. They even advertised together. With one stop, the advertisements tell us, a woman could have her silk stockings laundered and borrow a book or two. Announcing his Charleston circulating library in the *South Carolina Gazette* in 1772, Samuel Gifford appealed to "Ladies and Gentlemen."[49] After Annapolis bookseller William Aikman started a circulating library in 1773, Maryland entrepreneur Joseph Rathell designed a similar venture for the Baltimore area and urged both ladies and gentlemen to support him. Aikman sensed a threat, and in the *Maryland Journal and Baltimore Advertiser* of 30 October 1773, he announced "To the Ladies and Gentlemen of the Town of Baltimore" that he would make his Annapolis collection conveniently available to them.[50]

Only two circulating library catalogs printed before 1776 survive. John Mein's 1765 catalog lists 750 titles in more than one thousand volumes. Most of his books are listed among "History, Poetry, Novels, &c.," but he also had French books and books in medicine, divinity, law, husbandry, gardening, and mathematics. Works specifically appealing to women included the *Ladies' Complete Letter-Writer*; Hannah Glasse's *Art of Cookery*; Glasse's *Whole Art of Confectionary*; Elizabeth Rowe's *Letters from the Dead to the Living*; Sarah Fielding's *Governess; or Little Female Academy*; John Shebbeare's *Matrimony, A Novel*; Charlotte Lennox's *Harriot Stuart*; and *Letters of Lady Juliet Catesby*.[51] William Aikman's 1773 Annapolis circulating library catalog lists over eight hundred titles. Like Mein's library, the large majority of Aikman's books were history, voyages, poetry, and novels. By the middle of 1773, Aikman's collection had swelled to twelve hundred volumes "on the most useful sciences, history, poetry, agriculture, voyages, travels, miscellanies, plays, with all the most approved novels, magazines and other books of entertainment."[52]

Mein and Aikman, as proprietors of circulating libraries in the American colonies, had a good understanding of the tastes and needs of the American reading public. Their publishing ventures confirm their desire to promote reading among women. Two years after his circulating library catalog appeared, Mein published, for the first time in America, James Fordyce's *Sermons to Young Women* (Boston, 1767).[53] And two years after publication of his circulating library catalog, Aikman brought out John Gregory's *Father's Legacy to His Daughters* (Philadelphia, 1775); this was the first time that work had been reprinted in America.[54] Their circulating libraries taught Mein and Aikman what was popular, and both responded with more books for women readers.

Since circulating libraries were ephemeral ventures, many more may have existed than are known about from advertisements in colonial newspapers. Mein's Circulating Library catalog was also a sale catalog. One wonders how many other booksellers ran impromptu circulating libraries with stock that did not readily sell. Without additional evidence, we must rely on anecdote. New York entrepreneur Samuel Loudon, with his characteristic eye for profit, opened a circulating library in early 1774. After he had been in business for around ten months, he put an advertisement in the *New York Gazette* describing his success and announcing a new catalog. In the advertisement, he stated, "The ladies are his best customers, and shew a becoming delicacy of taste in their choice of books."[55]

Booksellers' catalogs provide additional evidence concerning women's reading habits. Boston booksellers Edward Cox and Edward Berry, whose business also involved selling jewelry, stocked many books for women. Their 1772 sale catalog lists: Martha Bradley's *British Housewife*; *Clio, or the Adventures of Mrs. Sanson*; *Culpeper's Midwifery*; *Lady's Compleat Letter-Writer*; *The Ladies Library*; *Memoirs of Several Ladies of Great Britain*; Laetitia Pilkington's *Memoirs*; and Marquise de Lambert's *Polite Lady; or, a Course in . . . Education*, among many others.[56] Cox and Berry, more than any contemporary bookseller, shaped their business to suit a female clientele. In addition, they published several important works for women, including William Cadogan's *Essay upon Nursing* (1772) and Susannah Carter's *Frugal Housewife* (1772).

Sale catalogs indicate the kinds of books available, but few sale records survive to show who bought what. The ledgers or "daybooks" which survive from the *Virginia Gazette* office for the years 1750–52 and 1764–66 consequently provide rare glimpses into colonial American book-buying habits and reading tastes. Although the daybooks do not list books purchased for cash, items from the *Virginia Gazette* office frequently were purchased on credit, and the daybooks list both who picked up the book and to whose account the purchase was credited. In some instances, this information can be interpreted as a record of buyers and readers. In 1764, Jane Vobe bought a copy of Marquise de Lambert's *Polite Lady* for "Nan," presumably her daughter. In 1765, Samuel Spurr bought a copy of Elizabeth Singer Rowe's *Friendship in Death; in Twenty Letters from the Dead to the Living* for his daughter.[57] Such conduct books and devotional poetry remained among the kinds of literature read most widely throughout the colonial period.

References in surviving poems, diaries, letters, and memoirs supply important comments about the colonial woman's reading habits and tastes. Anne Bradstreet's poetry provides the most prominent illustration. Since the Bradstreet family library, containing more than eight hundred volumes, was destroyed when the family's house burned, references in Anne Bradstreet's works provide the only clues about the library's contents. In her poetry, Bradstreet mentions Hesiod, Homer, Thucydides, Xenophon, Aristotle, Virgil, Ovid, Quintus Curtius, Pliny, and Seneca. Bradstreet's nineteenth-century editor, John Harvard Ellis, deprecatingly suggested that "there is no reason to suppose that she had read their works, either in the originals or in translations,"[58] but I disagree. Contemporary prejudice against the female pedant prompted colonial women writers to minimize rather than exaggerate the breadth of their reading. The Bradstreet library would have contained works by most, if not all, of the classical writers to whom she refers. Other Bradstreet poems specifically refer to modern works. "The Four Monarchies," based heavily upon Walter Raleigh's *History of the World,* also refers to James Ussher's *Annals of the World,* William Pember's *Period of the Persian Monarchie,* and Thomas North's translation of Plutarch's *Lives.*[59] Bradstreet's "Four Humours" was drawn largely from Helkiah Crooke's *Description of the Body of Man.* In her poem, "In Honour of Queen Elizabeth," she refers to John Speed's *Historie of Great Britain* and William Camden's *Annales; or, The History of . . . Elizabeth.*[60] Of course, she would have owned copies of Sidney's poetry and Du Bartas's works. The numerous comparisons made between Bradstreet and Du Bartas in the commendatory verses to her poetry suggest that Du Bartas was well known to her New England friends as well. Though these scattered references only hint at the breadth of the Bradstreet collection, the library apparently contained many ancient classics (including several in modern translation), modern histories of various parts of the world, poetry, and, of course, devotional works.

Surviving diaries and letterbooks provide much additional information about the kinds of books which found their way onto the colonial woman's bookshelf. Ann Bolton's diary contains much about her Philadelphia aunt, the early eighteenth-century writer and eccentric, Bathsheba Bowers, whose house was "furnished with books." Bowers "was a Quaker by profession," her niece related, "but so Wild in her Notions it was hard to find out of what religion she really was of. She read her Bible much but I think sometimes to no better purpose than to afford matter for dispute in which she was always positive. . . . But I must now proceed with the account of her Books. She had several wrote by a female hand filled with dreams and visions and a thousand Romantic Notions of her seeing Various sorts of Beasts and Bulls in the Heavens." The description suggests that, in addition to her writing activities, Bowers may have practiced conjuring. Bolton wrote: "Tho' my Aunt as I told you before was very religious yet very whimsical and thus were her Books suited to her humour—Tryon was one of her favorites in which was represented the hideousness of our Cannibal Natures in eating flesh fish or anything that had life in it." Of course, she refers to Thomas Tryon's *Way to Health, Long Life, and Happiness,* the work which once prompted Benjamin Franklin to briefly experiment with vegetarianism and which afforded him much amusement at his employer Samuel Keimer's expense. Bowers apparently was more dedicated to Tryon's beliefs than Franklin. Her niece relates that she ate no meat during the last twenty years of her life.[61]

Esther Edwards Burr's letters to Sarah Prince provide the single most extensive surviving literary criticism from a colonial woman. Burr was the daughter of Jonathan Edwards and, after 1752, the wife of Aaron Burr, Sr., pastor of a Presbyterian church in Newark, New Jersey, and president of the College of New Jersey (later Princeton University). Her marriage took her to New Jersey and away from her friend Sarah Prince, daughter of Boston bookman and divine Thomas Prince. The women agreed to correspond, and both kept journals in the form of letterbooks to each other. Prince's journal-letterbook apparently has not survived, but Burr's does, and it recently has been edited. Her husband traveled frequently, preaching and raising funds for the college, and her life in New Jersey was often lonely.[62] Reading and writing provided comfort. Books were storehouses for ideas, and they gave the two women common points of contact. Though they could not be with each other, Burr and Prince could share experiences by reading the same books.

The earliest bookish discourse reflected in the Burr letters concerns friendship. After reading Mary Jones's *Miscellanies in Prose and Verse,* Burr described how she felt: "She has a turn for poetry, is quite lively in some places, but in others flat which I wonder at. She has some fine strokes on friendship which shews a turn for it, but no turn for relegion. I believe her to be a Deist in principle. What a pity!" Prince responded, quoting a passage from Samuel Richardson's *Sir Charles Grandison* which discussed the quality of friendship; and Burr wrote back, quoting a poem from Mary Jones's *Miscellanies* which expressed similar sentiments. Female friendship is a key theme of Jones's book, and it became a theme within the correspondence of Burr and Prince. Burr next mused on the idea of friendship. Though she began with hope, her discussion ended with melancholy uncertainty: "I cant but hope my dear that the World is agoing to have better notions about friendship than they used to—it seems to me we did not use to meet with so many just thoughts on it as we do in late authors, or is it because friendship is going out of the World, and the judicious part of it see it, and are awake about it. If this is the case I wish they might awake others by what is printed."[63] Burr clearly recognized the value of print culture for disseminating ideas, and she saw books as bulwarks against encroaching immorality. Simultaneously, however, she saw the potential for books to disseminate new ideas which challenged established beliefs. Jones's Deist tendencies Burr clearly found threatening.

Reading further in Jones's *Miscellanies,* Burr became disgusted with some derogatory comments apparently concerning George Whitefield, and she refused to read further:

> Just now I meet with a paragraph in Miss Joans that has disgusted me extreamly, and beclouded all her witt and good sense. I have a good mind I'll read no farther but thro aside the book, but this you will say is prejudice. In one of her letters she undertakes to prove that there are such beings as *Demons,* and that men are often under the influence of em. One instance she mentions as . . . proof is Mr Whitefield and all the Methodists. She dont speak his Name but she says, "Some have left their ca[l]ling and all visible means of subsisstance, for the Kingdom of heavens sake, are now seting out for the Wilderness in order to be fed by the Ravens" and a quotation to the margin, "*Georgia*" and a great deal more that would be tedious to transcribe. She sets all zeal in religion in the most *abominable ridiculous* light.[64]

Jones actually referred to John Wesley, not Whitefield, as Burr surmised, but either way, she was sufficiently insulted to put the book away for some time—though she did not, as her remark suggests, permanently toss the book aside. In a letter to Prince three months later, Burr referred to a poem from Jones's *Miscellanies*: "I am perfectly satisfyed with my lot in life, and can say as Miss Joans in one of her poems to a Lady. 'The summit reached of Erthly joys.'"[65] Burr's most extensive bookish remarks concern Samuel Richardson's *Pamela,* discussed below in a separate chapter.

Sadly, Aaron Burr, Sr., died during the fall of 1757, and Esther Edwards Burr herself died six months later, at the age of twenty-six. Their children were placed in the care of Esther's brother, Timothy Edwards, who saw to their education. All evidence indicates that Sally Burr received the kind of education her mother would have wished for her. Timothy Edwards had his niece diligently attend her studies, and he urged her to read history because, he told her, it was "one of the Best means to open, enlarge, improve the Mind, & Clear it of Narrow & vulgar Prejudices."[66]

Eliza Lucas began keeping a letterbook shortly after her father, Lt. Col. George Lucas, had sent her and the rest of the family to South Carolina, while he remained stationed in Antigua. The business of running the Lucas plantation near Charleston fell to Eliza, only fifteen at the time they moved in 1738. Like any responsible eighteenth-century business-woman, she kept a letterbook to record her business activities, but the letterbook incidentally tracks her social and intellectual maturity. As she wrote to a correspondent in 1740, "I have a little library well furnished (for my papa has left me most of his books) in which I spend part of my time."[67] Other letters reveal her reading habits. She arose at five in the morning to attend her studies and read until breakfast time two hours later. After breakfast, she read French and practiced shorthand, and she read again each evening before bed.

Lucas's letters specifically mention many different books, often with brief critical comments. South Carolinian Charles Pinckney (whom she eventually would marry) recommended that she read Locke. Lucas took advantage of his suggestion during a time of mental disquiet. She wrote a friend: "I began to consider what alteration there was in this place that used so agreeably to sooth my (for some time past) pensive humour, and made me indiferent to every thing the gay world could boast; but found the change not in the place but in my self, and it doubtless proceeded from that giddy gayety and want of reflection which I contracted when in town; and I was forced to consult Mr. Lock over and over to see wherin personal Identity consisted and if I was the very same self."[68] Else-where, she found Virgil's comments on agriculture pertinent to South Carolina: "I have got no further than the first volume of Virgil but was most agreeably disapointed to find my self instructed in agriculture as well as entertained by his charming penn; for I am pursuaded tho' he wrote in and for Italy, it will in many instances suit Carolina."[69] Scat-tered through the letters are references to other prominent writers: Cervantes, Milton, Addison, and Samuel Richardson. Lucas's comments on Richardson's *Pamela*, like Burr's, will be taken up in greater detail in another chapter.

Lucas, more than any other colonial woman reader and writer, cared little about the kinds of restrictions society placed upon women's intel-lectual freedoms. One old neighbor lady hardly approved of the ambi-tious young woman's diligent studies. She told Lucas that reading would make her look old before her time. Lucas, however, believed that the old woman was mistaken: "What ever contributes to health and pleasure of mind must also contribute to good looks." The old lady was so persis-tent that she once tried to throw Lucas's copy of Plutarch's *Lives* into the fire and pleaded with Lucas never to read Father Malebranche's *Search After Truth*. Happily, Lucas ignored the old woman's example, and actively encouraged literacy in her community. She taught two of the family's slaves to read; and she planned, with her mother's approval, to have those two teach the remaining slaves.[70]

The correspondence of Philadelphia bluestocking Elizabeth Graeme (later Ferguson) reveals her enthusiasm for books and learning. Surviving letters to her show that others recognized her bookish interests. Graeme's fabled meeting with Henry Fielding during a trip to England may never have occurred; but she certainly was familiar with the author's writings. Her one-time suitor William Franklin alluded to Henry Fielding's *Tom Jones* in a letter to her. After presenting Graeme with a muff, Franklin wrote, "[As] she was often pleas'd to liken me to Tom Jones, and express herself much delighted with the Story of Sophia's Muff mentioned in that Novel, I could not help flattering myself that This might, in the same Manner, tend to raise or keep alive some Soft Emotions in my Favour. But now, alas, I see there is no intrinsic Merit in a Muff. It can have no avail where a Sophia's Breast is wanting."[71] Another of Graeme's correspondents, Eliza Stedman, alluded to Pope's *Essay on Man*.[72] Graeme's mother quoted Addison in a letter, telling her daughter that God's mercy "extends to all his works, as Mr Addison sets forth most clearly in the paper I gave you to read; and as I know he is very justly a favorite Author, I have Transcribed another Papar of his for your consideration."[73] The process of copying key passages from books and sharing them with other women allowed ideas from books to become more widely disseminated. This letter from mother to daughter provides an example of the interaction between manuscript and print culture.

A letter from Graeme's friend Hannah Griffitts shows that the two women exchanged books. Griffitts respected Graeme's reading tastes and was a little uncertain about making book recommendations to her better-read friend. Sending Graeme a copy of Alexander Dow's tragedy, *Sethona,* Griffitts wrote:

> I have sent you the books & if they afford you any entertainment it will make me happy. I was fearful of sending them lest you should condemn my taste in reading, and as I really know no person in whose esteem It would afford me greater pleasure to stand high than yours, it would be

a sensible mortification. There is part of the last leaf of *Sethona* torn off, but as there is but a few lines more & those of no consequence, I would not deprive you of the pleasure of reading the play. If it gives you as much as it did me, you will not regret the time. The other books are merely entertaining but I leave them to speak for themselves.[74]

Griffitts's specific comment about the copy of *Sethona* reveals much about the contexts of reading in early America. Books were precious things. Even when they became damaged, readers did not stop reading or sharing them. Her remark that the last few lines were "of no Consequence" suggests that it was unnecessary to read a whole work from beginning to end in order to appreciate it. The other books Griffitts recommended to her friend are "merely entertaining," while *Sethona* evidently is viewed as considerably more. Here Griffitts reflects the critical commonplace that the best literature both delights and instructs.

Elizabeth Graeme herself possessed a fairly large library. A Pennsylvania Supreme Court document mentions: "Four hundred Volumes many of which are not bound & of those which are[,] 130 are the property of different Gentlemen whose Names stand in them." The court record reveals her familiarity with colonial Philadelphia's literary men. They were willing to encourage her studies by loaning her books, and she was enthusiastic enough about the books that she was reluctant to return them. Only one known volume from Graeme's library survives, Le Maitre's *Traité du vrai merite de l'homme* (Amsterdam, 1742), a book Sarah Tabary had given her in 1769.[75]

Abigail Adams's letters reveal her intelligence, insight, and wide reading. Like Esther Edwards Burr, she often found analogies between what she experienced and what she read. After spending time with Samuel Adams and his wife, she wrote, "In them is to be seen the tenderest affection towards each other, without any fulsome fondness, and the greatest Complasance, delicacy and good breeding that you can immagine, yet seperate from any affectation—in them you might see those Lines of Thomson verified."[76] She then quoted a passage from James Thomson's *The Seasons*. Reading one thing led to another, and Thomson's poetry once sent her in search of Chesterfield's *Letters*: "I was led to the request from reading the following character of him in my favorite Thomson and from some spiritted and patriotick speaches of his in the Reign of Gorge 2."[77] When her husband John Adams was at Philadelphia for the Continental Congress, she wrote him asking for a copy of Chesterfield. He responded, "Chesterfields Letters are a chequered sett. You would not choose to have them in your Library, they are like Congreeves Plays, stained with libertine Morals and base Principles."[78] Her reply was submissive: "I give up my Request for Chesterfields Letters submitting intirely to your judgment, as I have ever found you ready to oblige me in this way whenever you thought it would contribute either to my entertainment or improvement."[79]

Abigail Adams also enjoyed reading histories, finding facts immediately pertinent to her own life. After reading Rollin's *Ancient History,* she saw its relevance to the American Revolution. "The loss of Ticondoroga," she wrote, "has awakened the sleeping Genious of America and call'd forth all her Martial fire, may it never again be lulld to rest till crownd with victory and peace. Good officers will make good Soldiers." She then quoted an episode from Rollin and explained, "This is a case I think very similar to our own, may it prove so in the end. Their are two ways says Rolin of acquiring improvement and instruction, first by ones own experience, and secondly by that of other men. It is much more wise and usefull to improve by other mens miscarriages than by our own."[80]

While her husband was away, Abigail Adams did whatever she could to help her children develop a fondness for books. As she was reading Rollin, she had their son, John Quincy Adams, read the work. She wrote her husband, "I have perswaided Johnny to read me a page or two every day, and hope he will from his desire to oblige me entertain a fondness for it."[81] The frustrations and inadequacies women felt concerning the education of their children near the end of the colonial period are most apparent in the correspondence between Abigail Adams and Mercy Otis Warren. Perhaps the two most articulate women in Revolutionary America, both found difficult the task of educating their children while their husbands were away on the business of forming a new country. Unable to seek their husbands' guidance, the two women relied on books. Mercy Otis Warren shared Abigail Adams's concern that their relative lack of education (compared to men) made it difficult for them to educate their children properly. She wrote back, "You ask assistance and advice in the mighty task of cultivating the minds and planting the seeds of Virtue in the infant Bosom, from one who is yet looking abroad for Every foreign aid to Enable her to the discharge of a duty that is of the utmost importance to society though for a Number of Years it is almost wholly left to our uninstructed sex."[82]

Autobiographical writings form another important source for understanding women's reading in colonial America. The *Memoirs* of Hannah Adams and Anne MacVicar Grant remain among the most important. Both women were born in 1755, grew up during the last two decades of the colonial period, and lived well into the nineteenth century. Their *Memoirs*, consequently provide insightful comments comparing the state of female education before and after the Revolutionary War. Hannah Adams recalled her early colonial education: "The country schools, at that time, were kept but a few months in the year, and all that was then taught in them was reading, writing and arithmetic. In the summer, the children were instructed by females in reading, sewing, and other kinds of work. The books chiefly made use of were the Bible, and Psalter."[83] Fortunately, Hannah's father was an avid reader and possessed an excellent library, so she had an opportunity to read much. The problem, she explained, was that her lack of education prevented her from reading the proper books. Adams, of course, was not alone. In fact, she had a small group of female friends who shared her literary tastes. She relates:

> I had a few dear friends, (for novels had taught me to be very romantic,) who were chiefly in indigent circumstances, and like myself had imbibed a taste for reading, and were particularly fond of poetry and novels. Most of them wrote verses, which were read and admired by the whole little circle. Our mutual love of literature, want of fortune, and indifference to the society of those whose minds were wholly uncultivated, served to cement a union between us, which was interrupted only by the removal of the parties to distant places, and dissolved by their death.[84]

Anne MacVicar Grant's *Memoirs of an American Lady,* less personal and more detached than Adams', nevertheless embodies much of her personal philosophy and includes important comments about reading. In the first part of her work, Grant writes, "Books are, no doubt, the granaries of knowledge: but a diligent, inquiring mind, in the active morning of life, will find it strewed like manna over the face of the earth; and need not, in all cases, rest satisfied with intelligence accumulated by others, and tinctured with their passions and prejudices."[85] Later, while admitting that she derived "unspeakable benefit and improvement" from her reading, Grant reasserts the idea that books alone are not enough for a well-rounded education. In a chapter titled, "Benefit of Select Reading," Grant states that

> a promiscuous multitude of books always within reach retards the acquisition of useful knowledge. It is like having a great number of acquaintances and few friends; one of the consequences of the latter is to know much of exterior appearances, of modes and manners, but little of nature and genuine character. By running over numbers of books without selection, in a desultory manner, people, in the same way, get a general superficial idea of the varieties and nature of different styles, but do not comprehend or retain the matter with the same accuracy as those who have read a few books, by the best authors, over and over with diligent attention."[86]

Grant's admonition to read books by the best authors over and over is a recommendation which the religious writers had frequently emphasized in the popular devotional manuals.

Published funeral sermons and their accompanying biographical sketches also provide important comments about women's reading. While post-mortem praise always must be viewed with caution, the eulogistic portrayal of women certainly illustrates a feminine ideal. Many of the eulogies stressed the woman's reading activities. Jane Colman Turell's husband Ebenezer recalled that, during her teens, she borrowed many books from friends and that she "had indeed such a Thirst after Knowledge that the Leisure of the Day did not suffice, but she spent whole Nights in reading. . . . When I was first inclin'd . . . to seek her Acquaintance (which was about the Time she entred her *nineteenth* Year) I was surpriz'd and charm'd to find her so accomplish'd." At the time, Jane Colman was "in a good measure Mistress of the politest *Writers* and their Works; could point out the Beauties in them, and had made many of their best Tho'ts her own: And as she went into more free Conversation, she discours'd how admirably on many Subjects!" Turell continued, "She had read, and (in some measure) digested all the English *Poetry*, and polite Pieces in *Prose*, printed and Manuscripts in her Father's well furnish'd Library." No inventory of Benjamin Colman's library survives, but it would have been one of the finest in early eighteenth-century Boston, containing a wide variety of authors, ancient and modern.[87]

In a biographical sketch published with *Victorina,* Cotton Mather's funeral sermon for his daughter Katherine, Thomas Walter wrote that her education led her to excel not only at housewifery but also at writing. Furthermore, "she became in her Childhood, a Mistress of the Hebrew Tongue. She also attained to a considerable Knowledge in the Sacred Geography."[88] In a funeral sermon for his daughter Deborah, Thomas Prince wrote, "As she grew up, he was pleas'd to restrain her from youthful Vanities, to make her serious, and move her to study the BIBLE and the best of *Authors* both of *History* and *Divinity*: Among the latter of which, Dr. *Watts* and Mrs. *Row's* Writings were very agreeable and familiar to Her."[89] After the death of Philadelphian Sarah Eve, an anonymous contributor to the *Pennsylvania Packet* wrote, "Her understanding was strong, her imagination brilliant, and her taste correct. These were improved by an intimate acquaintance with some of the best poetical and prose writers in the English language."[90] Martha Laurens Ramsay's obituary in the *Carolina Gazette* emphasized her learning: "Deeply read in all the solidity and elegancies of English literature, her mind, like a rich soil, continually improved by cultivation. . . . she had a thorough knowledge of the Latin and Greek."[91]

Colonial American portraiture provides convincing visual evidence to substantiate the lively interest women had in reading. Time and again, colonial American women chose to feature books in their portraits. In New York artist John Watson's painting of *Captain Johannes Schuyler and His Wife* (ca. 1725), Mrs. Schuyler is portrayed with a book, her arm across the open pages. John Smibert portrayed Sarah Boucher (1730) with a book in her lap, her finger marking the place where she had been reading. As Wayne Craven has noticed, the book, along with her eye contact, "gives a lively immediacy to the image, and the book further reminds us that she is an educated woman. The book and the chair create a setting that suggests to the viewer that Mrs. Boucher has been portrayed in the quiet privacy of some snug corner of her own comfortable home, engaged in some customary activity—reading a book from her library."[92] In her portrait, New Yorker Alida Schuyler Livingston is also pictured holding a book in her right hand, resting it on her knee with her index finger marking her place. Here, the book is no mere icon of wealth (though it is that, too); it represents the importance she attaches to learning. In 1753, Joseph Blackburn portrayed Mary Lea Harvey with an ornately tooled, paneled, and gilt book. The fine binding, like her lace collar and cuffs, are symbols of affluence, but her posture, facial expression, and the way she holds the book open show her in the process of reading. The meaning of her stern grimace seems unmistakable. She looks up from her book as if to say: "How dare you interrupt my reading to paint my picture."

CHAPTER 2

Devotional Books

During the mid-eighteenth century, South Carolina printer Peter Timothy issued Henry Heywood's *Two Catechisms: By Way of Question and Answer*. Heywood dedicated the work to four wives and mothers, Amarantha Farr, Frances Elliot, Elizabeth Elliot, and Elizabeth Williamson, in the hope that they would use the book to teach their children religious fundamentals and thereby make their homes "little Schools of Christianity" and their families "Nurseries for Christ's Church, and the Kingdom of the great God."[1] Though Heywood's was an eighteenth-century Baptist work, the domestic scene envisioned in his dedication had been enacted repeatedly within American families of all faiths since the early seventeenth century: a mother reading a shorter catechism aloud to her young children; the girls and boys getting it by heart even before they could read; and the older children silently reading a longer catechism, often turning their heads away from the page every few sentences to try and repeat the text without looking, and, when they gained enough confidence in their memories, asking their mothers to quiz them.

Catechisms were among the earliest books to reach the Plymouth Colony. William Brewster's 1617 Leyden edition of John Dod's *Plaine and Familiar Exposition of the Tenne Commandements,* for instance, includes a "methodicall short catechisme, containing briefly all the principall grounds of Christian Religion." The Clements copy is inscribed "Eliza Baldwin, hur book."[2] After the 1642 mandate requiring all New England children to learn the catechism, many were printed and imported. Dozens of Nathaniel Vincent's *Little Child's Catechism* were sent to Boston during the last two decades of the seventeenth century. Catechisms for every faith could be found throughout the colonies. Benjamin Franklin, recognizing a lucrative market, printed several and distributed them widely. He issued two editions of David Evans's *Short Plain Help for Parents* (1732 and 1740) and sent copies to booksellers in Massachusetts and South Carolina and others to his sister-in-law Ann Franklin to sell at her Rhode Island bookshop. He also printed several Presbyterian catechisms; two United Brethren catechisms, one in German and the other in Swedish; and a Baptist catechism.[3]

Catechisms were organized in a question-and-answer format to facilitate learning. Initially, mothers could read both questions and answers to their children; as the little ones began to memorize the answers, their mothers could simply ask them the questions. Often, children would have many, if not all, of the answers memorized before they could read. Learning to read, therefore, involved matching memorized sounds with their corresponding letters, syllables, words, and sentences. Literacy occurred when a mother stopped and a child started pointing out the words on the page. At this moment, the book transferred from the hands of the mother to the hands of her child. Both the reading process and the book as physical object, therefore, were linked inextricably with spirituality. Learning to read religious books was the same as learning to read.

Catechism reading often continued as the young reader progressed to more difficult texts. Just as children could memorize a catechism before they could read it, they could read it before they could understand it completely. Cotton Mather's story of five-year-old Ann Greenough, who "had an unspeakable Delight in *Catechising*" and would "put strange *Questions* about eternal things, and make *Answers* her self that were extreamly pertinent," seems apocryphal.[4] In his *Token for Children,* James Janeway recommended additional books for children while suggesting that they continue studying their catechism. Janeway also urged them to ask their parents about any parts of the Bible or the catechism that they did not understand.[5] To make sure that older children continued reading the catechism, most faiths had shorter and longer versions. After mastering the shorter catechism, the child or adolescent progressed to the longer catechism which asked more difficult questions and supplied lengthier answers. In this way, the older children could continue reading their catechism without having to read a "baby" book. The day a child graduated from the shorter to the longer catechism was a proud moment in her or his spiritual and intellectual life and in the lives of the parents.

Studying a catechism's principles was something both women and men could continue as adults. John Freame's *Scripture-Instruction* (Ephratra, Pennsylvania, 1754)—one copy of which belonged to Quaker

Rhoda Garretson—contained a publisher's preface which remarked: "The ultimate Design of reprinting these few Sheets, is for the Benefit of little Ones, tho' it is presumed that those who are adult, may not find it altogether unprofitable to them."[6] Samuel Willard's posthumous *Compleat Body of Divinity* (Boston, 1726) was a collection of "Two Hundred and Fifty Expository Lectures on the Assembly's Shorter Catechism." Willard had presented the lectures to "show the farther beauty[,] use and excellence of the [catechism's] Truths explain'd, by reducing them to a suitable Practice and applying them to the Hearts and Lives of his Hearers." Previously, Willard had explained the catechism to children; these lectures were designed "to exercise and entertain the Riper and stronger Minds, of more enlarg'd Capacities and more advanced Knowledge." *The Compleat Body of Divinity,* the most ambitious printing task then undertaken in British colonial America, was published by subscription, and several women are listed among those who subscribed to the weighty folio.[7] A woman's responsibility for educating her children guaranteed that she would continue reading and thinking about the catechism as an adult. After learning a shorter catechism as a child, a longer catechism in adolescence, and perhaps reading one of the many works explaining the catechism as a young woman, she returned to the shorter catechism as a mother. This cumulative attention to religious fundamentals profoundly influenced both her thought and her reading choices.

During the course of her life, the colonial woman experienced religious reading in many different contexts. Her first contact with the catechism occurred in a social setting—that is, as a child listening to her mother read. After learning to read, the child could then read in private. Other types of religious books—most notably hymnbooks and psalms—were experienced (sung or read) in large public assemblies, within families as either devotion or entertainment, and in private. Other books—the Bible, sermons, devotional manuals—were read within prayer groups. In seventeenth-century New England, some of these were all-female prayer groups.[8] Still other types of religious books were designed specifically for private reading as part of the woman's "closet devotions," a phrase used to denote any private religious practice.

The process of reading religious books complemented the other fundamental way in which colonial woman experienced religious discourse, hearing sermons. James Janeway urged children, "Hear the most power-ful Ministers, and read the most searching Books."[9] Richard Baxter, a nonconformist author whose works the young colonial woman might begin reading in her teens, similarly linked hearing sermons and reading religious books: "The Writings of Divines are nothing else but a preach-ing the Gospel to the eye, as the *voice* preacheth it to the ear." As such, religious books were a kind of surrogate minister; but, Baxter continued, reading had the potential to provide much more. Books had certain ad-vantages over preachers:

> you may read an able Preacher when you have but a mean one to hear. Every *Congregation* cannot hear the most judicious or powerful Preachers: but every *single person* may *read* the Books of the most powerful and judicious. . . . Books we may have at hand every day and hour: when we can have Sermons but seldom, and at set times. If Ser-mons be forgotten, they are gone. But a Book we may read over and over till we remember it: and if we forget it, may again peruse it at our pleasure, or at our leisure. So that good Books are a very great mercy to the world.[10]

Baxter, who recognized that potentially inadequate preaching existed in the English provinces and abroad, often sent his works to outlying ar-eas.[11] Books gave all readers the opportunity to experience the most pow-erful preachers whenever and wherever they wished.

While hearing sermons and reading religious books were both ways that the colonial American experienced religious discourse, the two ac-tivities differed significantly. Michael Warner has argued that early New England sermons were read as if the minister were present and speaking directly to the reader, but it is important to note that Warner takes his examples from locally printed versions of locally preached sermons.[12] If the reader knew the author, then she or he could imagine them speaking; since imported books made up the largest percentage of books circulated throughout the colonies, however, many American readers had no way of personally knowing the European authors they read. They could not read sermons written by English divines as the spoken word transferred to the printed page because they had never heard them preach.

Unlike the spoken sermon, the book allowed readers to shape reli-gious discourse to suit their own experience. Warner suggests that the process of reading religious books meant internalizing the printed document's message. In the case of religious reading, the argument goes, print culture constrained rather than emancipated the reader.[13] While the process of catechism reading involved such thoroughgoing internalization, other religious texts encouraged the reader to become more involved with the book. Reading was a more active process than listening to sermons, because it required much more decision-making. In his comparison of books and sermons, Richard Baxter wrote, "We may choose Books which treat of that very Subject which we desire to hear of; but we cannot choose what subject the Preacher shall treat of." The possibility of individual choice distinguishes the activity of reading a religious book from the activity of listening to a spoken sermon. Naturally, a reader's choice was limited by availability—largely determined by family and community—but involvement with the text cannot be ignored. Even when the choice of books was limited, people could choose what to read within each book. The cumulative catechism reading imposed a deep bias on the colonial reader's decisions about what to read; but otherwise she or he could choose what books or parts of books to read. Often religious writers supplied prefatory comments which detailed ways that their books could be read selectively. Isaac Watts, for example, stressed that readers of his *Psalms of David* could pick and choose psalms to "suit their own Case and Temper, or the Circumstances of their Families and Friends."[14]

Owning books also helped readers tailor religious discourse to their personal needs. In *A Token for Children,* James Janeway stressed the value of book ownership as he mentioned specific volumes which young readers should "get your Father to buy you."[15] One of the books Janeway recommended was Thomas White's *A Little Book for Little Children*, a work which first appeared in England in the 1670s and which was reprinted in Boston during the early eighteenth century. Like Janeway, White emphasized the importance of book ownership: "As you read (if the Books be your own) mark in the margin, or by underlining the places you find most relish in, and take most special notice of, and that doth most concern thee, that you may easily, and more quickly find them again."[16] Explaining how to read and annotate a text, White allowed young readers to individualize the religious discourse and shape the book to suit themselves. The colonial American learned at an early age how to read selectively.

The popularity of ballads among seventeenth- and eighteenth-century readers made verse an attractive way to present religious matters. John Flavel, who included several poems in his widely-read devotional work, *Husbandry Spiritualized*, suggested that people would read poetry anyway, so devotional writers might as well supply poetry which would help bring their readers closer to God. It was better to provide people with religious verse than to let them read the ballads and "filthy songs" which they were used to reading. Echoing Flavel, Cotton Mather wrote: "I am informed, that the Minds and Manners of many People about the Countrey are much corrupted, by foolish Songs and Ballads, which the Hawkers and Pedlars carry into all parts of the Countrey. By way of Antidote, I would procure poetical Composures full of Piety, and such as may have a Tendency to advance Truth and Goodness, to be published, and scattered into all Corners of the Land."[17] While I do not imagine that religious hymns completely supplanted bawdy songs among the general public, Mather's efforts at least gave people more choice.

Children's authors found religious poetry especially appropriate for young readers. In his collection of children's verse, Isaac Watts wrote, "There is something so amusing and entertaining in rhymes and metre that will incline children to make this part of their business a diversion." Watts also emphasized that his book would help children with their closet devotions. Memorized verse would be "a constant furniture, that they may have something to think upon when alone, and sing over to themselves. This may sometimes give their thoughts a divine turn, and raise a young meditation. Thus they will not be forced to seek relief for an emptiness of mind out of the loose and dangerous sonnets of the age."[18] Reading and memorizing religious verse facilitated meditation.

Nathaniel Crouch, whose pseudonymous history and adventure books were extremely popular among colonial boys,[19] also wrote *Some Excellent Verses for the Education of Youth* (Boston, 1708). Judith Sewall, the youngest daughter of Samuel and Hannah Sewall, acquired a copy after her sixth birthday. She inscribed her name on the title page and the last page, and she wrote elsewhere in the book. Practicing her penmanship at the bottom of page two, Judith copied the first line from the poem, "The Ten Commandments," which occurs on that page: "Worship thou shalt no God but me." "Verses for Little Children," a long poem in iambic tetrameter couplets, takes up most of the book.

From this poem, many colonial children read, memorized, and repeated the following lines:

> Though I am Young, yet I may Die,
> And hasten to Eternity:
> There is a dreadful fiery Hell,
> Where Wicked ones must always dwell:
> There is a Heaven full of joy,
> Where Godly ones must always stay. . . .

This dark message in light verse often was included in subsequent editions of the *New England Primer*.[20]

Versified biblical history also helped girls and boys learn religion. The most widely read work was *The History of the Holy Jesus*, a metrical version of the New Testament. First published in London during the early eighteenth century, the work went through countless American editions over the next hundred years. During the colonial period, it was reprinted in New Haven, New London, and Boston. Its ballad stanzas—quatrains with alternating four stress and three stress iambic lines—emphasize that the author, known only as "A Lover of Their Precious Souls," wished to exploit the ballad's popularity and to make the work appealing, easy to read, and easy to memorize.

The History of the Holy Jesus begins with introductory verses recounting Adam's fall, in which children are told:

> And thus he broke his Lord's Command,
>   And Death did thence ensue,
> And thus Death comes, my Children dear,
>   On every one of you.

The story of Jesus' life follows the brief introduction, and many curious woodcuts illustrate the book. One, titled "Wise Men come from the East, &c," consists of a group of Puritan men gazing through telescopes at a shooting star. Another, showing Christ teaching the multitude, portrays Christ dressed as a New England preacher. His multitude consists of Puritan men and women. Some editions of *The History of the Holy Jesus* append extra verses. The 1747 Boston edition includes two devotional hymns and "The Child's Body of Divinity," a twenty-six line poem using internally rhymed, iambic tetrameter, each line of which begins with a different letter of the alphabet. Both devices help make the poem easy to memorize. The P and Q lines, for example, read:

Putting our Trust, in Christ the Just.
Quickning Grace, he'll give always.

Later editions of the *History of the Holy Jesus* include other poetry. The 1771 Boston edition—one surviving copy of which is inscribed "Judith Brown"—includes "St. Paul's Shipwreck," a metrical paraphrase of Acts 26 and 27.[21]

Isaac Watts wrote the verses read most widely among colonial women. Watts's *Hymns and Spiritual Songs* (1707), a work designed "to promote the pious entertainment of souls truly serious, over the meanest capacity," remained in print well into the nineteenth century. After its first publication in 1715, Watts's *Divine Songs Attempted in an Easy Language for the Use of Children* joined the *History of the Holy Jesus* as the two most popular books of children's religious verse in early America. During the colonial period, *Hymns and Spiritual Songs* and *Divine Songs* were reprinted in Connecticut, Massachusetts, New Hampshire, New York, Pennsylvania, and Rhode Island and were widely owned by women throughout the colonies.[22] In his preface to *Divine Songs*, Watts emphasized that his work was intended to appeal to readers of all faiths: "You will find here nothing that savours of a party: the children of high and low degree, of the Church of England or Dissenters, baptized in infancy or not, may all join together in these songs. And as I have endeavoured to sink the language to the level of a child's understanding, and yet to keep it, if possible, above contempt, so I have designed to profit all, if possible, and offend none."[23] Watts's description of his children's book applies to many of the most widely read religious books. The most popular works often bridged denominations.

In the preface to *Divine Songs*, Watts tells parents how to use the book to teach their children to read. Parents could encourage their daughters and sons to read and learn the book's contents by having them memorize one song a week and promising them the book itself after they had memorized ten or twenty songs from it. Watts thus establishes a parallel between a child's heavenly reward, the focus of the *Divine Songs*, and the earthly reward, the book. Devotion and book ownership were inextricably linked. The more devout you became, the more books you would own.

Watts's songs themselves link reading with salvation, encourage children's literacy, and prescribe ways to read. Song VII, "The Excellency of the Bible," for example, ends with the stanza:

> Then let me love my Bible more,
>   And take a fresh Delight,
> By Day to read those Wonders o'er,
>   And meditate by Night.[24]

Watts clearly emphasized the "read, then meditate" pattern which had been and continued to be an important aspect of a Christian's devotions. Song VIII, "Praise to GOD for learning to read," ended with an equation between learning religion and learning to read.

> O may that Spirit teach,
>   And make my Heart receive
> Those Truths which all thy Servants preach,
>   And all thy Saints believe.

> Then shall I praise the Lord
>   In a more chearful Strain,
> That I was taught to read his Word,
>   And have not learnt in vain.[25]

Some books of religious poetry that the colonial woman read first as a child remained on her bookshelf and in her heart throughout her life. Laurel Thatcher Ulrich has located evidence in material culture to substantiate Watts's ongoing popularity. A mid-eighteenth-century bedhanging made by Mary Bulman of Maine contains a complete poem by Watts as an integral part of its decorative crewelwork. Painter John Greenwood portrayed Catherine Moffatt of New Hampshire with her left arm resting on a volume of Isaac Watts.[26]

Elizabeth Graeme, who began writing a metrical paraphrase of the Psalms in 1766, explains her interest in a preface to her own manuscript version: "The Psalms of David have ever been a very favorite subject of my meditations. When I was very young my worthy mother frequently made me read the Psalms to her, and I so early imbibed a fondness for them that like all other first impressions they are like to be lasting."[27] Graeme's comment shows her reading psalms in three different contexts.

As a child, she read them in a family (social) setting for both entertainment and education. Not only did Elizabeth amuse her mother, she also showed what she had learned. Also, she read the psalms privately to prepare for meditation, a practice she began as a child and continued as an adult. Finally, she studied them as a scholar, reading the Biblical text to create her metrical versions.

The colonial woman had a wide variety of metrical psalms to choose from, but by the end of the colonial period, Isaac Watts's *Psalms of David* (1719) had become the most widely read version. Benjamin Franklin printed the first American edition of Watts's *Psalms* (Philadelphia, 1729); later colonial editions were printed in Massachusetts, New York, Connecticut, and New Jersey.[28] Describing early American women's education, a veteran teacher writing in the early nineteenth century recalled that daily reading of the Bible, combined "with the use of Watts's *Psalms* (a book which, with all the defects it may have, contains a rich treasure of *poetry* and *thought* as well as *piety*) at home, at church, and in singing schools, I regard as having furnished, more than *all other books and instructions*, the means of mental improvement, for 40 years of the last century."[29] While Watts's *Psalms* was a steady seller through the eighteenth century, it is important to realize that children as well as young men and women read a wide variety of ephemeral literature (ballads, chapbooks, songbooks), evidence of which scarcely exists. Benjamin Franklin helps put things in perspective. In his "Apology for Printers," Franklin, whose edition of Watts's *Psalms* had not sold as quickly as he had hoped, wrote: "I have known a very numerous Impression of *Robin Hood's Songs* go off in this Province at 2 s. per Book, in less than a Twelvemonth; when a small Quantity of David's *Psalms* (an excellent Version) have lain on my Hands above twice the Time."[30]

Watts died in 1748, but his works continued popular for many decades. After his death, Connecticut poet Martha Brewster eulogized:

> Great Watts is set, that bright and glorious star,
> Which oft conducted strangers from a-far
> To come by faith and view their sav'or's seat,
> And pay their humble tribute at his feet.[31]

Besides Isaac Watts, other poets the young colonial woman was most likely to read during the early eighteenth century were Abraham Cowley,[32] John Milton,[33] Richard Blackmore,[34] and Elizabeth Singer

Rowe.[35] Later in the colonial period, James Thomson and Edward Young became favorites. These poets differ in terms of the poetic genres employed. Cowley wrote elegies, a biblical epic, and pseudo-Pindaric odes. Milton's epic, *Paradise Lost,* was the most highly revered poem in colonial America. Blackmore wrote epic poetry based on English history but steeped in Christian doctrine. Rowe composed pastoral verse, hymns, and biblical paraphrases. Young and Thomson wrote lengthy meditative verse evoking the pleasures of the imagination.

While the styles and genres of the most widely read poets differed, their works, by and large, provoked emotions involving the religious sublime. Reading these poets inspired lofty religious feelings. Jane Colman Turell's poem, "On Reading the Warning by Mrs. Singer," hints that she read Elizabeth Singer Rowe's poetry for its sublime aspects: "Each noble line a pleasing terror gives, / A secret force in every sentence lives." The colonial woman also read James Thomson's *The Seasons* and Edward Young's *The Complaint: or Night-Thoughts on Life, Death and Immortality* for the terror, wonder, and awe they evoked.[36]

Hannah Adams's recollection of her youthful reading is characteristic. In her *Memoir,* she admitted that, before she was twenty years old, "the religious works I perused were chiefly devotional poetry, and such works as Mrs Rowe's Devout Exercises."[37] Elsewhere in her *Memoir* she writes, "I was also an enthusiastic admirer of poetry; and as my memory, at an early period, was very tenacious, I committed much of the writings of my favorite poets to memory, such as Milton, Thomson, Young, &c. . . . Another source of my enjoyments in early life was an ardent admiration of the beauties of nature. This enthusiasm was heightened by the glowing descriptions of poetic writers, and I entered into all their feelings."[38] Poetry of the religious sublime allowed eighteenth-century readers to indulge themselves with poetry without feeling that they were spending their time frivolously. While ballads and scurrilous verse were frowned upon, poetry which evoked feelings of religious sublimity received hearty approval.

Of course there was much else in these poems to attract the colonial woman; I do not want to imply that the religious content was the only thing which drew her to poetry. In letters written during the colonial period, Abigail Adams, for example, frequently quoted her favorite poet, James Thomson. Though Adams appreciated Thomson's meditative religious verse, she enjoyed many aspects of his poetry. Asking Mercy Otis Warren for advice on how to educate her children, Adams alluded to

Thomson: "I must beg the favour of you to communicate to me the happy Art of 'rearing the tender thought, teaching the young Idea how to shoot, and pouring fresh instruction o'er the Mind.'" Writing to her husband during the spring of 1776, she revised a passage from Thomson to apply the poet's words to the Continental Congress. Whereas Thomson had queried, "Oh! is there not some patriot in whose power . . . ," Abigail Adams writes, "Oh are ye not those patriots, in whose power. . . ."[39] But Abigail Adams's literary tastes were exceptional. The religious sublime remained the shared characteristic of the poetry read most widely by colonial women.

While the Bible and religious poetry were read in both public and private contexts, other religious literature was designed to be read privately. This private or secret reading was a crucial part of the colonial woman's closet devotions, a term which goes back to Christ's "Sermon on the Mount": "When thou prayest, enter into thy closet, and when thou hast shut thy door, pray to thy Father which is in secret; and thy Father which seeth in secret shall reward thee openly" (Matt. 6:6). Practicing closet devotions was a threefold process: read first, meditate second, and pray third. After his mother's death in 1721, Thomas Foxcroft aptly eulogized that she spent "much time with her BIBLE. And in Private Retirement she would be often Reading, and Conversing with GOD in Meditation and Prayer, while the rest of the Family were in Bed."[40] As Isaac Watts emphasized in his works, reading religious works prepared Christians for meditation, and meditation prepared them for prayer, the culminating activity of closet devotions.

The Bible was the book most likely to be read by the colonial woman in that private place metaphorically known as the closet, but it was by no means the only one. Benjamin Colman recommended that his daughter Jane read the Bible and "other useful Books" as part of her "daily Hours of secret Reading or Devotion." Cotton Mather, paying tribute to early New England women, wrote, "They have replenish'd and accomplish'd their Minds with Reading the Word of God, and Books of the best Composition." Quaker Thomas Chalkley praised eleven-year-old Philadelphian Hannah Hill for attending her devotions rather than playing in the streets, and he held up Hannah's reading as an example for other children: "She had an extraordinary Gift in Reading of the Holy Scriptures, and other Good Books, in which she took much Delight." The "other" books which Colman and Chalkley mention include pious lives, sermons, eucharistic manuals, and practical devotional works. Without exception, ministers of every faith advised parishioners to acquire books which supplemented, revealed, exemplified, or exalted the Bible's teachings.[41]

The practice of closet devotions usually began shortly after the child had mastered reading on her own. Many children's books designed for the closet contained somber descriptions of exemplary children who died at a young age. The best known were James Janeway's *Token for Children* (1671), which presented a series of biographies of pious children; Janeway's *Invisible Realities* (1673), a spiritual biography of his brother John Janeway; and Englishwoman Sarah Rede's *Token for Youth,* which described the life and Christian experiences of her daughter Carteret. In 1677, before Janeway's *Token for Children* had been reprinted in America, Increase Mather described the work as a book "which many of you have in your houses." Numerous copies of both Janeway works were imported into Boston during the 1680s and 1690s, and all three books mentioned were reprinted in Boston during the eighteenth century. Cotton Mather highly recommended Janeway's *Token for Children*: "Some worthy men, have made Collections, of Histories, concerning *little* children, that have given wonderful Instances of an *Early Piety* before they left the world. The Excellent *Janeway*, has done excellently well this way, in his *Tokens* [*sic*] *for Children,* which little Books, I most affectionately Recommend unto the perusal of you all." American editions of Janeway's *Token for Children* included Cotton Mather's appendix, "A Token for the Children of New-England." Though these works could be most often found in colonial New England households, they were not unknown elsewhere in the colonies. Janeway's *Token for Children,* especially popular among the Quakers, was reprinted in New Jersey and Philadelphia. To cite one further example, Virginian Sarah Suggett owned a copy of *Invisible Realities.*[42]

It is easy to imagine colonial children reading and memorizing *The History of the Holy Jesus* or Watts's *Divine Songs,* but it is more difficult to imagine them willingly retiring to their rooms to read Janeway's somber tales which describe little children becoming aware, before their deaths, of their inherent sinfulness. One story, for example, tells about a child who "had such extraordinary meltings that his eyes were red and sore with weeping for his sins."[43] On the other hand, Janeway's *Token for Children* was not necessarily unattractive to children. Janeway wrote using a children's vocabulary, and he takes children seriously.[44] Still, it seems unlikely that, given a choice, children would have chosen to read these stories rather than the more pleasing verse works. The title word which both Janeway and Rede used, *token*, suggests that the books were intended as gifts which well-meaning adults could buy for their young relatives. An inscription in a surviving copy of the 1771 Boston edition of *A Token for Children* confirms the suggestion: "Elizabeth Francis her Book Given by her Aunt Scollay October 1st 1771."[45]

If these stories seem gloomy, that was their intention. They were written specifically to provoke sadness and fear within the hearts and minds of young readers. In a preface directed to his child readers, Janeway warned them of the torments of hell ("worse a thousand times than whipping") and urged them, in order to avoid such misery, to read *A Token* "over an hundred times." Near the end of *A Token for Children*, Janeway provided specific information about his intended effect. He asked his young reader: "How art thou now affected, poor Child, in the reading of this Book? Have you shed ever a Tear since you begun reading?"[46] In her *Token for Youth,* Sarah Rede explained Janeway's effect on her seven-year-old Carteret. Rede found her daughter alone in her room, reading Janeway's *Invisible Realities*: "She was all in Tears, she said to me, Oh! that I were such a Worm as this was! that God would give me Repentance unto Life! Oh! that I were in the Bosom of Jesus! Oh! that my Sorrow might be true Sorrow!"[47] These stories were designed to make young readers recognize the precariousness of earthly life and to coax them into repentance.

Funeral sermons for children and adolescents served much the same purpose. In *Devout Contemplation on the Meaning of Divine Providence, in the Early Death of Pious and Lovely Children* (Boston, 1714), a funeral sermon for Elizabeth Wainwright, who died at the age of fourteen, Benjamin Colman reminded Boston children of the similarity between Elizabeth's condition and their own. Judith Sewall, who was just two years younger than Elizabeth (the two may have been good friends), acquired her copy just after it appeared.[48] Local sermons describing the lives of recently deceased children let ministers make the sense of loss more tangible, and such funeral sermons were effective—if number of copies sold can be taken as a gauge of their effectiveness. *A Legacy for Children,* the story of young Quaker Hannah Hill's last days, went through three editions in 1714–17.[49] The anonymous *Early Piety; Exemplified in Elizabeth Butcher of Boston* (Boston, 1718), the story of a devout girl who died a month before her ninth birthday, sold quite well.

Less than a year after it appeared, printer Samuel Gerrish had exhausted the unusually large first edition. Samuel Sewall, who may have helped to subsidize publication, recorded: "Mr. Gerrish thinks he must Print Elisabeth Butcher over again next week, though he printed a Thousand of them."[50] The American Antiquarian Society's copy of the fourth edition (1741) is inscribed: "Prudence Wales 1751, She was born December the 12 1736, given her by Abigail Hall."

John Joachim Zubly's *Real Christians Hope in Death* (Germantown, Pennsylvania, 1756), one surviving copy of which is inscribed "Helena Forman," vividly describes death scenes of many different people. Zubly, a South Carolina Presbyterian, shaped his work to appeal to a wide audience; he even got an Anglican priest in Charleston to write the preface. Zubly further broadened his work's appeal by making it applicable to both men and women. About half of Zubly's examples describe women's experiences during their last moments on earth: a sixteenth-century Italian woman, Olimpia Fulvia Morata, "who excelled in Learning & yet much more in Piety"; Magdalene Henry, a woman born of Roman Catholic parents, but converted to the Protestant faith; an unnamed French Protestant woman (the longest account in the book); and Sophia Hunter Jaegerin.[51]

Eucharistic manuals—books describing the meaning of the Lord's Supper and telling the reader how to proceed before, during, and after taking communion—were widely read by colonial women. Jabez Earle's *Sacramental Exercises* was first printed at Boston in 1715 and was reprinted frequently during the next forty years. One of the American Antiquarian Society's copies of the 1729 edition is inscribed "Nathaniel Heaton his book 1742; Abigail Heaton his [*sic*] book." Another copy of the 1729 edition was owned by Sarah Clark Hurlburt and "given by her to her daughter Ruth." The American Antiquarian Society's copy of the 1730 Boston edition of Thomas Vincent's *Companion for Communicants* is inscribed "Lucy Withington's book." The same book also contains the autograph of Betsy Tileston. Matthew Henry's *Communicant's Companion,* reprinted at Boston several times in 1716–31, was also popular among New England women. The American Antiquarian Society's copy of the 1731 Boston edition is inscribed "Sarah Nutting her book." The evidence of these inscriptions suggests that the eucharistic manuals were not kept for as long as other devotional books. The reader obtained a copy before becoming a communicant; after she or he began taking the sacrament, the usefulness of the book diminished, and it was given or sold to a friend or relative.

Many young women began reading devotional manuals during their early teens and continued reading them throughout their lives. The manuals read most widely share two common features: useful advice and accompanying prayers. Lewis Bayly's *Practice of Piety,* the devotional work most popular throughout seventeenth-century America, contained prayers for many different occasions, as well as useful advice on reading the Bible, practicing closet devotions, singing psalms, and observing the Sabbath. Though Bayly was Bishop of Bangor, *The Practice of Piety* is usually considered a Puritan work.[52] Copies of the treatise had been sent to Virginia by the London Company even before the Plymouth Colony was settled. Jane Porge, of Northumberland County, Virginia, owned a copy at the time of her death in 1651. The Dutch translation, *Practijcke der Godtsalicheyt,* could be found in New York. John Eliot translated the work into Algonquin as *Manitowompae Pomantamoonk.* Bookseller Elkanah Pembrook imported many copies into Boston during the 1690s. Imports could not meet the demand for the work in early eighteenth-century New England, and an edition was reprinted at Boston in 1718.[53]

An abridgment from Lewis Bayly's *Practice of Piety,* entitled *Meditations and Prayers for Household Piety* (Boston, 1728), especially appealed to women and their families. The unique copy which survives at the American Antiquarian Society is inscribed "Hannah Allin." The book begins with the sentence: "If thou beest call'd to the Government of a *Family,* thou must not hold it sufficient to serve God, and live uprightly in thine own Person, unless thou causest all under *thy Charge* to do the same with thee."[54] Just as the conduct books emphasized that women were responsible for their children's education, this edition of Bayly stresses that women also were in charge of edifying their children's souls. Furthermore, the edition reiterates the notion that religious texts were read selectively. Bayly's was a long, sprawling work. The editor's choice of passages from Bayly's larger work provides the text of a selective and purposeful reading of *The Practice of Piety.*

The most popular seventeenth-century Anglican works were similar to Bayly's in organization and content, if not in denominational slant. Jeremy Taylor's *Rule and Exercises of Holy Living* (1650) and his *Rule and Exercises of Holy Dying* (1651), usually bound and sold together as "Holy Living and Dying," were undoubtedly the most elegantly written seventeenth-century devotional works. The two remained popular well into the eighteenth century. In December 1764, for example, Mary Grimes bought a copy of "Living and Dying" at the *Virginia Gazette* office for her daughter Sally.[55] Taylor designed the two works for both male and female readers. Several of his prayers and instructions, such as the rules of conduct and the complementary prayers for virgins, widows, married women, and parents, specifically apply to women.

Richard Allestree's *Whole Duty of Man,* like Bayly's *Practice of Piety* and Taylor's *Holy Living and Dying,* contains both practical advice and prayers. While its author was an Anglican divine, he deliberately obfuscated his identity and wrote in an impersonal style to make the work appeal to a wide audience.[56] The title page puffed the work as "necessary for all families" and mentioned that it had been designed for "the meanest reader." *The Whole Duty of Man* was read throughout the colonies. Several copies were imported into New England during the 1680s, and Boston bookseller Michael Perry had it in stock in 1700. In a survey of selected colonial South Carolina library inventories, Walter B. Edgar found twenty-seven copies of the work, and it could be had in North Carolina as well. Englishwoman Mary Degge willed her Virginia grandniece and namesake, Mary Degge, her copy. It was in great enough demand in Virginia to justify a Williamsburg reprint in 1746. The popularity of *The Whole Duty of Man* among eighteenth-century colonial women was further enhanced by the inclusion of generous excerpts in *The Ladies Library.*[57]

The works of John Bunyan held a special place among early American readers. *Grace Abounding,* Bunyan's spiritual autobiography, was reprinted numerous times in Boston during the first half of the eighteenth century. The work provided a model for many early American spiritual autobiographies. *Rest for a Wearied Soul* was Bunyan's admonition to his children to fulfill their religious and social duties. The work contained a hodgepodge of advice, aphorisms, and devotional verse. A surviving copy of the New London edition (1765?) is inscribed "Betsy Hynes's book." The American Antiquarian Society's copy of Bunyan's *Come and Welcome to Jesus Christ* (Boston, 1728) is inscribed "Sarah Gould." Bunyan's best-remembered work, *Pilgrim's Progress,* was also widely read.[58] Boston bookseller Michael Perry had multiple copies of a London edition for sale at the time of his death in 1700, and there were numerous Boston editions during the colonial period. A German translation was printed at Germantown, Pennsylvania, in 1755.[59] Bunyan's allegory was quite unlike the other popular devotional works. The others provided specific advice and prayers to facilitate devotion, but *Pilgrim's Progress* provided an allegorical narrative exemplifying the Christian's struggle. The devotional manuals told readers how to become good Christians, but *Pilgrim's Progress showed* them.

While the inscriptions in surviving volumes indicate the kinds of religious books read by the colonial woman, they provide little information concerning *how* she read. Furthermore, few surviving documents written by early American women describe their religious reading in any detail. Many women's autobiographical narratives indicate the importance of reading, without detailing the reading process. Thus, "Some Account of the Fore Part of the Life of Elizabeth Ashbridge" takes on great significance as a document showing one colonial woman in the process of reading. Ashbridge's religious experiences were far from typical, but her experimentation with many different faiths exposed her to many devotional practices. In the account of her spiritual conversion, her comments on books and reading are more than a documentary record. Ashbridge makes her reading experience an integral part of the narrative. The act of reading marks a crucial turning point in her story.

Before her mid-twenties, Elizabeth had been exposed to many different religions but had not really settled on any particular one. She was raised in the Church of England. Her father, a ship's physician, often was away during her youth, but her mother gave her an education good enough to enable Elizabeth to work as a schoolteacher later. At fourteen, she forsook her parents to marry a young man who died within six months of their marriage. Still estranged from her father even after her husband's death, Elizabeth went to Dublin, Ireland, where she boarded with some Quaker relatives, although, at the time, she did not consider adopting their faith. She did, however, meet some Catholics and was briefly attracted to their religion. Before she was twenty, Elizabeth left Ireland to come to America, where she was sold as an indentured servant. Three years later, she bought out the final year of her four-year indenture and obtained her freedom—which lasted only until she married a man who, though nominally a member of the Church of England, was callous, abusive, and often drunk. She quickly recognized his faults but resolved to do her duty to God, become an obedient wife, and cope with her situation. Baptized in the Anglican Church during her infancy, she felt the need for a grander, more memorable gesture after her marriage and was baptized among the Baptists, though subsequently she never worshipped closely in that faith. Her husband, a kind of itinerant schoolteacher, disliked staying in one place for too long. His restlessness next brought her in contact with some Presbyterians and, after another remove, back to the Church of England, which, she admits, she preferred above the other religions she had so far encountered.

When Elizabeth became anxious to visit a Philadelphia aunt and uncle whom she had never met before, her husband could see no harm in it, so he gave her leave to go. The relatives turned out to be Quakers; indeed, her aunt was a Quaker minister. Before Elizabeth had been at their home for long, she came across a curious book. Elizabeth writes:

> I had not been there three Hours before I met with a Shock, & my opinion began to alter with respect to these People.—For seeing a Book lying on the Table (& being much for reading) I took it up: My Aunt Observing said, "Cousin that is a Quakers' Book," for Perceiving I was not a Quaker, I suppose she thought I would not like it: I made her no answer but revolving in my mind, "what can these People write about, for I have heard that they Deny the Scriptures & have no other bible but George Fox's Journal, & Deny all the holy Ordinances?" So resolved to read, but had not read two Pages before my very heart burned within me and Tears Issued from my Eyes, which I was Afraid would be seen; therefore with the Book (Saml. Crisp's Two Letters) I walked into the garden, sat Down, and the piece being Small, read it through before I went in; but Some Times was forced to Stop to Vent my Tears, my heart as it were uttering these involuntary Expressions; "my God must I (if ever I come to the true knowledge of thy Truth) be of this man's Opinion, who has sought thee as I have done & join with these People that a few hours ago I preferred the Papists before? O thou, the God of my Salvation & of my Life, who hast in an abundant manner manifested thy Long Suffering & tender Mercy, Redeeming me as from the Lowest Hell, a Monument of thy grace: Lord, my soul beseecheth thee to Direct me in the right way & keep me from Error, & then According to thy Covenant, I'll think nothing too near to Part with for thy name's Sake. If these things be so, Oh! happy People thus beloved of God.[60]

Earlier in Elizabeth's narrative, print culture and the written word played a crucial yet ambivalent role. In the first paragraph of her account, she wrote that "whosoever reads the following lines, may take warning and shun the Evils that I have thro' the Deceitfulness of Satan been drawn into."[61] Though the account was not published in her lifetime, her words showed clearly that she intended the journal to be read by others. The numerous surviving manuscript copies attest to the work's popularity before its initial publication in 1774, nearly twenty years after Elizabeth's death. While the opening admonition attached much importance to the written word, Elizabeth, when describing her indentured servitude a few pages later, wrote, "Were it possible to Convey in Characters a sense of the Sufferings of my Servitude, it would make the most strong heart pity the Misfortunes of a young creature as I was."[62] This statement suggested that there are limits on what the written word can express.

Printed works, too, Elizabeth goes on to imply, have limitations. During her indentured servitude, her master, a member of the Church of England, "used to Pray every Night in his family, except when his Prayer Book was Lost, for he never Pray'd without it that I knew of."[63] Most likely, he read from the *Book of Common Prayer,* but the phrase "his Prayer Book" also might refer to a devotional manual such as Jeremy Taylor's *Holy Living and Dying* or Richard Allestree's *Whole Duty of Man.* To be sure, the Anglican prayers were eloquent, but, Ashbridge implied, devout Christians needed to be able to compose their own prayers. Prayer books caused people to rely too heavily on the printed word and thus made it difficult for them to pray without it.

Despite her second husband's cruelty and insensitivity, she made up her mind that obeying him was part of her duty to God. Reading helped. She wrote: "I now resolved to do my Duty to God; & Expecting I must come to the knowledge of it by the Scriptures I took to reading them with a Resolution to follow their Directions."[64] Also, she visited an Anglican priest who lent her "a Book of prayers, which he said was fit for my Condition," but, as she stated, "all was in Vain."[65] Although the book apparently had been ineffectual, it was not entirely clear why. Ashbridge clarified what she meant as she described a subsequent moment of intense hope and faith: "In an Instant my heart was tendered, & I dissolved in a flow of tears, abhoring my Past Offences, & admiring the mercy of God, for I now was made to hope in Christ my Redeemer, & Enabled to Look upon him with an Eye of Faith, & saw fulfilled what I believed when the Priest lent me his Book (Viz.) that if ever my Prayers would be Acceptable I should be Enabled to pray without form & so used form no more."[66] This quotation makes it clear that the prayer book which the priest had given her was unhelpful because its formulaic prayers, which were supposed to be "fit" for her condition, hindered rather than aided her devotion.

Early in her account, Elizabeth explained how she had developed a fondness for reading plays. This activity, she had been given to hope, would allow her to become an actress and live like a lady. In a way, her play-reading episode paralleled the prayer-book experiences. Just as she had read plays with the hope of improving her life, others read prayer books to heighten their devotion and thus improve their chances in the afterlife. Both, to her, seemed a sham. The plays were scripts which allowed readers to mimic life, and the Anglican prayer books provided scripts allowing their readers to mimic devotion. Enacting plays imitated reality; reciting written prayers enabled some cruel and un-Christian people—such as her former master and her husband—to imitate devotion. Rather than facilitating her devotion, such prayers seemed to bar her from genuine faith.

Ashbridge's overall attitude toward books, as expressed in the part of the account detailing her life prior to her Philadelphia visit, seemed to be that the printed word—except for the Bible—could not effect spiritual change. Asserting the inadequacy of books early in the account gave the anecdote of her reading experience at her aunt's home all the more impact.

The book occupied a prominent place on a table in the Quaker home, but her aunt's reaction to Elizabeth's reading it made clear that the book has not been placed there for house guests to pick up and glance at casually during a visit. Someone in the household—perhaps the aunt herself—had set the volume down in the middle of reading it. The work was Samuel Crisp's *Two Letters Written . . . About the Year 1702, to Some of His Acquaintance, upon His Change from a Chaplain of the Church of England, to Join the People Called Quakers*, most likely the 1722 London edition, a twenty-four-page pamphlet. Seeing Elizabeth reading and knowing that the book emotionally explains one man's conversion from the Anglican to the Quaker faith, her aunt realized its potential danger to the impressionable Elizabeth. It was not that her aunt did not want Elizabeth to become a Quaker. After all, the aunt was a Quaker minister. Rather, she realized the problems which would arise with Elizabeth's Anglican husband if Elizabeth were to convert to Quakerism. In practical terms, gaining another convert was not worth the emotional strife her conversion would cause between Elizabeth and her volatile husband.

Elizabeth was not dissuaded by her aunt's warning. Her fondness for reading encouraged her to take up the book; her curiosity and her continuing discomfort with the religions she had experienced encouraged her to continue reading. The aunt left her alone, and Elizabeth kept reading, but she soon became uneasy. Afraid she would be seen, she went into the garden. Here, Elizabeth conveys the essentially private nature of devotional reading. At home, she no doubt practiced her closet devotions. Away from home, she felt the need to carve out her own private space for reading, a place where no one could interrupt her devotions and where she could give vent to her emotions without others seeing her.

As Elizabeth read Crisp's work, which told the story of his conversion from the Anglican faith to Quakerism, she realized that her own attitude toward religion was much the same as his. After she had read the first two pages of Crisp's work, she explained, "My very heart burned within me and Tears Issued from my Eyes." In those two pages, Crisp revealed his desire to delve more deeply into the mysteries of God's Kingdom and described his present frustrations with his upbringing in the Church of England. Elizabeth, too, had been brought up in the Anglican Church and, though she preferred it to all the other faiths she knew, still found it inadequate. A few pages later, Crisp admitted that he had not previously read any Quaker books. Elizabeth, too, wrote that she had never read any of their works. To gratify his curiosity about the Quaker faith, Crisp explained that by chance he had located a copy of Barclay's *Works* at a London bookseller's. Elizabeth happened upon Crisp's work similarly—by chance. In other words, the conversion story she read was quite similar to the conversion story she was in the process of writing.

Alone in the garden, she was free to let the book have its effect, and it so emotionally overwhelmed her that she frequently paused to wipe the tears from her eyes. The book's emotional effect culminated in what Ashbridge calls "involuntary Expressions." These expressions are clearly the most deliberate invention within the anecdote. In other words, it seems unlikely that an involuntary exclamation could be sustained for multiple sentences. Still, there is little doubt that the book had profoundly changed her in a way that no other book ever had. She read it straight through before going back inside.

That Sunday, excited about her newfound interest in the Quaker faith, Elizabeth attended a Quaker meeting. She was somewhat disappointed. She thought, "How like fools these People sit, how much better would it be to stay at home & read the Bible or some good Book, than to come here and go to Sleep."[67] At this point in her spiritual development, the power of the written word had become more persuasive than the spoken word—especially when that spoken word was punctuated by the long silences typical of the Quaker meeting. Although later she would learn to enjoy the Quaker meeting and ultimately would become a minister, the printed word had acquired a power for her which it had not formerly possessed. Before, books had represented rigid formulas with little applicability to life. Crisp's work, on the other hand, had showed her that the printed word, in the form of a touching personal story of religious conversion, could have a profound impact.

For Elizabeth Ashbridge, the narrative's personal approach made it preferable to the devotional manuals. While the manuals, written in the third person, prescribed behavior and provided accompanying prayers to facilitate such behavior, the conversion narrative, told in the first person, explained how one individual lived life. Writers such as Taylor and Allestree told their readers, "Here is what you should do to become a devout Christian"; but Samuel Crisp told his readers, "Here is what I did to become a devout Christian." Elizabeth Ashbridge found the "I did" to be much more persuasive than the "you should."

The practice of closet devotions did not change appreciably during the eighteenth century. Its intensity oscillated—lessening in the early decades of the century, increasing during the mid-century Great Awakening—but the read-meditate-pray pattern held. What did change was the closet reading material. To be sure, the Bible remained the book read most widely, and devotional manuals continued popular; but other kinds of books, too, started to be read in the closet. The dividing line between belletristic essays and religious literature had blurred, and devout books with literary pretensions, as well as works advocating rational, commonsense approaches to religion, came to be read widely in and out of the closet.

Throughout colonial America, the author most popular during the early decades of the eighteenth century was Archbishop John Tillotson.[68] New England divine Benjamin Colman cited Tillotson more often than any other writer, and Colman's own works became quite popular with eighteenth-century New England women. Like Tillotson, Colman believed that good prose helped make good Christians. Colman broke with the rigid pattern of the Puritan sermon and made religious discourse more like an Addisonian essay. Instead of relying solely on textual exegesis,

Colman used witty tropes and dramatic scenes to illustrate his spiritual messages.[69] The subscription list to Ebenezer Turell's *Life and Character of the Reverend Benjamin Colman* (Boston, 1749) indicates Colman's lasting popularity among New England women. Subscribers included Rebecca Amory, Mary Bennett, Hannah Glover, Mary Johnston, and Prudence Prentice.

Not only did Colman's prose style make his writings attractive, but also his message itself differed significantly from the somber ones characteristic in the seventeenth century. Whereas Janeway deliberately had written to make children weep in the face of their inherent wickedness, Colman daringly suggested that laughter was permissible, and he wrote several sermons on the subject. Colman's *Government and Improvement of Mirth* (Boston, 1707), a work designed especially for young people, clearly signals a shift in attitude. An inscription in the Clements copy of the first edition indicates that the volume formerly was in the possession of Sarah Allen and had been given to her by Pheby Sampson.[70] In the work, Colman emphasized the compatibility of mirth and religion. Mirth was perfectly acceptable, so long as it did not lead to excesses such as filthiness, foolish talking, or jesting. "A chearful Spirit, or Pleasantness of Temper," Colman argued, was a gift of God "to be used to his glory."[71] Mirth was also useful to "refresh and recruit tir'd nature in its work," to preserve health, foster friendship, and increase love among Christians.

William Law's *Serious Call to a Devout and Holy Life* (1728) provides a good touchstone for early American devotional practice. More than any other writer, Law, an Anglican divine, embodied the diverse religious attitudes and practices that were experienced in English-speaking communities during the seventeenth and eighteenth centuries. His beliefs straddled both centuries, and his *Serious Call* captured elements of each. Law echoed seventeenth-century Puritan devotional practice, yet he wrote with the same Addisonian flair and liberal belletristic sensibility that Colman exhibited. Law significantly influenced John Wesley and George Whitefield, who in turn had an important impact on religious attitudes in America.

The charm of Law's *Serious Call* derived partially from his picturesque Theophrastian characters. His most vivid creations were the characters of Flavia and Miranda, "two maiden sisters that have each of them two hundred pounds a year." Each sister spends much of her money on books. Flavia "buys all books of wit and humor, and has made an expensive collection of all our English poets. For she says, one cannot have a true taste of any of them without being very conversant with them all." Miranda, on the other hand, "is sometimes afraid that she lays out too much money in books because she cannot forbear buying all practical books of any note, especially such as enter into the heart of religion and describe the inward holiness of the Christian life. But of all human writings, the lives of pious persons and eminent Saints are her greatest delight. In these she searches as for hidden treasure, hoping to find some secret of holy living, some uncommon degree of piety which she may make her own."[72] The devout colonial woman fit somewhere between the two extremes of Flavia and Miranda. Like Miranda, she often read practical religious books and lives of pious people, but she also knew the polite writers whom Flavia preferred.

The Great Awakening led women to attend more diligently to their faith and their studies, and this renewed diligence prompted a change in the colonial woman's reading material. George Whitefield abhorred Tillotson's writings, and he actively discouraged his listeners from reading the archbishop's sermons. On his travels through the southern colonies in 1740, Whitefield recorded a story of the wife of a wealthy South Carolina planter "who once had been 'a great admirer of Archbishop Tillotson' but now had 'her eyes . . . opened to discern spiritual things' and could no longer put up with 'such husks, fit only for carnal, unawakened, unbelieving Reasoners to eat.'"[73] With equal vehemence, Whitefield tried to discourage people from reading the still-popular *Whole Duty of Man,* although he had to admit that he himself had been influenced by the work.[74]

Whitefield encouraged colonial women not only to read recent evangelical authors, but also to reread long-standing colonial favorites. Thomas Prince described his daughter Deborah's experience:

When Mr. *Whitefield* came and preached in the *Fall* of the *Year ensuing*; she . . . was excited to a livelier View of Eternity, to a greater Care of her immortal Soul, to a stricter Search into Herself, and a more earnest Labour after vital Piety and the Power of Godliness, and to make them more the Business of her Life. And now such Experimental and Searching Writers as Mr. *Shepard* of *Cambridge,* Mr. *William Guthry* of *Scotland,* Mr. *Flavel* and *Mead* of *England,* Mr. *Stoddard of North-Hampton,* and Mr. *Mather* of *Windsor* in *New-England,* &c., were more diligently read and highly valued.

Deborah Prince's experience was hardly unique. Her father explains that she shared the experience "with Multitudes of Others."[75] Jane Dunlap was profoundly influenced by Whitefield, as shown by her *Poems on Several Sermons, Preached by . . . George Whitefield* (Boston, 1771). In the poem which begins the collection, Dunlap paid tribute:

> Most worthy man, of thy dear name,
> In love I'll mention make,
> Both for thine own, and for thy works
> And for thy masters sake.
>
> Dear Whitefield's name I'll not forget,
> That name to me so dear,
> That's made me glad, and also sad,
> And cost me many a tear.

Literary sentimentalism, which emerged concurrently with the evangelical movement and shortly after the popularity of the religious sublime peaked, greatly shaped woman's devotional reading, starting in the 1750s. Sentimentalism diluted the sublime. Sentimentalists blurred the differences between the sentiment and the sublime and essentially blended the two together. The notion of sublimity began to be applied to anything in art or nature which strongly excited the feelings.[76] The one author who excited the religious feelings of colonial American women (and men) more than any other during the second half of the eighteenth century was James Hervey.[77]

After Hervey's *Meditations and Contemplations* appeared at midcentury, it could be found from New England to Georgia.[78] Hervey had designed the work specifically for female readers. Addressing his dedicatory epistle to a young woman, "Miss R—— T——," he told her that the following reflections originally had been written for "a Lady of the most valuable Endowments: Who crowned all her other endearing Qualities, by a cordial Love of CHRIST" but who "lives no longer on Earth; unless it be in the Honours of a distinguished Character, and the bleeding Remembrance of her Acquaintance."[79] The dedicatory epistle makes Hervey's work suitable for women of all ages: young women such as Miss R—— T—— who aspire to lead a devout life and older women such as the "Lady" who led a devout life.

While modern readers may find it difficult to understand Hervey's immense popularity, it becomes more comprehensible when seen within the context of early American devotional practice. Hervey helped revitalize the colonial woman's closet devotions. Imagining one's inherent sinfulness had become increasingly difficult by the mid-eighteenth century. Readers needed tangible, concrete subject matter upon which they could focus their religious meditations. Hervey provided many examples of everyday subjects which could be used as a basis for spiritual meditation. One spring evening in 1755, Esther Edwards Burr, for example, wrote in her journal, "How extreamly the silence of the Night resembles the silence of the grave. Mr Hervy has most butifully painted in his Contemplations on the nig[ht]."[80] Of course, Burr had no way of knowing what the silence of the grave was like, but she did know what the silence of the night was like—especially on those nights when her husband was away tending to college business and after she had put her daughter Sally to bed. Reading Hervey, she could take time on those quiet, lonely nights to listen to the night and imagine the silence of the grave.

Sentimentalism achieved its literary pinnacle with the works of Laurence Sterne. *Sermons of Mr. Yorick* (1760) was Sterne's most widely read work, but his other works achieved popularity near the end of the colonial period. His *Sentimental Journey through France and Italy* was reprinted in Boston in 1768—one surviving copy is inscribed "Eliza A. Whittemore."[81] *Letters from Yorick to Eliza* were published at Philadelphia in 1773. Philadelphia printer James Humphreys issued Sterne's multivolume *Works* (1774), one copy of which survives with the inscription "Elizabeth Seccombe, Brookline." Humphreys also issued the third and fourth volumes of the *Works* separately, as the two-volume *Sermons of Mr. Yorick*. Several copies of "Yorick's Sermons" were sold at the *Virginia Gazette* office during the mid-1760s.[82] *Tristram Shandy*, however, was much less popular among colonial women readers. Abigail Adams wrote:

> I have read Sterns Sermons and Yoricks Sentimental journey [and] his Letters to Eliza, but I never read *Shandy* and I never will. I know it would lessen my opinion of him, I know it would sink him in my Esteem. It is not in humane Nature, to regard those we dispise.
>
> What I have read are the purest of his works, even in these there are exceptionable passages, but so intermixed with a rich Stream of Benevolence flowing like milk and Honey, that in an insensible heart, he

creates the sensations he discribes—in a feeling one, he softens, he melts, he moulds it into all his own.

Possessed of an exquisite Sensibility, a universal phylanthropy, what a perverse Genius must he have to hazard those fine powers and talents for a wicked wit, that admits of no defence, and almost calls in Question the stability of his understanding. *Shandy* should have considerd that true wit

"Was not a tale, was not a jest
Admir'd with Laughter at a feast
Much less could that have any place
At which a Virgin hides her face."[83]

While many colonial women may have read Yorick's *Sermons*, others could have heard them from the pulpit. It was commonplace for lay readers to rely on the work when there was no preacher nearby. One time, North Carolinian Penelope Dawson wrote, the local minister did not show up on Sunday morning, and so a law student (and later associate justice of the United States Supreme Court), James Iredell, "with his usual good nature obliged us so far as to Officiate in Mr. Bruce's stead and gave us an excellent discourse out of Yoricks' Sermons."[84] Describing frontier life at Fort Pitt, Benjamin Franklin wrote with wry pleasure: "The People have Balls for Dancing, and Assemblies for Religious Worship, but as they cannot yet afford to maintain both a Clergyman and a Dancing-master, the Dancingmaster reads Prayers and one of Tristram Shandy's Sermons every Sunday."[85]

To be sure, Sterne's blatant plagiarism of Tillotson's *Sermons* partially accounts for the popularity of "Yorick's Sermons." Sterne's generous borrowing seems especially ironic in light of Benjamin Franklin's "Silence DoGood, No. 4," in which Silence envisions "The Temple of Theology" where she sees "*Plagius* . . . diligently transcribing some eloquent Paragraphs out of *Tillotson's Works, &c.* to embellish his own."[86] But Sterne did not get his sentimentalism from Tillotson, and sentimentalism, more than anything else, is what made Yorick's *Sermons* popular. In one sale catalog, James Rivington puffed the work by explaining that Sterne "aims at mending the Heart; inculcating every moral Virtue . . . these Discourses are universally read and admired, they are Elegant without the Affectation of appearing so, and Familiar without Meanness."[87] North Carolinian Margaret Macartney, voicing the attitude of many American women during the late colonial period, wrote to a correspondent: "I am quite of Sterne's opinion, 'the tender sensations are the most valuable parts of humanity, and whoever endeavors to detract them from the soul, endeavors to rob her of the most precious gift of Heaven.'"[88]

When it came to coping with adversity and death, women traditionally bore a greater share of the burden than men, and many books specifically designed to help the reader cope with loss circulated among colonial women. Several copies of John Flavel's *Token for Mourners* (1674) were imported into Boston during the last two decades of the seventeenth century, and the work was reprinted in Boston at least four times during the first three decades of the eighteenth.[89] In this book, Flavel described Christ's advice to a distressed mother bewailing the death of her only son. In *Companion for the Afflicted* (Boston, 1701), a work based on a talk given at a private meeting, Cotton Mather provided similar advice. His intimate tone and homely prose, however, made the work more appealing to the colonial woman than more public modes of discourse.

William Sherlock's urbane and witty treatise, *Practical Discourse Concerning Death* (1689), originally written as a series of sermons for lawyers of the Temple, was the most widely read Anglican treatise on the subject. Describing the contents of an English "lady's library" in *The Spectator* 37, Joseph Addison listed "*Sherlock* upon Death."[90] Later, Addison would call the work "one of the strongest Persuasives to a religious Life that ever was written in any Language" (*Spectator* 289). Sherlock's *Practical Discourse Concerning Death* went through many English editions during the colonial period, and it was reprinted at Williamsburg in 1744. Over thirty copies were sold in 1750–52 at the *Virginia Gazette* office, making it the book most frequently sold there except for the almanac. Other copies could be found in the Carolinas and Georgia.[91] Yet another work, William Dodd's *Reflections on Death*, appeared near the end of the colonial period and remained a steady seller for the next half-century.

Inscriptions in surviving copies of these works provide key evidence concerning book circulation and its relation to mourning. The American Antiquarian Society's copy of the 1725 Boston edition of Flavel's *Token for Mourners* is inscribed "Mary Huntington's book. Given her by her Aunt Belcher." Huntington's aunt may have given her the book after the death of a child. One copy of Mather's *Companion for the Afflicted* survives with the inscription "Eunice Borllinggames Book Given to hur by hur Mother Chandler in the year 1749." It had been forty-eight years since the book was printed, but it still made an appropriate gift during times of sorrow. Chandler herself may have been given the book when she experienced some affliction earlier in her life, and now she was passing it along to help another during a time of loss. The Clements copy of William Dodd's *Reflections on Death* (Boston, 1773) is inscribed "This book given to Mrs. Mercy Davis at the funeral of Elizabeth Coburn." Books about how to cope with death, the inscription indicates, often were presented during times of mourning. Every book presented carried the implicit message from its giver: I understand and want to help you cope with your loss.

One of the religious books Priscilla Carter may have read in the 1770s was the anonymous Anglican work, *A Lady's Religion*. The work is listed in the inventory Philip Vickers Fithian made of her father's library, and it was also available to other colonial readers.[92] The anonymous editor of the third edition of *A Lady's Religion* explained in his preface that he first read the book at a woman's request: "When I heard the Title of the Book, *A Lady's Religion, &c.*, I expected to find in it, Formularies of Devotion, Prayers for particular Days, Directions for Closet Exercises, Confessions of a List of Sins, and Receipts for Saintship," but instead he found "a most rational Treatise." For the editor, *A Lady's Religion* represented a considerable advance over prior religious books for women. Instead of the practical manuals and pious lives normally associated with women's devotional reading, *A Lady's Religion* contained a well-organized, thoughtful, and well-presented religious treatise. To the modern reader, however, the editor's comments are unsettling. Though he praised the treatise for its rational presentation of religion, he also praised it because it told women neither more nor less than they needed to know. It told them "what in Religion was truly Good, and what accidentally so; what she ought not to be satisfy'd without, and what she might innocently not concern herself with; in a Word, what would carry her to Heaven safely, and what answer'd no other Purpose, than either to furnish Matter of Dispute for wrong-headed quarrelsome Divines, or to distinguish Religious Sects, or to employ the idle Hours of Devotees."[93] What the editor was really applauding was the way the book imposed limits on a woman's knowledge. For him, the book was worthwhile as much for what it told as for what it did not tell its female readers. Such attempts to circumscribe woman's knowledge are even more apparent in connection with conduct books.

CHAPTER 3

Conduct Books

During the early 1770s, Mary Cary Ambler took a journey from Fauquier County, Virginia, to Baltimore in order to get herself and her children, Sally and Jack, inoculated against smallpox. As it turned out, the trip took much longer than expected. The doctor's first attempt to inoculate them failed, and he had to send to Philadelphia for more serum. The diary which Ambler kept during the experience ably conveys her frustration at waiting for the inoculation to take effect. Fortunately, Mrs. Chilton, the woman with whom she was staying, had books enough for her guest to read. One day Mary Ambler recorded in her diary, "A Rainy Day (very dull) if it were not for Books & knitting . . . would be at a great loss how to fill up the Day."[1]

After the day-to-day account, Ambler's diary contains miscellaneous information from the trip, including money she spent, a topographical description of Baltimore, and a passage which she transcribed from one of the books she had read, James Fordyce's *Sermons to Young Women* (1765), the women's conduct book read most widely during the last decade of the colonial period. Mary Ambler introduced the extract with the note: "From Mr Fordyce's Sermons to Young Women. this Paragraph is transcribed for the use of the Copi[e]st & She begs her Daug[hte]r to observe it well all her Life." She then copied the following passage concerning a women's proper conduct: "If to Your natural softness You join that christian meekness, which I now preach; both together will not fail, with the assistance of proper reflection and friendly advice, to accomplish you in the best and truest kind of breeding. You will not be in danger of putting yourselves forward in company, of contradicting bluntly, of asserting positively, of debating obstinately, of affecting a superiority to any present, of engrossing the discourse, of listening to yourselves with apparent satisfaction, of neglecting what is advanced by others, or of interrupting them without necessity."[2]

This one episode indicates a variety of reading situations which took place in early America. First, it indicates the practice of sharing books, so common among early American women. Mrs. Chilton's hospitality clearly extended to letting her house guest borrow books from her own collection. Though Ambler was married and had two children, her introductory note to the extract from Fordyce shows that she recognized that the advice for young women also applied to her. Even more, she saw that Fordyce's words applied to her daughter. Once she had transcribed the passage into her diary, Ambler could return and reread the passage whenever she wanted. Furthermore, the transcription guaranteed that, even if her daughter Sally never saw a copy of Fordyce's book, she at least would be able to read a key passage from it. Clearly revealing Ambler's desire for Sally to read the diary once she got older, the introductory note provides further evidence that the volumes on the colonial woman's bookshelf were not limited to printed works. Such cherished manuscript works as a mother's diary made for important reading. Also, by admonishing her daughter to follow the advice in the introductory note, Ambler appropriates Fordyce's words and makes them her own. She thus gives her daughter advice which has a double authority. It comes not only from a minister's sermon but also from her mother.

Understood within their social contexts, the conduct books American women read during the seventeenth and eighteenth centuries often spoke with such multiple voices. Loosely defined as any writing which gives advice concerning how to behave, conduct literature could speak from the point of view of a minister, a mother, a father, or a peer. The voice of women's conduct books, however, must be recognized not only as the narrative voice inherent within the text itself, but also as a voice refracted through the framework of early American society. More than any other type of book in early America, conduct manuals were acquired as gifts. The purchaser, in other words, was not necessarily the consumer. Most often, parents bought such books for their adolescent daughters. As a mother's or father's gift, a book would be endowed with authority beyond the written text. Through the act of giving, givers sanction a book's message and make it their own.

Richard Allestree's *The Lady's Calling* (1673) was the earliest seventeenth-century women's conduct book which frequently could be found on the colonial woman's bookshelf. Though published anonymously, *The Lady's Calling* established its authority on the title page, which showed that it was written "by the Author of the Whole Duty of Man." Like *The Whole Duty of Man, The Lady's Calling* was written in an impersonal style, so as to make the work appeal to readers of all faiths. Despite the aloof narrative stance, the text makes clear that Allestree believes what he advocates. In *The Lady's Calling,* he appears firmly committed to his religious and moral purposes.[3] That kind of commitment is absent from some later conduct books which were little more than hastily assembled hackwork.

In one form or another, *The Lady's Calling* sold well throughout the colonial period. An anonymous editor, capitalizing on the popularity of Allestree's books, published *The Whole Duty of a Woman,* a work largely plagiarized from *The Lady's Calling,* with an additional section including recipes for meals, medicines, and perfume. In 1700, Boston bookseller Michael Perry had multiple copies of *The Whole Duty of a Woman* in stock. *The Ladies Library* contained generous excerpts from *The Lady's Calling.* In 1722, Mary Degge of Virginia inherited *The Lady's Calling* from her aunt. Since Daniel Dulany's Maryland library contained a copy at the time of his death in 1753, any or all three of his wives may have read the work.[4]

The Lady's Calling was divided into two parts, dealing with the virtues a woman should possess and the roles she should fulfill. The first part indicated that a woman should be modest, meek, compassionate, affable, and pious. Elaborating upon these feminine virtues, Allestree often juxtaposed them to masculine attributes. Women should cultivate meekness because they are inferior to men. Women more easily could be compassionate and pious, because they did not share their husbands' weighty public responsibilities. Running a household, the author implied, was a comparatively easy job which allowed women plenty of extra time for their closet devotions. The second part of *The Lady's Calling* detailed a woman's duties as virgin, wife, and widow. A wife's greatest duty, of course, was to obey her husband and patiently tolerate his faults. Her greatest responsibility was to care for her children, providing for both their physical and their mental well-being. Allestree put women in a difficult position, however. While stressing their responsibility for educating children, he never emphasized that women themselves needed to be educated. Apart from a brief reference to women's learning in his preface, Allestree never broached the subject. He rarely mentioned reading, except to caution young women against the influence of evil books and to admonish bespectacled old women who indecorously read romances.

After its publication, Lord Halifax's *The Lady's New-Year's-Gift, or, Advice to a Daughter* (1688) circulated widely throughout colonial America. While Halifax's prose is more graceful than that seen in the other conduct books, the work's literary merits alone cannot account for its attractiveness to contemporary readers. Unlike Allestree's anonymous and largely impersonal work, *The Lady's New Year's Gift* speaks from an intimate point of view. Halifax wrote the work for his daughter Elizabeth as a present, but his advice concerning religion, marriage, behavior, and conversation was pertinent to many young colonial women. The fatherly advice gives the work its force. The female reader, as Kathryn Shevelow has convincingly shown, responded to Halifax's advice in much the same way as she would have responded to advice from her own father.[5] Halifax's fatherly advice became the advice of every father who gave the work to his daughter.

Like Allestree, Halifax devoted little space to the subject of women's reading. Not surprisingly, his remarks concern how reading could facilitate piety. In this way, Halifax anticipates *A Lady's Religion*. Though books could help a woman with her devotions, she should avoid those which might bring her faith into question: "In respect that the Voluminous Enquiries into the *Truth,* by Reading, are less expected from you. The *Best* of *Books* will be direction enough to you not to change; and whilst you are fix'd and sufficiently confirm'd in your own *Mind,* you will do best to keep vain *Doubts* and *Scruples* at such a distance, that they may give you no disquiet."[6] In other words, she should read the Bible and such devotional books as *The Whole Duty of Man,* but she should not read any theological works which might challenge her religious notions or make her think too deeply.

Such advice became part of the feminine ideal in colonial America. After Mary Lloyd's death, Ebenezer Pemberton published her *Meditations on Divine Subjects* (New York, 1750), prefixing a biographical sketch. He wrote: "She read the sacred Pages, and other religious Tracts, not so much to encrease her *speculative Knowledge,* and gratify the Inclinations of an *inquisitive Mind;* as to learn the self-denying Mysteries of the Cross of CHRIST,—*detach* her Affections from the *Creature,* and *unite* them more vigorously to the ORIGINAL SOURCE of Perfection and Blessedness."[7] In other words, Mary Lloyd's avid reading properly came from her piety, not from her desire for knowledge.

François de Salignac de la Mothe Fénelon, archbishop of Cambray, wrote an important women's educational treatise, *Traité de l'education des filles* (1687), but he was better known as the author of *L'Avantures de Télémaque* (1699), the French book read most widely in colonial America.[8] Since reading French was an accomplishment expected of the well-to-do colonial woman, many—like Philadelphian Sally Logan—read the work in the original. Others read it in the English translation, *The Adventures of Telemachus*. The book was sometimes used to teach French. Boston booksellers Edward Cox and Edward Berry stocked copies in French and English, as well as ones with parallel English and French texts. James Rivington had parallel text editions for sale in New York and Philadelphia.[9] Perhaps the book's most prominent colonial woman reader was Elizabeth Graeme, who translated the work into English verse. In the preface to her manuscript translation, Graeme explained that *Telemachus* had been one of her favorite books ever since childhood.[10] Written for Fénelon's pupil, the young Duke of Burgundy, the book is a fictional retelling of the adventures of Ulysses' son, designed to help guide the young leader. However, the work also contains a section which describes the proper feminine virtues. In conversation, Telemachus discusses the accomplishments of his love, Antiope. She is an exemplar of modesty, reserve, and diligence. She expertly manages her father's household. She is not self-conscious about her beauty or her intelligence. Her lively imagination is checked by her discretion. The summary of these feminine virtues comes not from a cleric or a father, but in the voice of Telemachus, the young woman's attractive suitor.

The respect the colonial woman had for Fénelon's *Telemachus* helped to popularize *Traité de l'education des filles,* a work Fénelon had been prompted to write because of the deplorable state of women's education in the late seventeenth century. Like Allestree, Fénelon made his book as objective as possible so that it would appeal to a wide audience. Though the work of a Catholic archbishop, the treatise contains little that a Protestant could have opposed. Fénelon apparently permitted women to study a wider range of subjects than did his contemporaries. A woman should learn how to write and keep accounts, and she should acquire a basic understanding of the law. Fénelon saw nothing wrong with teaching her Latin but suggested that she must cultivate an enjoyment of reading before she studied languages. Histories of Greece and Rome could provide her with examples of virtuous conduct. While Fénelon seems to allow women a considerable breadth of reading, his educational plan ultimately sought to constrain rather than expand woman's intellectual freedom. Fénelon's treatise was motivated by his wish to divert the woman from the salon and return her to the home, to turn her away from polite society and toward the domestic sphere. To be sure, he wanted women to learn how to keep accounts and know the basics of law, but he wanted them to know these things to help them manage their estates.[11]

Fénelon condemned the female pedant who ostentatiously displayed her learning but could not apply it practically. Women's minds, he suggested, were fundamentally different from those of men. While women were more inquisitive than men, their minds were weaker. They might seek knowledge, but they might not be able to handle it. Furthermore, there were certain realms of learning women need not understand: "They are not destined to govern the state, to make war, or to minister in holy things; so they may pass by certain extended fields of knowledge that belong to politics, the art of war, jurisprudence, philosophy, and theology."[12] Fénelon put no stock in the idea of knowledge for knowledge's sake. If a woman was curious about politics, it hardly mattered. She could not participate in politics, so there was no need for her to read about it.

In colonial America, Fénelon's *Traité de l'education des filles* was found most often in George Hickes's English translation, *Instructions for the Education of a Daughter* (1707). Hickes added a postscript to his translation which specifically recommended what books a woman should read. Besides the Holy Scriptures, she should also read such devotional works as *The Whole Duty of Man*; William Cave's *Primitive Christianity*; Robert Parsons's *Christian Directory,* a work which had gone through countless editions since its first appearance in 1585; Augustine's *Meditations*; and Robert Boyle's *Some Considerations Touching the Style of the Holy Scriptures,* as well as Boyle's *Martyrdom of Theodora.* The only poetry Hickes mentioned was Abraham Cowley's "Davideis," an epic based on the biblical history of David, and Cowley's "Pindarique Odes." Hickes also suggested two works written by Mary Astell, *A Serious Proposal to the Ladies* and *Christian Religion.* The latter work had been published just a few years before Hickes's translation appeared. Of course, Hickes mentioned *The Lady's Calling* and Halifax's *The Lady's New Year's Gift.* His recommendations are still limited, but they do mark an advance over Fénelon. While Fénelon permitted women to read history as a way of seeing "examples of virtuous conduct," Hickes allowed women to read history for no reason other than curiosity: "If she be curious, her time will not be lost in turning over the best Histories and Memoirs."[13]

Fénelon's *Dissertation on Pure Love* (1735), though not precisely a conduct book, provided its readers with much additional information about how to behave. The book was especially appealing to female readers because it contained many letters written by Jeanne Marie Guyon concerning her religious principles. South Carolinian Martha Laurens, for example, once asked to borrow a friend's copy of the work, promising to "take great care of the book."[14] Guyon was an attractive figure, and her biography also was popular. Philadelphian William Logan gave his daughter Sally a copy of *The Life of Lady Guion* (Bristol, England, 1772).[15] The feminine voice of her epistles within Fénelon's *Dissertation* makes the advice for young women more persuasive. Many editions of the work were published through the 1760s, including one at Philadelphia (1738) and another at Germantown, Pennsylvania (1750).[16] Overall, Fénelon's works strongly influenced colonial American thought concerning women's education.

The earliest homegrown woman's conduct book was Cotton Mather's *Ornaments for the Daughters of Zion* (Cambridge, Mass., 1692). The first edition was exhausted within two years, and a second appeared in 1694. Mather still had plenty of copies on hand eight years later, but he made diligent efforts to circulate the work. At the funeral of his first wife, Abigail, in 1702, he presented copies of *Ornaments* to many women "who 'first and last' waited upon his·wife during her long sickness."[17] When George Whitefield came across a copy of *Ornaments* decades later, he admired it and recommended it highly. Whitefield's enthusiasm for the work prompted a new edition in 1741.[18]

Ornaments for the Daughters of Zion is organized as a sermon. It begins with a biblical text and moves through doctrine to application, which latter consists of seven different counsels. The last and largest counsel provides advice for the maid, wife, mother, and widow. Describing the attributes of the "virtuous maid," Mather provided some specific pointers about reading: "Such is her *Devotion,* that while she *prudently* avoids the reading of *Romances,* which do no less naturally than generally inspire the Minds of young People with *Humours,* that are as *Vicious* as they are *foolish*; on the other Side, she *piously* reads the Bible every Day."[19] In the section discussing the virtuous maid's industry, Mather wrote, "Such is her *Industry,* that she betimes applies herself to learn all the Affairs of *Housewifery,* and besides a good Skill at her *Needle,* as well as in the *Kitchen,* she acquaints herself with *Arithmetick* and *Accomptantship,* (perhaps also *Chirurgery*) and such other Arts relating to *Business,* as may enable her to do the *Man* whom she may hereafter have, *Good and not Evil all the Days of her Life.* If she have any Time after this to learn *Musick* and *Language,* she will not loose her Time, and yet she will not be proud of her *Skill.*"[20] While Mather's comments appear to limit a woman's activities to domestic concerns, it is important to note that many of the skills Mather listed were learned from books. Reading and writing were taught before arithmetic; Mather's suggestion that women learn accounting presupposes that they already knew how to read.[21] Mather had clear priorities concerning women's reading, however. He allowed the young woman the possibility of studying languages—Latin, Greek, and Hebrew—but she should pursue such erudition only after learning those accomplishments which would allow her to serve her *Man.* Then and only then should she seek knowledge for its own sake.

The women's conduct book most widely circulated during the first half of the eighteenth century was *The Ladies Library* (1714). Historically attributed to Sir Richard Steele, the work now is known to have been compiled by George Berkeley.[22] It was advertised for sale from Massachusetts to South Carolina, and it shows up in subscription library catalogs and inventories of private libraries throughout the colonies. For example, Walter B. Edgar found it listed several times in his survey of selected South Carolina estate inventories. In a letter to his wife Deborah, Benjamin Franklin recommended that their daughter Sally read the work "over and over again."[23]

The Ladies Library consists of unacknowledged excerpts from conduct books and Anglican devotional manuals and is organized similarly to *The Lady's Calling.* The first volume is subdivided into separate sections describing the virtues that a woman should possess and the vices she should avoid, and it includes chapters concerning employment, wit, delicacy, recreation, dress, chastity, modesty, meekness, charity, envy, censure, ignorance, and pride. The second volume describes a woman's duties as daughter, wife, mother, widow, and mistress. Berkeley's sources include: *The Lady's Calling,* Halifax's *The Lady's New Year's Gift,* Fénelon's *Instructions for the Education of a Daughter,* Astell's *Serious Proposal to the Ladies,* Richard Lucas's *Practical Christianity,* and Jeremy Taylor's *Rule and Exercises of Holy Living,* among others. When the work first appeared, Richard Royston, who owned the rights to Jeremy Taylor's works, complained about Berkeley's blatant plagiarism, but such liberal borrowing was widespread. Many editors and booksellers took for granted that popular didactic materials were in the public domain.[24]

Berkeley made no attempt to revise the appropriated texts to apply their advice specifically to women. In the preface to the work, Sir Richard Steele wrote: "In Matters where both Sexes are equally concern'd the Words Man and Men are made use of, but the Matter does not for that Reason the less relate to Women, or argue that the Work is not principally intended for the Information of the Fair Sex." Since the work retains the masculine pronouns of its sources, much of its advice was helpful regardless of the reader's gender. Men could and did read and benefit from *The Ladies Library*. Jonathan Edwards, for example, made use of the work, and many Harvard undergraduates read it.[25] Nevertheless, Berkeley had shaped the book for a female audience. In the preface, Steele explained that the work itself had been given to him by a woman friend who compiled it as "a Guide to her own Conduct, and if thought worth publishing, to be of the same Service to others of her Sex, who have not the same Opportunities of searching into various Authors." Steele's female friend, a fictional persona created by Berkeley, serves an important narrative function. His sources—with the exception of Mary Astell's *Serious Proposal*—speak in a masculine voice, but the various extracts are introduced and framed by the words of the female friend, a woman with "a Strong Propensity to Reading" who believes that "it is a great Injustice to shut Books of Knowledge from the Eyes of Women." The feminine voice thus co-opts the masculine sources and makes them her own.

In the introductory chapter, she relates how she spent one day perusing the polite writers—Otway, Milton, Dryden—and came across nothing but blatantly misogynous comments. She writes, "I could not have believed from their general and undistinguished Aspersions that many of these Men had any such Relations as Mothers, Wives or Sisters."[26] As a result, she explains, she will avoid the "polite" writers and restrict herself to "more solid Authors." She concludes her introduction: "I resolve therefore to confine my little Studies, which are to lead to the Conduct of my Life, to the Writings of the most eminent of our Divines, and from thence, as I have heard young Students do in the study of a Science, make for my own private Use a Common-Place, that may direct me in all the relations of Life, that do now, or possibly may, concern me as a Woman."[27] The pretense that this work was one woman's common-place book made it attractive to female readers. Commonplace books most often were kept by ambitious college men bent on a course of self-improvement. This female commonplace book suggests that women, too, could take advantage of such opportunities for reading and self-improvement. In addition, Berkeley's female persona gives the work a sense of intimacy. She created the work for her own use and now has decided to share her private experience with other women.

Ned Ward, the Grubstreet poet and essayist, also recognized the value of writing from a female perspective, and his works which address women's issues were well known in early America. During the first half of the eighteenth century, it was common knowledge—if Alexander Pope can be believed—that Ward had a large American readership. In the *Dunciad*, Pope deprecatingly wrote that, in "Ape-and-monkey" climes, vile tobacco was traded for Ward's "viler rhymes." Footnoting the reference, Pope stated, "Great numbers of his works were yearly sold into the Plantations."[28] One of Ward's books which could be found on the colonial woman's bookshelf was *Female Grievances Debated: In Six Dialogues Between Two Young Ladies,* an anonymous work published in London around 1710. Demand for *Female Grievances Debated* remained high enough to warrant a Boston edition some years later. In Virginia, both Frances Parke Custis and Martha Washington may have read the work.[29]

By presenting his material as a prose dialogue between two young women, Eliza and Mariana, Ward made *Female Grievances Debated* appeal to women readers. Even his title emphasized the book's feminine perspective. Other conduct books asserted that women should quietly accept their lot in life, but *Female Grievances Debated* let women know that it was acceptable to voice complaints. The work presented a discussion of love and marriage, defining love, distinguishing it from lust, describing how to tell whether a man or a woman was in love, condemning those who married for money, and proposing taxes for men who neglected to marry. While *Females Grievances Debated* was a breezy work, it nevertheless advanced some important concepts. At one point, Mariana told Eliza, "I am easily perswaded to believe that our Sex are very much imposed upon and cheated out of their *Natural Liberty.* For, since we are furnished by *Nature* with the same *Propensity* to *Love* as *Men,* I think it is but reasonable we should enjoy an equal Freedom of declaring our Minds whenever we see Occasion, without Incurring the least Reflection for so Innocent a Discovery."[30] Mariana's phrase, "*Natural Liberty,*" invoked the seventeenth-century Whiggish thinkers from James Harrington to Algernon Sidney and John Locke; her words asserted that natural law applied equally to women and men.

An additional Ward work concerning women's issues could be found on the colonial woman's bookshelf. This was *Nuptial Dialogues and Debates; Or, A Useful Prospect of the Felicities and Discomforts of a Marry'd Life* (1710). Patrons of the Hatboro, Pennsylvania, Union Library often borrowed it, and the Library Company of Philadelphia owned two copies. The work was widely available for purchase, and a new Boston edition was advertised around the middle of the eighteenth century.[31] *Nuptial Dialogues* presented a series of brief verse dialogues between stereotypical husbands and wives—a melancholy gentleman and his merry bantering wife, a salacious monarch and his barren consort, a surly drunkard and an inflexible termagant. The work appealed equally to male and female readers; the couples were evenly matched in debating ability. Both husbands and wives made valid criticisms of their spouses' behavior and worthily defended their own actions. While a seemingly humorous work, the last dialogue in the collection reveals its underlying didactic purpose: "Familiar Chat between a loving Couple, concerning their own Happiness."

In the 1740s, Benjamin Franklin published *Reflections on Courtship and Marriage* (Philadelphia, 1746), a work which became popular both in America and abroad. Franklin sent copies to Elizabeth Timothy to sell at her Charleston, South Carolina, bookshop, as well as to booksellers in New York and Maryland. London and Edinburgh editions appeared in 1750, and a second Philadelphia edition was published in 1758.[32] Some attribute *Reflections on Courtship and Marriage* to Franklin while others assert he did not write it.[33] Neither the style nor the viewpoint was similar to Franklin's. From the Silence DoGood essays to the *Autobiography,* Franklin's own writing evinced a progressive attitude toward women's education, while *Reflections* echoed a more customary stance toward women's learning. Like Fénelon, the writer of *Reflections* attributed the shortcomings of young women to inadequate education; but also like Fénelon, the writer condemned the female pedant, "whose Brain is loaded with a Heap of indigested Stuff, and is eternally throwing up her confused Nonsense, in hard Words ill pronounced, jumbled Quotations misapplyed, and a Jargon of Common-Places; in order to let you know she is a Women of Reading."[34] Despite such an indictment, the work emphasized that women should read more than they do. Franklin's reason for publishing *Reflections on Courtship and Marriage*, I believe, involves the work's conceptual framework. While earlier conduct books were religiously based, *Reflections* was a secular work.[35]

Eliza Haywood's *The Female Spectator*, one of the most important books which could be found on the colonial woman's bookshelf, originally was issued in monthly parts from April 1744 to May 1746, but it could be found much more often in one of the later collected editions. Copies were available from New England to Georgia throughout the last three decades of the colonial period.[36] Though much more than a conduct book, *The Female Spectator*'s primary didactic purpose was to influence the behavior of its female readers. Unlike so many of the other conduct book writers, Haywood sought to expand rather than circumscribe the woman's sphere. To be sure, she provided numerous anecdotes and characters to emphasize the traditional feminine virtues—modesty, charity, chastity—but, most significantly, she emphasized the importance of reading. Haywood's paean to books is worth quoting in full:

> What clods of earth should we have been but for reading!—how ignorant of every thing but the spot we tread upon!—Books are the channel through which all useful arts and sciences are conveyed.—By the help of books we sit at ease, and travel to the most distant parts; behold the customs and manners of all the different nations in the habitable globe; may take a view of heaven itself, and traverse all the wonders of the skies.—By books we learn to sustain calamity with patience, and bear prosperity with moderation.—By books we are enabled to compare past ages with the present; to discover what in our fore-fathers was worthy imitation, and what should be avoided; to improve upon their virtues, and take warning by their errors.—It is books which dispel that gloomy melancholy our climate but too much inclines us to, and in its room diffuses an enlivening chearfulness.—In fine, we are indebted to books for every thing that can profit or delight us.[37]

Later in *The Female Spectator*, Haywood elaborated upon the importance of reading and encouraged women to learn history, geography, and the natural sciences.

In 1753, *The Whole Duty of a Woman* was first published in London. It is important to distinguish this work from the similarly titled work published over a half century before. While different from the older work, the new *Whole Duty of a Woman* was reactionary. The work indicates that the forward-looking ideas of Eliza Haywood and Benjamin Franklin were far from being universally accepted. Its heavy-handed, conservative stance toward a woman's place is more backward than most seventeenth-century conduct books. Its author, William Kenrick, was an enterprising hack writer with a keen understanding of what the reading public wanted. He never shied away from sensationalism or slander in order to sell books. *The Whole Duty of a Woman* struck a note different from Kenrick's scurrilous earlier treatises lambasting London's leading men of letters, but the work reflected the same impulse to profit from the labor of others. When viewed among Kenrick's sensational pamphlets, *The Whole Duty of a Woman* appears much less like the serious work of a stern moralist attempting to shape the behavior of young eighteenth-century women and much more like hack work capitalizing on profitable trends. Kenrick's title links his book with Allestree's still-popular *Whole Duty of Man,* and his pseudo-biblical style owed a debt to Robert Dodsley's widely read *Oeconomy of Human Life.* Based on the number of reprints and bookseller's advertisements, *The Whole Duty of a Woman* enjoyed considerable colonial success. The work was first reprinted at Boston in 1761, and it was often reprinted throughout the remainder of the eighteenth century.[38]

Like the earlier works, *The Whole Duty of a Woman* was subdivided into sections providing advice on such topics as vanity, affectation, chastity, virginity, marriage, education, and religion. The title page claimed that the book was written "by a Lady." Kenrick's persona was a fallen woman who sorely regretted having lost opportunities to achieve feminine virtue: "O that I could overtake the wings of time! O that I could recall the pleasures of my youth! for the days of my womanhood have been days of many sorrows; the tears of misfortune have bedimmed the lustre of mine eye; the lily is fallen, and the rose-bud is blown and withered on my cheek."[39] Kenrick's reactionary attitude toward a woman's limitations, his female persona, and his pseudo-biblical style clashed, creating a discordant narrative stance. Using the first person plural would have helped to create a sense of camaraderie between Kenrick's female persona (narrator) and its female readers. Instead, the narrator addressed readers in the second person and thus created a distancing effect which diminished the credibility of the female persona. Consider the following diatribe on women's education:

It is not for thee, O woman, to undergo the perils of the deep, to dig in the hollow mines of the earth, to trace the dark springs of science, or to number the thick stars of the heavens.

Let the kingdom rule itself, let the wise-men and the counsellers enact laws, and correct them; the policy of government is a hidden thing, like a well of water in the bottom of a deep pit.

Thy kingdom is thine own house, and thy government, the care of thy family.

Let the laws of thy condition be thy study, and learn only to govern thyself and thy dependants.[40]

The book continued to be sold through much of the eighteenth century, but I have located no evidence to show how colonial women reacted to this book. It may have been more often purchased by well-meaning fathers than read by normally obedient daughters. Colonial men continued to find messages like Kenrick's agreeable. In 1753, the same year *The Whole Duty of a Woman* was first published, a poem called "Advice to the Fair Sex" appeared in the *Boston Gazette*. The speaker of the poem recommended: "To a wise Husband ev'ry Thought submit, / Nor trust a *Female Forwardness* of Wit."[41]

Besides those books discussed so far, a number of other conduct books could be found on the colonial woman's bookshelf: the Quaker Moses West's *Treatise Concerning Marriage: Wherein the Unlawfulness of Mixt Marriages Is Laid Open* (Philadelphia, [1738]), one surviving copy of which is inscribed: "Elizabeth Bowne";[42] Edmund Moore's *Fables for the Female Sex* (1744), a work which Jenny Byrd and her sisters may have read in Virginia and which was reprinted at Philadelphia in 1762;[43] John Taylor's *Value of a Child; Or, Motives to the Good Education of Children* (Philadelphia, 1753), a letter from a father to a daughter who had just borne a son; *The Accomplish'd Woman* (1753), an English translation of Jacques du Bosc's *L'honneste femme*, a work which asserted that the woman's temperament made her better able to study the arts and sciences;[44] John Hill's *On the Management and Education of Children: A Series of Letters Written to a Niece* (1754), a work published under the pseudonym Juliana Seymour, which both Abigail Adams and Mercy Otis Warren read;[45] *The Young Lady Conducted; From Her Leaving the School to Her Entering upon the World* (1754), a series of dialogues written by a parent for a daughter's edification;[46] *The Young*

Gentleman and Lady Instructed (1759), a work largely derived from the *Spectator* and from Locke's *Some Thoughts Concerning Education;*[47] *The Two Mothers; or the History of Antigone and Phronissa; Shewing How Antigone Laughed at Her Good Old Grandmother, and Married Her Daughters, before Sixteen to a Laced Coat and a Fashionable Wig—and How the Wiser Phronissa Instructed Her Daughters in Reading, Dressing, Singing, Dancing, Visiting, &c., in Order to Make Them Happy and Useful in the Rising Age* (Boston, 1759);[48] Thomas Marryat's *Female Conduct* (1760), a lengthy poem which, among other things, recommended reading history, geography, Shakespeare, and Milton;[49] James Hervey's *Treatise on the Religious Education of Daughters* (Boston, 1762), a copy of which could be found in the Mather library;[50] the Abbé d'Ancourt's *Lady's Preceptor; or, A Letter to a Young Lady of Distinction, upon Politeness* (Woodbridge, New Jersey, 1762); Anne Thérèse de Marguenat de Courcelles, Marquise de Lambert's *Polite Lady; or, A Course in . . . Education,* a series of letters between a fictional mother and daughter which emphasized the importance of women's education;[51] and Jeanne-Marie Leprince de Beaumont's *Instructions for Young Ladies on Their Entering into Life, Their Duties in the Married-State, and Toward Their Children* (1764).[52]

Historical and biographical treatments of women taught conduct through example. Many early histories provided specific examples of women's roles in history. Nahum Tate's *A Present for the Ladies: Being an Historical Account of Several Illustrious Persons of the Female Sex* (1693), a late-seventeenth-century work which could be found in early America, was not organized chronologically like a history or a collection of biographical sketches, as the title suggested.[53] Instead, it was organized like *The Lady's Calling.* The historical women whom Tate chose to mention lost their individual personalities as their virtues were discussed piecemeal under various headings. Like *The Lady's Calling* and *The Ladies Library,* the work contained a second section describing women's roles, this time in the form of a poem, "The Character of an Accomplish'd Virgin, Wife, and Widow." George Ballard's *Memoirs of Several Ladies of Great Britain* (1752) was read widely during the second half of the eighteenth century. Ballard specifically included women who had been "celebrated for their writings or skill in the learned languages, arts and sciences."

A work frequently borrowed from the Hatboro, Pennsylvania, Union Library was *Biographium Foemineum: The Female Worthies; or, Mem-*

oirs of the Most Illustrious Ladies of All Ages and Nations (1766), a collection of alphabetically arranged biographical sketches.[54] While not as overtly didactic as Tate's *Present for the Ladies, The Female Worthies,* as the work became known, implicitly conveyed notions of the feminine ideal similar to those of the conduct books. The women portrayed within the work were "eminently distinguished for their magnanimity, learning, genius, virtue, piety, and other excellent endowments." The author asserted that the British women of a century and a half before had been much more learned than those of the mid-eighteenth century: "Queens, princesses, and ladies of quality, then, found the most agreeable amusements in their closets, in the study of languages, and in scientific and philosophical enquiries. The muses were their delightful companions, and the *Belles Lettres,* the garden from whence they plucked the finest flowers to adorn their minds, and add a lustre to all their noble qualities."[55] Mid-eighteenth-century women, the author implied, had fallen from the standards set by their forebears, but it might be possible for them to recapture the earlier enthusiasm for learning.

The Ladies Complete Letter-Writer (1763), a work which could be found from Boston to Williamsburg during the last decade and a half of the colonial period,[56] differed from the other advice books in both format and focus. While it sought to teach women how to write letters for every occasion on a variety of subjects, the collection, taken as a whole, also could be read as a conduct book. The title page puffed it as "a collection of letters, written by ladies, not only on the more important religious, moral, and social duties, but on subjects of every other kind that usually interest the fair sex: the whole forming a polite and improving manual, for their use, instruction, and rational entertainment." The work was published anonymously, and, while its editor is not generally acknowledged, the collection was assembled by the minor British novelist and one-time American traveler, Edward Kimber.[57]

According to Kimber's preface, *The Ladies Complete Letter-Writer* was the first book of its kind. Letter-writing manuals were commonplace, and examples of letters written by women had been published in periodicals and other books, but Kimber's was the first letter-writing manual compiled specifically for women. He selected the letters from a variety of published sources, including works by Eliza Haywood. Kimber chose the letters not only to provide examples of good letter writing, but also to serve as conduct literature: "Most of those I have made choice of, at the same time that they render the Fair Reader Mistress of an elegant Stile, are fraught with such Instructions as cannot fail of having the best Effect upon her Mind; inculcating the Practice of every Moral and Social Duty, and tending to make her happy, by making her wise and virtuous."[58] In addition, Kimber supplied "many Original Letters never before published," explaining "as they are not the Issue of my own Pen, but supplied by the Friendship of Persons of approved Sense and delicate Manners."[59] Kimber's earlier novels reveal that he was a master of pseudo-veracity, and his remarks here also seem feigned. An accomplished litterateur, Kimber most likely composed many letters himself. He, too, recognized the importance of the female voice for inculcating virtue.

In his introduction, Kimber described how easily women could learn good letter writing: "The Epistolary Stile and Manner may be as easily acquired, as the Knowledge of any Branch of Domestick Employment or Oeconomy."[60] He also supplied specific directions as to how the book should be read and used: "By frequently perusing, copying, and imprinting the Language of them on their Memories, they will soon learn to express themselves with Grace and Freedom upon all Manner of Subjects."[61] In other words, simply reading the book was not enough. In order to internalize fully the letters' style and content, the reader needed to copy and recopy them.

To further improve their writing style, Kimber suggested that women peruse "the most approved Writings in their native Tongue, as the Lucubrations of the *Spectator, Tatler, Guardian, Rambler, Connoisseur,* and *Adventurer.*"[62] The recommendation may have been inspired partially by a woman he met in Maryland. After falling into the Chesapeake Bay and nearly drowning, he was nursed back to health by a young African woman whom he later commemorated in the poem "Fidenia." In a footnote to the poem, Kimber described Fidenia as "a very beautiful Negro Girl, aged 16, from *James* River in *Guinea,* who, by every superior Accomplishment, seems far beyond any of her Kind. She learnt the *English* Tongue in three Months Time, and in four, read the *Spectators* and *Tatlers* with inimitable Grace."[63]

The first letter in the collection, "From Lady * * * to her Daughter, a Girl twelve Years old, under the Care of her Grandmother in the Country," remains Kimber's most intriguing, both for its content and its placement as the first letter. In the introduction, Kimber had explained that he selected the letters "to come home to every Occasion that can, almost, arise, in the Course of their Lives, as Daughters, Wives, Mothers, Relations, or Friends."[64] The comment suggested that the letters would be organized chronologically according to the different phases in a woman's life. As a model letter, however, the first one was directed to mothers with adolescent daughters. As conduct advice, on the other hand, it was more pertinent to their daughters. The first letter thus signals Kimber's intent to make the book both a letter-writing manual and a conduct book.

The first letter is important also because it embodies the attitudes of three generations of women. After all, the mother is writing to her daughter who is staying with her grandmother. The mother writes: "I am certain you will be kept to your Music, Singing and Dancing, by the best Masters the Country affords; and need not doubt, but you will very often be told, that good Housewifery is a most commendable Quality. I would have you indeed neglect none of these Branches of Education; but. . . ."[65] In other words, the mother recognizes that *her* mother will encourage the traditional female accomplishments, but she (the girl's mother) also wants to make sure that her daughter receives a better education than she herself received in adolescence. The mother tells her daughter to "devote two Hours, at least, every Day, to Reading." Then she recommends some specific types of reading: "Poetry, if it be good, . . . very much elevates the Ideas, and harmonizes the Soul; and well-wrote Novels are an Amusement, in which sometimes you may indulge yourself; but History is what I would chiefly recommend;—without some Knowledge of this, you will be accounted at best but an agreeable Trifler.—I would have you gay, lively and entertaining; but then I would have you able to improve, as well as to divert the Company you may happen to fall into."[66] Finally, the mother suggests that her daughter learn the sciences as well.

After its first publication in 1765, James Fordyce's *Sermons to Young Women,* the work which Mary Ambler read with such enthusiasm during her stay in Baltimore, quickly became the best-known woman's conduct book in colonial America. Literary tastes had changed significantly since Allestree had published *The Lady's Calling.* Most important, the sentimental novel had emerged as a dominant literary genre. Aware of his literary competition, Fordyce shrewdly recognized that he had to make his work compete with other books being read by young women at the time, such as Samuel Richardson's *Pamela* and Frances Moore Brooke's *History of Lady Julia Mandeville.* Of course, the novels which intricately detail the emotions and virtues of their heroines often them-

selves were read as conduct books.[67] After all, both Fordyce and the novelists were attempting to explore a woman's emotions, thoughts, and sentiments, in order to reveal the inner workings of the heart. Fordyce essentially codified the kinds of feminine behavior that the novels' heroines
exemplified. Explaining his approach in the preface to the *Sermons*,
Fordyce wrote that young women no longer would tolerate a "dull discourse" and that there were "few hearers who will attend to that by
which their hearts are not engaged, or their imaginations entertained."
Rather than simply entertaining the imagination, he sought to "engage
the heart, with a view to mend it."[68]

Fordyce's sentimental stance helped to make the book a huge success. When Boston booksellers Cox and Berry included an advertisement
for Fordyce's *Sermons* in their 1772 sale catalog, they emphasized as the
work's main attraction his sympathetic narrative voice:

> Though this Author is a professed advocate for that sex, which leads
> the world, he does not however address them in the usual strains of
> flattery and adoration, but in the sober and impartial stile of friendship.
> He entertains the highest idea of their importance and destination; and
> does not consider them in that debasing light in which they are too of-
> ten considered, as formed only to be domestic drudges, and the slaves
> of our pleasures; but as intended to be reasonable and agreeable com-
> panions, faithful and affectionate friends, the SWEETNESS and the CHARM
> OF HUMAN LIFE. There are no compositions of this kind in the English
> language in which are to be found greater delicacy of sentiment, cor-
> rectness of imagination, elegance of taste, or that contain such pictures
> of life and manners. *Happy the Mothers who follow his Maxims in
> forming the taste and manners of their daughters! Happy, thrice happy
> the daughters who are blessed with such mothers.*

Copies of Fordyce's *Sermons to Young Women* could be found
throughout the colonies. The book shows up in estate inventories from
Massachusetts to the Carolinas. At his death in 1768, Boston bookseller
Jeremy Condy had the work in stock. Massachusetts attorney Francis
Dana owned a copy of Fordyce's *Sermons*. North Carolinian James
Reed's estate inventory shows a copy of Fordyce's *Sermons to Young
Women*. Subscription libraries—the New York Society Library, the Li-
brary Company of Philadelphia—had copies on their shelves. The bor-
rowing records of the Hatboro, Pennsylvania, Union Library shows that

its copy often was checked out during the 1760s and the 1770s. The title is frequently listed in bookseller's advertisements.[69] Shortly after its publication, British bookseller William Strahan highly recommended Fordyce's work to Philadelphia bookseller David Hall—who soon had it for sale.[70] The *South Carolina Gazette* was one of many colonial papers that advertised Fordyce's *Sermons* during the 1760s. The work was reprinted in Boston by John Mein in 1767; one copy from that printing, inscriptions tell us, was owned by Susan L. Phillips, Phoebe Foxcroft, and Lucretia Huntington.[71]

Surviving diaries and letters indicate that Fordyce's recommendations were read and heeded by colonial women, whether mothers, daughters, or sisters. In 1766, Francis Hopkinson wrote his sister Ann in Philadelphia, sending her a copy of Fordyce.[72] The following year Abigail Adams wrote her sister Mary Smith Cranch that she was reading Fordyce's *Sermons to Young Women* and promised to send the work to her as soon as she had finished it. She wrote, "I cannot say how much I admire them, and should I attempt to say how justly worthy they are of admiration I fear I should not do justice to this most Excellent performance."[73]

Fordyce's work became so well known that the colonial woman was virtually required to know the work. While courting Hannah Johnston in 1772, James Iredell recorded reading Fordyce's *Sermons to Young Women*. His diary signals the influence of Fordyce's sentimentalism. Iredell gushed: "I have been reading . . . Fordyce's Sermons, which I admire and love above all things—How elegant, how just, how noble his Sentiments!—Excellent Man! May your Writing be productive of the universal good they are calculated to occasion—and Oh! what Rapture do I feel in reading him, when I compare my dear Hannah with his Standard of female Excellence!—My dear, lovely Girl, what Bliss have I not in expectation with you?"[74] Did Hannah Johnston know she was being compared to Fordyce's example of the ideal woman? Did other men compare women to Fordyce's feminine ideal? If so, the women had better read Fordyce to know what they were up against.

In his sermons, Fordyce included extensive comments concerning the proper books women should read. Poetry was acceptable, so long as the verses paid strict attention to decorum. History and biography were worth reading because they provided examples of "passions operating in real life and genuine characters; of virtues to be imitated, and of vices to be shunned; of the effects of both on society and individuals; of the mutability of human affairs."[75] Works of imagination such as fables, visions, and allegories also were sanctioned by the Reverend Fordyce because "Fancy sports under the control of Reason; Dramatic writings also, where truth of character and purity of thought are preserved." Ultimately, however, Fordyce fell back on the viewpoint which had been part of the woman's conduct book since before *The Lady's Calling,* phrasing it even more bluntly than had some earlier writers: "Your business chiefly is to read Men, in order to make yourselves agreeable and useful." Despite this reactionary statement, Fordyce allowed women more latitude in reading than many previous conduct book writers. Even while learning how to "read Men," Fordyce tells his female readers, "in this study, you may derive great assistance from books."[76]

Near the end of the colonial period, another women's conduct book gained considerable attention throughout America: John Gregory's *A Father's Legacy to His Daughters.* First published in London in 1774, copies quickly reached America. On 14 November 1774, Annapolis bookseller and publisher William Aikman announced that he had received "The celebrated Dr. Gregory's Legacy to his Daughters, just published." The shipment of books came at a particularly appropriate time— just in time for the Christmas season.[77] Aikman found the work in great enough demand to have it reprinted for him in early 1775. Like previous women's conduct books, the first American edition of Gregory was promoted as a gift book which fathers could purchase for their daughters. Aikman sold two different versions, both of which were marketed as gift books. The less expensive version was available "bound and gilded." The more expensive was available "thrown off on a superfine writing paper, elegantly bound and gilt."[78] The work was also reprinted in New York in 1775 by Samuel Loudon and Frederick Shober. Loudon had a keen eye for money-making ventures. His involvement in printing the work confirms its salability.

Gregory's narrative stance was much the same as Halifax's had been nearly a century before. The former appeared as an aging man imparting last-minute advice to his young daughters. Yet Gregory had to do more than Halifax in order to imbue his message with authority. He had to invoke the image of the daughters' long-deceased mother. Since their mother died young, they had been unable to benefit from her prudent advice. His advice was not his own, he suggested; instead, it was his wife's: "As my sentiments on the most interesting points that regard life and manners, were entirely correspondent to your mother's whose judgment and taste I trusted much more than my own."[79] It was this rhetorical device which gave Gregory's voice authority. He then proceeded to supply advice on religion, behavior, leisure, friendship, love, and marriage. While Gregory did not object to women's reading, he reiterated the cautions against female pedantry which Fénelon and the anonymous *Reflections on Courtship and Marriage* also had emphasized: "Be even cautious in displaying your good sense. . . . it will be thought you assume a superiority over the rest of the company. But if you happen to have any learning, keep it a profound secret, especially from the men, who generally look with a jealous and malignant eye on a woman of great parts, and a cultivated understanding."[80]

The availability of Fordyce's *Sermons* and Gregory's *Father's Legacy* during the last decade of the colonial period hints that women had greater opportunity to read than ever before. Yet the very books which signaled increased opportunities to read also represented attempts to circumscribe woman's intellectual freedom. Some colonial women bristled at such restrictions. The ideas expressed in "Impromptu, on Reading an Essay on Education," a poem published in the *Virginia Gazette* on 11 February 1773, provide one indication of this attitude. The anonymous author, known only as "a Lady," wrote:

Yes, women, if they dar'd, would nobly soar,
And every art and science would explore;
Though weak their sex, their notions are refin'd,
And e'er would prove a blessing to mankind.[81]

CHAPTER 4

Housewifery, Physick, Midwifery

When the second supply reached Jamestown in 1608, it brought the Virginia colony's "first gentlewoman and woman-servant . . . Mistresse Forrest, and Anne Burras her maide." Other women soon reached Virginia, but their daily experience proved to be very similar to the men's. Unable to rely on servants, the women found themselves unprepared to do their own work. Like Jamestown's early gentlemen, they lacked practical, everyday survival skills. Books, they realized, contained information necessary to help them stay alive and healthy. While the combination of a high literacy rate and a high mortality rate among the early Jamestown colonists had created a good supply of books, practical works were scarce commodities. The colonists eventually wrote the London Company, asking it to send books on husbandry and housewifery. In 1620, they received Gervase Markham's *Country Contentments, in Two Bookes* (1615), which contained Markham's *The English-Housewife,* the first housewifery book known to have reached the American colonies.[1]

Markham was an enterprising author who often republished the same works under different titles. After appearing as the second book of *Country Contentments, The English-Housewife* was published as the third part of *A Way to Get Wealth* (1625) and published separately in 1631. Markham's various works continued to be read in America throughout the seventeenth century and into the eighteenth. Yet their popularity cannot be attributed simply to Markham's talent for marketing his books under various guises. He wrote in an engaging style and provided useful information concerning not only cookery, but also the cultivation of herbs and the preparation of medicinal remedies.[2]

As with the conduct books, the narrative voice of each housewifery book helped to determine its popularity. The savvy Markham recognized that it was incongruous for a man to write such a book, and he rhetorically shaped his work accordingly. He established camaraderie with his female readers with the self-effacing remark: "Thou mayst say (gentle reader) what hath this man to doe with hus-wifery, he is now out of his element . . . to express more in one book than can be found exprest in two women." Markham playfully denigrated himself and simultaneously elevated the position of his women readers. The comment suggests that his book was intended not to supplant, but rather to supplement, the traditional network of mothers, daughters, and friends for the circulation of household hints. For first-generation American women, Markham's approach was especially important. In a new country, away from friends and relations, these earliest female immigrants were cut off from their traditional sources of knowledge concerning how to feed and cure their husbands, their children, and themselves. Markham further appealed to his women readers by distancing, or at least feigning to distance, himself from the work. He took the position of editor rather than author. His "receipts," as they were known then, or recipes, as we call them now, were not his own; he simply had collected them from a prominent woman. "I shall desire thee therfore to understand," he told readers, "that this is . . . an approved manuscript . . . belonging sometime to an honorable personage of this kingdome, who was a singular amongst those of her ranke for many of the qualities here set forth."[3]

In the first chapter of *The English-Housewife*, Markham blurred the distinction between conduct books, devotional works, and cookery books, as he emphasized the inward virtues every housewife should possess. Of course, she must be pious, but she must also be courageous, patient, hardworking, watchful, pleasant, loyal, compassionate, quick-witted, and "generally skilful in all the worthy knowledges which do belong to her vocation."[4] Cookery was a principal duty of the woman. Evoking the language of the marriage ceremony, Markham stated that, without knowledge of cookery, a wife "can then but performe halfe her vow, for she may love and obey, but she cannot serve and keepe him with that true dutie which is ever expected."[5] Like the conduct book writers, Markham emphasized that a woman's principal duties involved serving her husband.

Another popular seventeenth-century work found in the colonies was William Rabisha's *The Whole Body of Cookery Dissected, Taught, and Fully Manifested* (1661). Though not written specifically for women,

Rabisha's work is important to the history of colonial American cookery because it was written for a general audience rather than for professional cooks. A long-time professional cook himself, Rabisha told readers that his peers would "open their mouths against me, for publishing this Treatise," because it would teach the art of cookery to "every Kitchenwench." Rabisha compared cookery to such skilled scientific pursuits as astronomy, mathematics, navigation, and surgery; and he criticized practitioners who guarded their craft's inner secrets. Emphasizing that cooking was both art and science, Rabisha gave it much greater status than Markham had given it. Cookery was not merely something a woman learned so as better to serve her husband; it was also a form of self-expression.[6]

Hannah Wolley's *A Queen-Like Closet, or Rich Cabinet Stored with All Manner of Rare Receipts for Preserving, Candying and Cookery* (1670) was the most important seventeenth-century cookery book to reach the American strand. London bookseller Robert Boulton sent copies of the work to Boston, and later Boulton sent copies of "Rich Cabinet," which may have been additional copies of the *Queen-Like Closet* or its similarly titled sequel, *Queens Closet Opened.*[7] In *A Queen-Like Closet,* Wolley specifically addressed a wide female audience. The title page characterizes the book as "very Pleasant and beneficial to all Ingenious Persons of the Female Sex," and Wolley addressed it "To all Ladies, gentlewomen, and to all other of the female sex who do delight in, or be desirous of good accomplishements."[8] She used straightforward, unadorned prose to make her cookery book understandable to all female readers. She refused to confound "the brain with multitudes of words to little or no purpose, or vain expressions of things which are altogether unknown to the learned as well as the ignorant." Her book, she asserted, was "imparted for the good of all the female sex."[9]

Virginians Anne Mercer and Maria Taylor Byrd both knew Richard Bradley's *Country Housewife and Lady's Director* (1727), and the work was popular elsewhere in colonial America. By the time it was advertised in the *American Weekly Mercury* in 1740, it had gone through six editions.[10] While Bradley was a fellow of the Royal Society and the first professor of botany at Cambridge, he made his work both practical and approachable. Bradley's *Country Housewife* was more like Rabisha's and Wolley's cookery books and less like the work of an earlier Royal Society fellow, John Evelyn's *Acetaria: A Discourse of Sallets* (1699) which had used salad-making as the subject of a scientific treatise. Bradley dedicated the work to the "Ladies of Great Britain" because "the principal Matters contained in it are within the Liberty of their Province." Furthermore, he claimed, "the Women have the Care and Management of every Business within doors, and to see after the good ordering of whatever is belonging to the House." Instead of emphasizing his own learning, Bradley gave his work authority by using the same rhetorical device Markham had used over a hundred years before—in other words, by depicting himself as the editor of the recipes he had collected from women friends. He wrote: "I may call myself rather their Amanuensis, than their Instructor; for the Receipts which I imagine will give the greatest Lustre or Ornament to the following Treatise, are such as are practiced by some of the most ingenious Ladies, who had Good-nature enough to admit of a Transcription of them for publick Benefit."[11]

The colonial success of Bradley's *Country Housewife* was eclipsed by another work first published the same year, E. Smith's *Compleat Housewife* (1727). The London edition was imported into the major cities and advertised in the newspapers throughout the colonies during the next few decades. Virginia printer William Parks reprinted the *Compleat Housewife* (Williamsburg, 1742), editing the text to suit the local audience.[12] Immediately after Smith's preface, Parks appended the comment:

> THUS ends the Author's Preface: The Printer now begs Leave to inform the Reader, that he hath Collected the following Volume from a much larger, printed in *England,* which contain'd many Recipes, the Ingredients or Materials for which, are not to be had in this Country: He hath therefore collected only such as are useful and practicable here, and left out such as are not so, which would only have serv'd to swell out the Book, and increase its Price.

Clearly, Parks's emphasis on practicality and thrift made the edition particularly American. Though his prefatory comments did not mention his supplying any extra recipes, he did provide an indigenous fever remedy made of Virginia snakeroot. New York printer Hugh Gaine, who had a reputation for shrewdly publishing popular self-help books, advertised a new printing of the *Compleat Housewife* in the early 1760s, and the work appears among the titles in booksellers' advertisements and library inventories throughout the colonies.[13]

The title page tells us it was written by "E. Smith," but the work's author remains a mystery. The *National Union Catalog* suggests "E" might stand for Elizabeth.[14] To be sure, the work was written from a woman's perspective. The preface began with a tongue-in-cheek remark about how books responded to fashion: "It being grown as unfashionable for a Book now to appear in Publick without a Preface, as for a Lady to appear at a Ball without a Hoop-petticoat, I shall conform to Custom for Fashion sake, and not through any Necessity." The preface, a typical eighteenth-century progress piece, traces the invention, development, and rise of cookery. At first, cookery was unnecessary, but when humankind progressed from a vegetable diet to an animal diet, cooking developed. Importantly, Smith refuted the notion that Esau was the first cook; instead, she asserted, he learned to cook from his mother Rebecca. Cookery slowly evolved into a science and eventually into an art. Like Rabisha's, Smith's prefatory remarks elevated cookery to the status of both an art and a science. Her title, *Compleat Housewife,* like Markham's, implied that cookery was a skill necessary for the woman who would properly serve her husband and family.

Smith had a good sense of her readers' needs and a good understanding of the book as a physical object. She confined herself "within the Limits of Practicalness and Usefulness" and created a volume that would "neither burthen the Hands to hold, the Eyes in reading, nor the Mind in conceiving." Not only would it be written in easily understandable prose, she implied, but also it would be easy to handle. Smith expressed her disappointment with earlier cookery books, as "many of them to us are impracticable, others whimsical, others unpalatable, unless to depraved Palates." Smith's use of the word "us" shows she identified with her female readers and understood the difficulties they might have had with other cookery books. She also criticized the techniques of writers like Markham and Bradley—in other words, of those who simply copied recipes from others without "the Copiers ever having had any Experience of the Palatableness, or had any Regard to the Wholsomness of them." Smith stressed that her book was the product of her own experience. Like Wolley, Smith aimed the work at both the well-to-do and the "lower sort." Her recipes for both frugal and sumptuous meals suggested a balance between the two economic classes; but her recipes for medicinal cures, like Wolley's, seem to have been directed especially to the well-to-do woman. The remedies in her book, Smith stated, were "very proper for those Generous, Charitable, and Christian Gentlewomen that have a Disposition to be serviceable to their poor Country Neighbours." With this advice, Smith retained the spirit of such women's conduct books as *The Lady's Calling,* which had recommended charity as one of the woman's principal virtues.

Twenty years after Smith's *Compleat Housewife* appeared, Hannah Glasse first published her *Art of Cookery* (1747), a work which would become the most popular cookery book during the last three decades of the colonial period. James Rivington puffed it as "a great Improvement on all the Books on this Subject ever yet published."[15] Both Glasse's persona and her sense of her audience made the work appeal to early American readers. While Wolley and Smith had tried to appeal to both the well-to-do and the "lower sort," Glasse directed her book specifically to average women: "every servant who can but read, will be capable of making a tolerable good cook, and those who have the least notion of Cookery cannot miss of being very good ones." Instead of using the "high polite style," she used the everyday language of the common folk. Like Rabisha, she stressed cookery an art in itself rather than as a task a woman performs in the service of her husband. Glasse specifically directed the book toward a female audience: "The great cooks have such a high way of expressing themselves, that the *poor girls* are at a loss to know what they mean." She was unconcerned with pleasing gentlemen, especially those who preferred French cooks: "If gentlemen will have *French* cooks, they must pay for *French* tricks." She wrote that she would be satisfied as long as her female readers liked her work: "I only beg the favour of every lady to read *my Book* throughout before they censure me, and then I flatter myself I shall have their approbation."[16]

Glasse's *Art of Cookery* could be found throughout the colonies. During the 1764–66 period, at least twenty-seven copies were sold at the *Virginia Gazette* office.[17] William Fitzhugh bought a copy of Glasse's *Cookery* there for Polly Chiswell. His account was debited, but she picked up the book. The Bolling family and the Mercers both acquired copies the same month. The *Georgia Gazette* and the *South-Carolina Gazette* advertised the work during the 1760s. In March 1772, the Annapolis firm of Wallace, Davidson, and Johnson imported half a dozen copies. In Boston, Mein's Circulating Library had a copy of Glasse's *Art of Cookery* and a copy of her *Art of Confectionary.*[18]

Other cookery books could be found on the colonial woman's bookshelf after 1747, but none was as popular as Glasse's. In 1760 and 1761, the New York papers advertised "Harrison's Cookery"—that is, Sarah

Harrison's *House-Keeper's Pocket-Book, and Compleat Family Cook* (1755); and Martha Bradley's *British Housewife; or, The Cook, Housekeeper's, and Gardiner's Companion*, a posthumously published work over seven hundred pages long. In 1764, Virginian Catherine Blaikley received her copy of "Harrison's Cookery," for which she had waited some time. The book inadvertently had been left out of an earlier shipment from England. Besides Blaikley's, at least nine other copies of "Harrison's Cookery" were sold at the *Virginia Gazette* office from 1764 to 1766, and Mein's Circulating Library in Boston had a copy of the work as well.[19]

Madam Johnson's Present; or, The Best Instructions for Young Women in Useful and Universal Knowledge also could be found from Boston to Williamsburg.[20] Though popularly known as "Johnson's Cookery," *Madam Johnson's Present* was much more than a housewifery book. It began with "A Short Dissertation on the Benefits of Learning, and a Well-Directed Female Education" and also contained directions on how to learn spelling, reading, writing, and arithmetic "without the Help of a Master." It provided many sample letters, much like those Edward Kimber included within *The Ladies Complete Letter-Writer.* Furthermore, *Madam Johnson's Present* contained a long list of spelling words.

The spelling list, titled "The Young Woman's Instructor for the Right Spelling of Words Used in Marketting, Cookery, Pickling, Preserving, &c.," remains the most intriguing part of the whole book. The *et cetera* in the title allowed a wide variety of words. In fact, many of the included words had nothing to do with the tasks normally involved in managing a household. Taken as a whole, the alphabetically-arranged list conveyed Johnson's notion of the woman's social and intellectual sphere. Besides *anchovies* and *artichoak-bottoms*, the A-list included the words *astronomy* and *atom*, a clear indication that the realms of the telescope and the microscope should be part of a woman's knowledge. Besides *cambrick* and *camomile, chitterlings* and *collyflower,* the C columns listed *charity* and *chastity*, two crucial virtues the conduct books had emphasized. The Cs also listed behaviors to avoid: *coquet* and *cuckold*. Between *damask* and *dumpling*, Madam Johnson listed *denominator, diamond, distich, dower, doxology,* and *dragon.* Such words convey a knowledge of arithmetic, literature, religion, and the business of marriage. H, I, J: *hartshorn-jelly, imbroidery, jac-a-lan-thorn; horn-book, intellect, journal.*

Scholar comes between *scallion* and *scollop*. W: *wages, walnut, wedlock, Westphalia, whipt-cream, Whitsunday, widow, winding-sheet, woman, womb, writing*.

One further cookery book deserves mention. Unlike Smith and Glasse, Susannah Carter felt no need to include a preface with her *Frugal Housewife, or Complete Woman Cook* (1772). In a way, her title page said everything her potential readers needed to know about the work and its author: it was written by a woman and directed toward frugal cooks. When the work was reprinted in Boston (with copper plates by Paul Revere), Boston booksellers Edward Cox and Edward Berry gave it a full-page advertisement at the back of their 1772 sale catalog, noting: "Any Person by attending to the Instructions given in this Book, may soon attain to a competent Knowledge in the Art of Cookery, &c.—And it likewise contains more in Quantity than most other Books of a much higher Price."[21] The prominent attention that Cox and Berry gave to the *Frugal Housewife* confirms that women were an important part of their book-buying clientele.

Printed works formed only a portion of the cookery books which could be found on the colonial woman's bookshelf. Women often made their own manuscript cookbooks. Surviving manuscript volumes show that colonial American women took advantage of both folk and literary traditions to create their own personal works. (Many more manuscript volumes have not survived, while others no doubt remain cherished in family sideboards and have not yet become available for scholarly perusal.) By 1763, Bostonian Anne Gibbons Gardiner had compiled an extensive manuscript volume of her favorite recipes. As a testament to her own diverse reading, she borrowed her recipe to dress trout from Isaac Walton's *Compleat Angler*. Martha Dandridge began a manuscript recipe collection soon after she married Daniel Custis, continued the work after she married George Washington, and eventually made it a wedding present to her granddaughter, Eleanor Parke Custis.[22] Martha Washington may have taken some of her recipes from the *Compleat Housewife*, a copy of which could be found at Mount Vernon. Eliza Lucas Pinckney kept her own manuscript cookery book, and so did her daughter, Harriot Pinckney Horry. Harriot took some of her recipes from her mother's manuscript cookbook, and her mother had taken some of her recipes from Hannah Glasse's *Art of Cookery*.[23]

Sometimes print and manuscript recipes could be found within the same volume. Women often had their cookery books bound with blank leaves to allow them space to add their own recipes. In one surviving copy of Sarah Harrison's *House-Keeper's Pocket-Book,* a contemporary owner added many of her own recipes. For example, one printed page of the book contains a basic cheesecake recipe. On the adjacent manuscript page are recipes for orange cheesecake and almond cheesecake. Clearly, the owner of the volume was supplementing and expanding upon the original recipe. On another printed page is a recipe for "whipt syllabub." The adjacent manuscript leaf contains an alternate syllabub recipe. The printed version begins, "You must have a Quart of cream and a Pint of Sack." Instead of sack, the manuscript recipe uses "Mountain Wine." For the enterprising housewife, the volume indicates, sack was not a "must" at all.[24] While the earliest Jamestown women lacked the traditional network of friends and relatives, as well as sufficient quantities of housewifery books, both folk and literary traditions had become well established by the end of the colonial period. These manuscript recipes suggest a healthy interaction between folk and print cultures, signaling the vitality of both.

As the numerous medicinal recipes within these cookery books suggest, housewifely duties included treating injuries and caring for the sick. While the cookery books provided a variety of medical cures, the colonial woman had other books from which she could get medical advice. The books most widely used by early American women were those which supplied practical hints. The overall medical knowledge the colonial woman received from books was a curious mixture of astrological advice, antiquated lore, and homegrown folk remedies.

The almanac—which reached a greater colonial audience than any book other than the Bible—usually contained remedies and cures for a wide variety of ailments. Ironically, almanacs were so ubiquitous that few contemporaries thought it necessary to mention that they owned one or describe how they read or used their almanacs. To be sure, some used them simply as calendars and paid little attention to the additional information the almanac had to offer, while others read and used the tidbits of wisdom. The most frequent medical "information" supplied by the almanacs was astrological advice. Most contained a cut illustrating a "man of signs"—a man's body showing Zodiac signs keyed to whichever part of the body a given sign influenced. The almanac's "man of signs" helped to perpetuate the Renaissance notion that the human body was analogous to the makeup of the whole universe—an idea which, in the view of medical professionals, long since had become scientifically untenable.[25] A verse accompanying the diagram in John Foster's 1678 *Almanack* shows one way in which the "man of signs" was interpreted:

> The Head and Face the Ram doth crave,
> The Neck and Throat, the Bull will have,
> The loving Twins do rule the Hands,
> The Brest and Sides in Cancer bands. . . .

The texts of these early American almanacs, too, imparted such astrological advice. John Tully's 1692 Boston *Almanack*, for example, contained several pages describing the interrelations between diseases and the positions of the planets.[26]

The almanac perpetuated the Galenic theory of the four humors, long after it had been discarded by university-trained physicians. Sickness, according to Galen, came from disturbances among the four humors: blood, phlegm, black bile, and yellow bile. Health could be restored only when the balance among the four humours was restored through such cures as bleeding, purging, and sweating. Almanacs often promulgated astrological advice in conjunction with Galenic treatments. Another key medical influence on the almanacs, the teachings of Paracelsus, marked an advance over Galen. Paracelsus attacked Galen's general theory of humors and argued instead that medicinal remedies should be applied to specific ailments. Paracelsus also advocated the "doctrine of signatures," the idea that plants, animals, and minerals were marked by a sign indicating their medical use. Furthermore, Paracelsus argued that, in a country where a disease arises, nature produced its cure nearby. In practical terms, indigenous American flora contained the remedies for indigenous American agues. While Paracelsus had repudiated the teachings of Galen, Paracelsian remedies often were advocated alongside Galenic treatments within the colonial American almanacs.

The contents of late-seventeenth-century Boston almanacs illustrate the various attitudes toward astrology, Galen, and Paracelsus. John Tully's 1694 *Almanack*, for example, described which remedy worked best under which Zodiac sign. Purging worked well when the moon was in Pisces, vomiting under Taurus, and glysters when the moon was in

Aries, Cancer, or Virgo. Christian Lodowick's *New-Englands Almanack* for the following year provided Paracelsian cures—that is, specific remedies for specific ailments. Lodowick supplied cures for cholic, worms in children, jaundice, loosenesses, toothache, and many others. He also included an essay criticizing astrological or Galenic medicine and addressed further criticisms toward a "pagan Tully," whose "Physical observations in his late Almanack, about letting blood, Purging, &c. when the Moon is in such and such a Sign, are things disclaimed by the greatest part of Physicians."[27] In his 1696 almanac, John Tully responded with an essay, "Concerning Astrology & Meteorology," in which he answered Lodowick's criticisms; in subsequent almanacs, however, Tully silently dropped his section on astrological medicine. Though Tully apparently was influenced by Lodowick's forward-thinking attitudes toward medical practice, there were plenty of other almanac-makers who believed (or at least catered to the public belief) in the influence of the stars.

Early American almanacs also began supplying locally derived folk remedies before the end of the seventeenth century. The earliest to list specifically indigenous cures was Daniel Leed's 1694 New York *Almanack,* which described the virtues of "Indian corn." Titan Leed's 1713 *American Almanack* described the medicinal properties of tobacco, a plant that long had been recognized for its curative powers. Titan Leeds's 1729 *American Almanack* described how to make the "Decoction of Seneka Rattlesnake Root," and Benjamin Franklin included the Indian cure for rattlesnake bite in his *Poor Richard's Almanac* for 1737 and 1740.[28]

The almanacs facilitated cultural exchange among Native Americans, African slaves, and European settlers. Actually, the Indian medicinal approach resembled the Paracelsian approach. Like Paracelsus, the Native Americans had their own doctrine of signatures. Snakeroot was used to cure snakebite, because the plant's root resembled the snake's rattle.[29] While the English colonists long had derived medicinal cures from local Indians, the almanacs helped disseminate indigenous remedies to a wider audience. Both John Jerman's 1741 *American Almanack* and Franklin's 1741 *Poor Richard's Almanac* contained John Bartram's description of *ipecacuanha,* the "true Indian Physick." The 1763 *Father Abraham's Almanack* called the Seneca rattlesnake root "a successful Method of cure in the annual Epidemick Fevers in America, which all the Chymical and Galenical preparations of the Shops cannot come near."[30] John

Tobler's 1765 *South-Carolina and Georgia Almanack* contained "An Indian Remedy for inveterate Ulcers":

> An Indian came to a person that had an ulcer which no European could
> cure: the Indian doctor performed his cure in the following manner;
> first, he made a strong decoction of the root of sassafras, in which he
> bathed the ulcerated leg, then took some grains of rotten Indian corn,
> well dried, beaten to powder, and the soft down that grows upon the
> turkeys rump, with this he quickly dried up the filthy ulcer, and made a
> perfect cure.[31]

While it is unknown how many industrious housewives ever concocted
this sassafras, corn, and turkey-feather poultice, the recipe authorizes the
American Indian as a valid source of knowledge.

African remedies, too, were widely disseminated via the almanacs.
Jonas Green's 1751 *Maryland Almanack* contained the Negro Caesar's
cure for poison and rattlesnake bites. Francisco Guerra has called that
remedy the first reference to Negro medical practices being used by the
white population, but the exchange of medical information between African slave and American colonist already was well established by the time
Green's almanac appeared. Cotton Mather, in *The Angel of Bethesda,*
described how Africans cured smallpox—a remedy that he had heard
from his own servant as well as from several other slaves.[32] Still, the almanac made the African-American remedies more influential. Caesar's
cures, as well as those advocated by other Africans, were reprinted in
American almanacs during the next several years. Theophilus Grew's
1753 *Virginia Almanack* and John Tobler's 1757 *Pennsylvania Town
and Country-Man's Almanack* included Caesar's cures for poison and
rattlesnake bites. Tobler's 1759 *South-Carolina Almanac* included
Caesar's cures and another cure for rattlesnake bite from "the Negro
Sampson."[33] Overall, African and Native American cures helped the settlers break away from the complex European medical tradition and begin prescribing specific remedies for specific ailments.[34]

The volume of homespun medicine used most widely in the southern
and middle colonies was John Tennent's *Every Man His Own Doctor;
Or, The Poor Planter's Physician,* a work designed "to lead the Poorer
Sort into the *pleasant Paths of Health*; and when they have the Misfortune to be *sick,* to shew them the cheapest and easiest Ways of *getting*

well again." The work was first published at Williamsburg in 1734, and it immediately became popular. Benjamin Franklin, who reprinted the work for distribution in Pennsylvania, Delaware, and New Jersey, noted that "Great Numbers" of the Williamsburg edition had been "distributed among the People both in Virginia and Maryland, and 'tis generally allow'd that abundance of Good has been thereby done."[35] Convincing evidence shows that women made up a significant portion of the readers of Tennent's pragmatic work. The unique copy of William Hunter's reprint of *Every Man His Own Doctor* (Williamsburg, 1751) which survives at the American Antiquarian Society is bound with a copy of William Parks's reprint of E. Smith's *Compleat Housewife* (Williamsburg, 1742). Hunter advertised a new edition of Smith's *Compleat Housewife* in 1752 and 1753,[36] bound with *Every Man His Own Doctor*; but the unique copy shows that Hunter acquired surplus sheets of Parks's edition of Smith's *Compleat Housewife,* bound them up with his new edition of *Every Man His own Doctor,* and sold the two together as a "new edition" of the *Compleat Housewife.* Londa Schiebinger has argued that, in Europe at mid-century, medical recipes dropped out of cookery books,[37] but the association between these two works in the surviving volume provides one indication that, in colonial America, the concoction of medicines remained the woman's responsibility.

Every Man His Own Doctor was further popularized by Benjamin Franklin. It is hardly surprising that Franklin found *Every Man His Own Doctor* attractive. Tennent's first sentence clearly shows that he and Franklin shared similar beliefs. The work begins: "The most acceptible Service we can render to GOD, is Benificence to MAN." Not only did Franklin print several editions of the work, but also he incorporated it into his 1748 and 1753 editions of *American Instructor.* The latter work, written by the Englishman George Fisher and published anonymously, first appeared in London with the title *The Young Man's Best Companion.*[38] Franklin changed the title to make it more appealing to an American audience. Eliminating the gender-specific term from the main title, Franklin made this practical book appeal to both men and women. The expanded contents of Franklin's *American Instructor* confirm his desire to cater to female readers. It included: "Instructions for Marking on Linnen; how to Pickle and Preserve; to make divers Sorts of Wine; and many excellent Plaisters, and Medicines, necessary in all Families."[39]

The estate inventory of John Eustace, a North Carolina doctor, provides further evidence that women used *Every Man His Own Doctor.* After Dr. Eustace's death, his wife Margaret inherited his fine library. The inventory of the doctor's library lists his excellent collection of medical books—the best in colonial North Carolina—separately, but *Every Man His Own Doctor* is not listed among them. Instead, it is listed among the practical household books.[40] Most likely, the Eustace copy of Tennent's work had been Margaret Eustace's book all along. Even where there was a doctor in the house, the Eustace inventory shows, there was still room for the housewife to concoct her own home remedies.

Every Man His Own Doctor also became known in England, if Mary Morris's similar work is any indication. Morris's collection of recipes "for the cure of most disorders incident to human bodies" was published with the sixth and later editions of Sarah Harrison's *House-Keeper's Pocket-Book, and Compleat Family Cook* and subsequently sold in the American colonies from New York to Virginia. The inclusion of Morris's work as part of Harrison's further brings into question Schiebinger's assertion that medicinal recipes dropped from cookery books after the mid-eighteenth century. Morris, apparently bristling at Tennent's gender-specific title, named her own work "Every One Their Own Physician." In her introduction, Morris wrote, "Physic has long been deemed an Art not to be acquired but by Men of Learning only; but the Exorbitance of their Fees, and the Extravagance of Apothecaries Bills, has made Family Receipts much esteemed; more especially when they are well chosen, and adapted to the Cure designed, by *Reason* and *Experience.*"[41] Though published in Great Britain, "Every One Their Own Physician" was compiled with American readers in mind. The recipes included "The Negro Caesar's cure for the bite of a rattle-snake," a recipe which would have been superfluous to the book's British readers. At the *Virginia Gazette* office in Williamsburg, at least fifteen copies of Tennent's work were sold on credit during the 1750–52 period, while only one was sold during the 1764–66 period. Ten copies of "Harrison's Cookery" containing Morris's "Every One Their Own Physician" were sold on credit at *Virginia Gazette* office during the later period.[42] The evidence suggests that, by the mid-1760s, Mary Morris's work was supplanting Tennent's among women in colonial Virginia.

Nicholas Culpeper's medical works could often be found on the colonial woman's bookshelf. Multiple copies of both his *English Physician* (1652) and his *London Dispensatory* were being sold in Boston during the last third of the seventeenth century.[43] In 1708, a work attributed to Culpeper and titled *English Physician* was published at Boston, the first medical work to be printed in America. Although the work was attributed to Culpeper, its contents were largely American in origin.[44] A Boston edition of Culpeper's *London Dispensatory* appeared in 1720. Susanna Fisher of Salem County, New Jersey, owned a copy of the *London Dispensatory* at the time of her death in 1721.[45] A 1721 Boston almanac advertised the work, and excerpts from Culpeper often were reprinted in other almanacs.[46] Surviving copies show that Culpeper's books were cherished by colonial women and handed down from one generation to the next. The Boston Medical Library's copy of the 1667 London edition of Culpeper's *London Dispensatory* was owned by Elizabeth Greenleaf, the wife of the parson-physician Daniel Greenleaf; she had her own apothecary shop in Boston. She passed her copy of Culpeper's *London Dispensatory* to her daughter Grace in 1764. Two years later, Grace presented the volume to her sister.[47] The Boston Medical Library's copy of the 1720 edition is inscribed "Rachel Martin, Her Book, Given Her by Her Mother Jest before her Deth, March 13th Day 1765."[48] Her mother died five days later. The inscription indicates that one of her last wishes was for her daughter Rachel to continue as the family's healer.

Toward the end of the colonial period, medicine became less an activity for lay practitioners and more the province of physicians. The increasing professionalization of medicine meant that many of the newly imported medical books were designed for university-educated physicians rather than housewives. Some popular writers reacted against such exclusivity with practical manuals emphasizing traditional home remedies. The two most important books stressing this back-to-basics approach were John Wesley's *Primitive Physick; Or, An Easy and Natural Method of Curing Most Diseases* (1764); and William Buchan's *Domestic Medicine; Or, The Family Physician: Being an Attempt to Render the Medical Art More Generally Useful, By Showing People What Is in Their Own Power Both with Respect to the Prevention and Cure of Diseases,* which first appeared at Edinburgh in 1769 and was reprinted at Philadelphia in 1772.[49] Wesley stated in his preface that, since the development of medical theory, "Medical books were immensely multiplied; 'til at length Physick became an abstruse science, quite out of the Reach of ordinary Men." He further complained that there were too many medical books and that they were "too dear for poor Men to buy, and too hard for plain Men to understand." His collection, unlike the numerous other contemporary medical books, would contain "only safe and cheap and easy Medicines."[50]

Buchan's *Domestic Medicine* became a special favorite of Abigail Adams. She first read the work thoroughly on board a ship bound for England during the mid-1780s, but she had known about the work beforehand, because she recalled that Mercy Otis Warren owned a copy. Recommending the work to her sister, Mary Smith Cranch, Abigail Adams showed that the book was useful for more than simply curing ailments. It also provided a philosophical outlook which helped to prevent sickness. She wrote:

> Nature abounds with variety, and the mind unless fixed down by habit, delights in contemplating new objects, and the variety of Scenes which present themselves to the Senses, were certainly designd to prevent our attention from being too long fixed upon any one object; and this says a late celebrated medical writer; greatly conduces to the Health of the animal frame. Your studious people and your deep thinkers, he observes, seldom enjoy either health or spirits. This writer I recommend to your perusal; and will tell you that you may borrow it of our Friend Mrs. Warren, tis Buchans domestick Medicine. I have read him since I came to Sea with much pleasure.[51]

Delivering babies remained a woman's responsibility through most of the colonial period, and childbirth was an important social event for women. Besides the midwife, an expectant mother's female friends, relatives, and neighbors joined together at the crucial time in support, comfort, and celebration; or, all too often, in commiseration.[52] The importance of this social network, however, has kept scholarly attention from focusing on the influence of books on midwifery practice. To be sure, books alone were not sufficient to teach a woman how to be a midwife, but they provided important supplemental information. Prefacing his translation of François Mauriceau's *Accomplisht Midwife*, Hugh Chamberlen described the appropriate relationship between practical experience and book knowledge: "I design not this Work to encourage any to practise by it, who were not bred up to it; for it will hardly make a Midwife, tho it may easily mend a bad one."[53]

Among the most popular midwifery books in colonial America were several pseudo-Aristotelian works: *Aristotle's Masterpiece, Aristotle's Compleat and Experienc'd Midwife, The Problems of Aristotle, Aristotle's Legacy,* and *The Works of Aristotle.* Many copies of these works were imported into the colonies, and they were often reprinted in America during and after the colonial period. Containing much astrological medicine and some outlandish folk remedies, these works nevertheless provided useful gynecological information and helpful practical advice concerning conception, pregnancy, and childbirth.[54]

The pseudo-Aristotelian works' popularity cannot be attributed entirely to women's reading. Boys and men sometimes read them as pornography.[55] Thomas Langhorn, a traveling salesman (seriously!), used what he read in "Aristotle" to try and seduce Elizabeth Holmes, a young Massachusetts woman. In the official complaint she lodged against him, Holmes stated, "He said that Arristottle saith that if the seed be thin the woman will not conceive but there are many ways to thicken it and then shee may." Holmes then related several more bawdy remarks she had heard from Langhorn and concluded, "Hee said that most of the storeys he told mee Hee had out of Arristottle."[56] Jonathan Edwards once conducted an investigation concerning the reading of obscene books by members of his church. He titled his transcript of the proceedings, "Papers concerning young men's reading midwives Books." Edwards's manuscript showed that men were reading the books as pornography, but it implicitly suggested that the books did have a valid readership—that is, women. The tremendous popularity of these works adds a splendid irony to the knowledge of early American intellectual history. A sentence beginning "According to Aristotle" was more likely to be an opening for a bawdy story than an introduction to philosophic discourse.

Nicolas Culpeper's *Directory for Midwives* (1656), like the pseudo-Aristotelian works, blended folk remedies, astrology, and occult practices with some genuine anatomical detail. His approach to childbirth, however, was practical, empirical, and sound. Overall, he advocated a passive rather than an active or "interventionist" approach to childbirth. The latter approach gained favor in later midwifery books.[57] In selecting "A Guide for Women" as the subtitle of his *Directory for Midwives,* Culpeper suggested that the book also was intended as a general gynecological treatise, in addition to being a midwives' how-to book. Like Culpeper's *English Physician* and *London Dispensatory,* his midwifery book was distributed widely throughout the colonies from its first publication and went through many editions during the colonial period.[58] Dedicating the work to the midwives of England, Culpeper once more emphasized the importance of spreading medical advice in English instead of Latin, so that general readers could put the knowledge to use. In the dedication, Culpeper characterized the midwife and incidentally commented on the reading of midwifery books: "a Midwife ought to be as quick-sighted as *Argus,* her wits must be in her Head, for her Books are at home: *Hippocrates* was never better skill'd in the Rules of Physick than a Midwife ought to be." In other words, the midwife should use books to help better her skill, but she must completely internalize everything she read. There would be no time for fumbling through pages at the moment of truth. Culpeper told midwives that, if they made use of the practical information, "you wil find your Work easie, you need not cal for the help of a Man-Midwife, which is a disparagement, not only to your selves, but also to your Profession."[59]

The only midwifery book made in America during the colonial period is much different than the pseudo-Aristotelian works or Culpeper's practical treatise. Cotton Mather's *Elizabeth in Her Holy Retirement* (Boston, 1710) was more similar to John Oliver's *A Present to Be Given to Teeming Women, by Their Husbands or Friends, Containing Directions for Women with Child* (1663; Boston, 1694), which Mather cited in his own work. All too often, pregnancy was a life-threatening time for an expectant mother, and Mather believed that a woman should ponder her spiritual condition during the final hours of pregnancy. The most expedient way to get his treatise to its intended audience, Mather realized, was to let midwives distribute the work. Ideally, Mather hoped, pious midwives would furnish their patients with copies of *Elizabeth in Her Holy Retirement,* "by whom they know an Hour of Travail and Trouble to be Expected. Certainly the Handmaids of the Lord, will receive thus as a Messenger from HIM unto them!" There's no way to know how well Mather's scheme worked, but in 1721, the first edition long since exhausted, Mather resolved, "I will move a godly Midwife, to procure a new Edition of my little Essay, entituled, *Elizabeth in her Holy Retirement:* that it may be scattered thro Town and Countrey; and occasion be taken from the Circumstances of them who are expecting an Hour of Travail, to quicken their Praeparation for Death, and the Exercise of all suitable Piety."[60] Not only did midwives try to bring babies safely into this world, but they also, if Mather's scheme worked, helped to spread piety and literacy.

Mather reused much of *Elizabeth in Her Holy Retirement* in his medical opus, *The Angel of Bethesda*. Revising the earlier text, Mather added a few practical folk remedies for coping with childbirth. The most notable item he added was a recipe to improve the nurse's milk:

> Potage made with *Lentiles,* or *Vetches,* does it. So does Powder of *Earth-worms,* well-cleans'd and dried. A Dram in any Proper Vehicle. So does, *Milk* turn'd with *Beer.*
> Here's an *Infallible,* and I hope, not an *Unacceptable.*
> Take *Chickens;* make a Brothe of 'em. Add thereto *Fennel* and *Parsly*-Roots: and butter the Roots with New Butter. Having so done, Eat all the Mess.
> But above all, Try this. Drink for a few Days, twice or thrice a Day, the Water wherein *fresh Fish* has been boiled. This will fetch back the Nurses *Milk,* when it is gone: and will so supply her *Breasts* that they shall be better to the *Infant* than the richest *Clusters of the Vine.*

After supplying the recipe, Mather wrote, "Hoc mea me Conjux Experta docere Volebat," that is, "This my expert wife taught me."[61]

Although its popularity never came close to the pseudo-Aristotelian works or Culpeper's *Midwifery,* François Mauriceau's *Les Maladies des femmes grosses et accouchées* (Paris, 1668) was, clinically speaking, the most important seventeenth-century midwifery book to reach the colonies. Mauriceau was "the first to write on tubal pregnancy, epidemic puerperal fever, and the complications that arise in labor from misplacement of the umbilical cord." Overall, the work contained "the best summary of the knowledge and practice of obstetrics of the era."[62] While Mauriceau advanced new theories about childbirth in France, new techniques were developed in England by the Chamberlen family. Peter Chamberlen had invented obstetrical forceps, but he had forbid his descendants from publishing the forceps secret. Though the Chamberlens did not reveal their secret, eventually it became known in the eighteenth century. The Chamberlen forceps—or "hooks," as they were more crudely called—epitomized the difference between the passive and the active or interventionist approach.

Hugh Chamberlen's translation of Mauriceau's book, *Accomplisht Midwife* (1673), helped the work become known throughout colonial America. A later English version of Mauriceau's work, *The Diseases of Woman with Child*, circulated throughout the colonies.[63] While Mauriceau had designed the book for both surgeons and midwives, Chamberlen, in the preface to his translation, took a deprecating stance toward midwives: "I have carefully rendred into *English* for the Benefit of our Midwives; of whom many may yet very well admit of an additional Knowledge."[64] The passive approach prevailed in colonial America through the mid-eighteenth century, but Chamberlen's interventionist approach took precedence after mid-century. Culpeper's *Directory for Midwives* had emphasized that seeking a man-midwife's help was disgraceful to her profession, but Chamberlen says quite the opposite: "Nor can it be so great a Discredit to a Midwife (let some of them imagine what they please) to have a Woman or Child saved by a Man's Assistance, as to suffer either to die under her own Hand, altho delivered . . . it will justify her better to wave her imaginary Reputation, and to send for Help to save the Woman and Child, than to let any perish, when possible to be prevented."[65] The interventionist approach, graphically symbolized by the obstetrical forceps, signaled a fundamental difference between female and male attitudes toward childbirth.

William Smellie deserves credit for popularizing the interventionist approach and for the ascendancy of man-midwives in both England and America. In England, Smellie developed a reputation for his public lectures and his birth-simulating machine, which was made from leather, beer, and a baby doll. In America, Smellie's method became widely known after the publication of his *Treatise on the Theory and Practice of Midwifery* (1752–56). Indeed, Smellie had developed a significant enough reputation that, even before publication, his approach to childbirth had become known in the colonies. After Boston physician William Douglass learned of Smellie's techniques, he roundly censured him in two treatises: *A Letter to Dr. Smellie, Showing the Impropriety of His New Invented Wooden Forceps; As Also the Absurdity of His Method of Teaching and Practising Midwifery* (1748) and *A Second Letter to Dr. Smellie* (1748?). The two replies to Smellie confirm Dr. Alexander Hamilton's characterization of Douglass—"a man of good learning but mischievously given to criticism and the most compleat snarler ever I knew"[66]—but Douglass's tracts indicate that midwifery had become a practice which deserved attention from stern medical men.

Throughout much of the colonial period, the midwifery books provided women (and men) with basic gynecological information as well as advice about how to care for newborn babies. As the colonial period ended, however, midwifery books, like the medical books, had become works for members of the medical profession. In their place, other books emerged to provide basic gynecological information. For example, *The Ladies Physical Directory; or, A Treatise of All the Weaknesses, Indispositions, and Diseases Peculiar to the Female Sex, from Eleven Years of Age to Fifty or Upwards*, a work which Virginian Anne Mercer knew,[67] was designed so that "women and maids of the meanest capacity may perfectly understand the symptoms, nature, and true cause of their own illnesses, and readily know how to manage themselves and all their infirmities." William Cadogan's *Essay upon Nursing and the Management of Children, from Their Birth to Three Years of Age* (Boston, 1772), the most important treatise on the subject to appear during the colonial period, provided a generation of young mothers with sound, useful information.

CHAPTER 5

Facts and Fictions

Ann Eliza Bleecker told "The History of Maria Kittle," a gruesome, thrilling, and sentimental story of one woman's brutal captivity during the French and Indian War, as a letter to her friend Susan Ten Eyck. Publication of the narrative, written during the 1770s, was delayed until the 1790s, when it came out as part of Bleecker's posthumous works. Nevertheless, Bleecker intended it for a broader audience than just her friend Susan, and it undoubtedly circulated in manuscript well before it appeared in print. She began the work by telling her reader: "However fond of novels and romances you may be, the unfortunate adventures of one of my neighbours, who died yesterday, will make you despise that fiction, in which, knowing the subject to be fabulous, we can never be so truly interested."[1] The remark, of course, was a deliberate ruse. "The History of Maria Kittle" was not a true story at all. Although it contained some elements of veracity, it was a fictional work. Still, Bleecker's opening comment reveals much about the early American woman's attitudes toward both fictional and factual narratives.

Most importantly, Bleecker reflected ambiguity toward fiction. Noting her reader's fondness for novels and romances, she testified to the continuing popularity of both. Suggesting that true adventure stories greatly surpassed fictional ones, Bleecker seemed to elevate the factual narrative far above the fictional. Her remark, however, was ironic, since she elevated the factual only to give her fictional account the semblance of truth. Instead of glorifying the factual, she was merely playing upon the prejudice against fiction which many American readers retained throughout the colonial period and well into the nineteenth century.

Linking novels and factual accounts, Bleecker suggested that both could provide analogous reading experiences. Indeed, novels and travel books could be grouped together because, quite simply, they tell stories, or, if you will, both were forms of narrative discourse. Most offered readers a protagonist with whom to identify and a set of intriguing events to experience vicariously. Novels and travel books also were similar in that they differed greatly from the other types of literature read by early American women. Each of the types of literature discussed so far—devotional works, conduct books, domestic manuals—provided useful and specific information. Their main purpose was to instruct. Novels and travel narratives, on the other hand, were read primarily for pleasure. This is not to say they did not instruct. Most of the period's novels remained heavily didactic, and travel books were full of information about diverse peoples and cultures throughout the world. While didactic novels and travel narratives fulfilled Horace's dictum, "to delight and instruct," that same maxim made the factual accounts much more respectable than fiction. A true story could instruct better than a fictional one. In the eighteenth-century hierarchy of literature, as Ann Bleecker well realized, fictional works—despite their didacticism—retained a place below nonfictional works such as biography, history, and travels.

Even among fictional narratives, the delight-and-instruct paradigm helped to determine a hierarchy. For most colonial Americans, the words "romance" and "novel" had imprecise, often overlapping meanings. In *Ornaments for the Daughters of Zion,* Cotton Mather cautioned young women against reading "*Romances,* which do no less naturally than generally inspire the Minds of young People with *Humours,* that are as *Vicious* as they are *foolish.*" Ebenezer Turell found that his sister-in-law Abigail Colman's reading tastes had "run her too soon and too far into the reading of *Novels,* &c. for which God in his righteous Providence afterwards punished her by suffering her to leave her Father's House, to the Grief of her Friends and the Surprise of the Town."[2] Harsh punishment, indeed. Though Mather used the word "Romances" and Turell used "Novels," both men referred to the same types of books—that is, works of fiction which unduly inflamed a young woman's passions and imagination. Mather, Turell, and their contemporaries were not against such works specifically because they were fictional. After all, the most popular French book throughout the colonies was a fictional work, Fénelon's *Adventures of Telemachus.* The key distinction between *Telemachus* and the works to which Mather and Turell deprecatingly refer is that Fénelon's work had a clear didactic purpose, while romances did not. The romance, or, as it was sometimes called before the mid-

eighteen͏   ͏vel, was scorned because it delighted without
instruct͏

The best way to understand how novels were read and received among
early American women is to take a careful look at the contemporary reception of Samuel Richardson's *Pamela*. No other single book elicited as
much written comment from colonial women as *Pamela*. While Eliza
Lucas Pinckney, in her surviving letterbook, mentioned reading several
different works, none received such detailed critical comment as *Pamela*.
Similarly, Esther Edwards Burr often described books she had read in
her letters to Sarah Prince, but none received treatment as extensive as
that accorded *Pamela*. Even Abigail Adams, who generally preferred histories and travel narratives, could not help but discourse upon *Pamela*.
The various comments made by these three women, as well as surviving
remarks about the book made by contemporary male readers, allow us
further to understand the colonial woman's reading process.

Samuel Richardson, printer, shrewdly calculated what would and
would not be acceptable within the literary marketplace. He knew that
the reading public, both at home and in the colonies, might be reluctant
to accept a fictional work. Richardson therefore made the title page of
Pamela; or, Virtue Rewarded a masterpiece of indirection. Nowhere is it
mentioned that the book is a work of fiction. Instead, it is puffed as a
conduct book and a collection of familiar letters "published in order to
cultivate the principles of virtue and religion in the minds of the youth of
both sexes." For those potential readers who suspected that the work
might be fiction, Richardson emphasized that *Pamela* was a "narrative
which has its foundation in truth and nature." Richardson deflected the
arguments of those who recognized the work as a fiction, by stressing its
instructive aspects: "At the same time that it agreeably entertains, by a
variety of curious and affecting incidents, [it] is intirely divested of all
those Images, which in too many Pieces, calculated for Amusement only,
tend to inflame the Minds they should Instruct." In other words, it was
not a romance. Benjamin Franklin, printer, who had no qualms about
retitling *The Young Man's Best Companion* as *The American Instructor*
in order to make the work more appealing to a local male and female
audience, and whose distinguishing feature as a printer was a clean, un-
cluttered title page, shrewdly retained Richardson's lengthy title when he
reprinted *Pamela* in 1744.[3]

Well before Franklin printed *Pamela,* numerous copies of Richardson's

London edition had reached America. Indeed, Franklin's reprinting was largely unsuccessful, because English editions were plentiful throughout the colonies. *Pamela* was so popular that every copy sent to America was read by about half a dozen people. Throughout the winter of 1741–42, a Philadelphian observed, "*Pamela* was in everybody's mouth and happy the person who could procure a reading."[4] The work could be found at booksellers' shops throughout the colonies. In South Carolina, for example, Elizabeth Timothy had copies of *Pamela* on sale at her shop during the mid-1740s.[5] *Pamela*'s tremendous popularity prompted English spoofs, copycat works, and sequels. The spurious continuations, *Pamela's Conduct in High Life* and *Pamela in High Life; or, Virtue Rewarded,* were written in much the same style as Richardson's original. When Dr. Alexander Hamilton attended a book auction in Boston during the summer of 1744, he noticed that *Pamela* and *Anti-Pamela* (*Anti-Pamela; or, Feign'd Innocence Detected* [1741]) were among the best-selling books.[6] Eliza Haywood, the work's probable author, capitalized on the vogue for Richardson to tell the story of lustful Syrena Tricksy, who sought numerous illicit love affairs.

While Richardson had not intended to continue Pamela Andrews's story, the spurious sequels forced him to take pen in hand to tell the story of Pamela's life as "Mrs. B." The two-volume continuation by Richardson appeared in late 1741. *Pamela,* "the Sequel," was popular with its eighteenth-century readers, who simply could not get enough of the virtuous young title character. The continuation strikes modern readers as awkward, because both Pamela and her paramour Mr. B already had proven their virtue and gotten married by the end of the original two-volume *Pamela*. Since she had already endured her trials and Mr. B had already submitted to her charms, there was little left for them to do in the continuation but exemplify their virtue, hardly the substance of an intricate plot or an exciting tale. Richardson's biographers explain: "The leading characters, because they are virtuous, can make no serious mistakes, and because their virtue has been rewarded, they can meet with no serious mishaps. The great fault of the continuation of *Pamela* is that there was nothing which could happen in it."[7]

The plot, which centers on the domestic bliss of Mr. and Mrs. B, was indeed meager. Their son, "Billy B," was not born until a third of the way through the second volume of the continuation. After his birth, Mr. B. gave Pamela a copy of John Locke's *Some Thoughts Concerning Education* and asked her to record her thoughts on the book. Pamela's subsequent discourse on Locke takes up sixty pages! The liveliest episode occurred when Pamela and Mr. B attended a masquerade ball. She went as a Quaker, while he went as a Spanish don. Mr. B met a saucy nun at the masquerade, who turned out to be a Countess. Afterwards, the Countess entered the lives of the B family, and Pamela believed the rumors she heard about the Countess's being a firm advocate of polygamy. Pamela became extremely jealous and eventually confronted her husband. As it turned out, Mr. B's friendship with the Countess was purely platonic.

The continuation is seldom read now. To most late-twentieth-century readers, the title of the work, *Pamela*, means the original two-volume version from 1740; modern critical readings of the novel rarely take the continuation into account. In order to understand the early American response to *Pamela*, however, it is important to realize that, when eighteenth-century readers wrote about *Pamela* after 1741, they referred to the four-volume work consisting of both the original two-volume edition and the two-volume continuation, included as volumes three and four. Although the editors of Lucas's and Burr's letterbooks failed to notice, clues within these women's letters reveal that both Lucas and Burr read *Pamela* in its four-volume version. Lucas mentioned Pamela's criticism of Locke, and Burr referred to the episode with the Countess.

Eliza Lucas read *Pamela* in 1742, when she was in her late teens, long before her marriage to Charles Pinckney. Like many colonial readers, Lucas shared *Pamela* with a friend. After finishing the work, she sent it to her frequent correspondent, Mary Bartlett. Along with the book, Lucas sent a letter in which she provided a lengthy critique of *Pamela*. Lucas started with a brief comment about the book's heroine, "She is a good girl and as such I love her dearly, but . . ."[8] She then began her critique: "I must think her very defective and even blush for her while she allows her self that disgusting liberty of praising her self, or what is very like it, repeating all the fine speeches made to her by others when a person distinguished for modesty in every other respect should have chose rather to conceal them."[9] Lucas suggested that the author could have let the complimentary speeches come from the pen of another character. Pamela's lack of modesty, according to Lucas, caused her to fall short of being the paragon of feminine virtue that she was supposed to represent. After all, Lucas explained, "Those high compliments might have proceeded from the partiallity of her friends or with a view to encourage her and make her aspire after those qualifications which were ascribed to her, which I know experimently to be often the case." Lucas's key word is *experimently*. Her evaluation of Pamela's behavior and character were based on her own experience. She had known other young women whose development had been encouraged by the positive remarks of their superiors and thought that the praise bestowed on young Pamela's behavior might have been similarly motivated.

Lucas next anticipated her correspondent's objection to her critique and answered it: "But then you answer she was a young Country Girl, had seen nothing of life and it was natural for her to be pleased with praise and she had not art enough to conceal it. True, before she was Mrs. B. it be excuseable when only wrote to her father and mother, but after she had the advantage of Mr. B's conversation and others of sence and distinction I must be of a nother oppinion." Lucas recognized the difficulty and proposed a solution. Pamela could include the praising speeches within her own letters to show her naiveté early in the book, but after she married Mr. B., the praise should be voiced in the letters of another. The author could there show development of character. Here, Lucas revealed her remarkable understanding of the way the epistolary narrative worked. Fictional characters should show growth, maturation, and development. Pamela Andrews's personality, it seemed, was static. Of course, Lucas may have been relying on the book's didactic stance for her criticism. After all, if *Pamela* were designed to cultivate the principles of virtue and religion, then the title character should be shown in the process of becoming more virtuous.

Either way, Lucas was indicting Pamela not as an individual but as a fictional creation. Her criticism was directed more toward the author than his protagonist. Writing her critique, Lucas recognized that she might be overstepping the bounds of propriety, and she briefly assumed a humbler stance. She imagined Mary Bartlett's reaction to what she had written so far and replied: "Here you smile at my presumption for instructing one so farr above my own level as the Authour of Pamella . . . but, my Dear Miss Bartlett, contract your smile into a mortified look for I acquit the Authour." Lucas then transformed her criticism of the author into a criticism of his subject matter: "He designed to paint no more than a woman, and he certainly designed it as a reflection upon the vanity of our sex that a character so compleat in every other instance should be so greatly defective in this." To be sure, Lucas was merely reflecting the prevailing critical notion, "True wit is nature to advantage dressed," but her final deprecatory remarks toward the female sex are disappointing after her otherwise thorough critique.

After these lengthy remarks, Lucas told Mary Bartlett: "I have run thus farr before I was aware for I have nither capacity or inclination for Chritisism." Her comments were genuine. Although she had mentioned books and reading several times in earlier pages of her letterbook, nowhere else had she provided such an extensive literary critique. She may have disagreed with the way Richardson handled Pamela, but she nevertheless found the book compelling and thought-provoking. Lucas attributed her newfound inclination for criticism to Pamela's own behavior. After all, Pamela had set the "example by critisizeing Mr. Lock and has taken the libirty to disent from that admirable Author." Lucas's words suggested that she indeed had read *Pamela* as a conduct book. In other words, she appears to have taken Pamela's extensive critique of Locke's *Some Thoughts Concerning Education* as a behavior which could and should be imitated. "If Pamela can criticize Locke," she implied, "then I can criticize Richardson."

Pamela's implicit advice differed greatly from the advice promulgated by the conduct literature read by colonial women. While the conduct books advised women that it was permissible for them to read, those works continually stressed that women should not display their learning. In the four-volume *Pamela,* its exemplary title character devoted sixty pages to discussing a work she had read, John Locke's educational treatise. Pamela Andrews's reading and, more importantly, her critical remarks about her reading set a standard of behavior which allowed eighteenth-century women to discuss their own reading more freely, without censure.

Still, the fictional Pamela's behavior and the real behavior of Eliza Lucas and other colonial American women should not be equated. After all, Lucas's comments do not seem entirely sincere. Just because Lucas seems to have adopted a behavior which Pamela exemplified, it cannot necessarily be inferred that Lucas derived her behavior from Pamela's. Lucas's remarks suggest that some eighteenth-century women may have followed Pamela's example, but Lucas herself was too strong-willed to let her own behavior be guided by that of a fictional character. To be sure, Lucas applauded Pamela's comments about virtue and religion, and she would have agreed that such virtuous precepts should be followed; but Lucas did not see Pamela as a paragon of virtue whose behavior could be mimicked slavishly. Taken as a whole, Lucas's comments toward Pamela were ambivalent. When Pamela immodestly repeated the compliments of others, Lucas censured her; but when Pamela exemplified suitable feminine behavior, Lucas approved. Before coming to the book, Lucas had already internalized her own code of female behavior. Where Pamela's actions concurred with Lucas's personal code of conduct, Lucas approved, but where Pamela's did not, she disapproved.

Esther Edwards Burr came to *Pamela* at a different time in her life and at a different time in the history of the work than did Eliza Lucas. While Lucas had read *Pamela* in 1742, before she was married, Burr read the book during the mid-1750s, when she was twenty-three, married, and the mother of a child. Burr's comments about *Pamela* survive in her journal, which she kept in the form of a letterbook to her friend Sarah Prince. During the intervening period, Richardson had published *Clarissa* (1748), and that work had become widely known throughout colonial America. Multiple copies were sold at the *Virginia Gazette* office, for example; and Esther Burr's father, Jonathan Edwards, approved the book. Edwards wrote: "Clarissa A Romance in several volumes highly commended in the Scots Magazine of Novem. 1749 as tending much to promote virtue and piety."[10] Burr read *Pamela* after she had read and immensely enjoyed *Clarissa*. Whereas Lucas made her comments about the book after she had read all four volumes, Burr wrote a variety of judgments about *Pamela* while she was in the process of reading the work. It is important to note that, in the decade and a half after *Pamela* first appeared, the book's authorship was not universally known; and Burr refers to "Mr. Fielding" as the work's author. Clearly, she recognized the book as a work of fiction, but it did not particularly matter to her whether Henry Fielding or Samuel Richardson had written the work.

Burr borrowed *Pamela* and began reading it on 10 March 1755. She had liked *Clarissa* so well that she doubted whether *Pamela* would be as good. She wrote Sarah Prince: "I remember you said that in your opinnion it [*Pamela*] did not equel her [Clarissa]. Your judgment my dear has a very great influence on mine. Nay I would venture to report that such a Book surpast such an one, if you said so, If I had never laid my Eyes on 'em—but forall I intend not to be so complaisant but I will have a judgment of my own."[11] Burr's prior enjoyment of *Clarissa,* as well as Sarah Prince's opinion of *Pamela,* established the set of expectations which Burr brought to the work. She began reading *Pamela* with a general notion that the book would be something like *Clarissa* but somehow not as good. Viewed objectively, the two works presented similar situations. Pamela Andrews and Clarissa Harlowe were both innocent young women who were approached by older, wealthier, persistent suitors. Clarissa, Esther Burr knew, had been raped by Lovelace and ended up dying rather than submit to the reality of a life with him. Pamela, on the other hand, successfully resisted Mr. B until he proposed an equitable solution and the two married. Clarissa, in other words, never compromised herself by willfully submitting to the advances of her suitor.

Even with her prejudice against the book, due to her friend Sarah Prince's comments, Esther Edwards Burr found *Pamela* compelling. The day after she started reading, her letterbook indicates, she had made it well into the second volume. She wrote to Prince: "Pray my dear how could Pamela forgive Mr. B. all his Devilish conduct so as to consent to marry him? Sertainly this does not well agree with so much virtue and piety. Nay I think it is a very great defect in the performance." Here, Burr directly criticized the author's "performance." It was incongruous that Pamela Andrews, who was supposed to be a model of virtue and piety, would ever consent to marry the "Devilish" Mr. B. Burr also questioned the book's implicit message: "Is'n't it seting up Riches and honnour as the great essentials of happyness in a married state? Perhaps I am two rash in my judgment for I have not read it half out tho' I have enough to see the Devil in the Man." She continued reading.

After she had spent three days reading *Pamela,* Burr's judgment remained basically unchanged. She expressed to Prince her continuing disgust with the work's author: "He has degraded our sex most horridly, to go and represent such virtue as Pamela, falling in love with Mr. B in the midst of such foul and abominable actions." While Richardson seemed to portray his heroine as a model of virtue, Burr saw her as quite the opposite. No virtuous woman ever willfully would submit to such a match. By telling the story of such a woman, the author degraded all women. It would be better to have Pamela die, like Clarissa, Burr believed, than to have her submit to Mr. B. She continued, "I could never pardon him [the author] if he had not made it up in Clarissia. I guss he found his mistake, so took care to mend the first opportunity." As Burr saw the novel, *Pamela* represented the author's first, botched attempt to tell a story of the relationship between a virtuous young woman and an aggressive suitor, whereas *Clarissa* later told the same story successfully.

Burr's letters indicate that her reading pace slowed considerably as she began volumes three and four, the continuation. While she had read almost completely through the first two volumes in three days, it took her an additional month to read the continuation. Although she did not read volumes three and four with the same intensity she devoted to the first two volumes, Burr did find much to admire: "I think there is some excelent observations on the duties of the Married state in *Pamela*. I shall repent my pains I guss." A few days later, she reiterated, "I am highly pleased with some of *Pamelas* remarks on Married life, as well as her conduct in it—She was more than Woman—An *Angel imbodied.*" By the time Burr reached the place in volume four where Pamela and Mr. B attend the masquerade, and Mr. B begins flirting with the Countess, her disgust with the author of *Pamela* returned in force. She wrote Prince: "To day I have [been] reading an account of Mr *B's* going after the *Coun[tess]* of _____. This appears very strange to me considering the [title] of the Book, which is, *Virtue rewarded*—I could but ju[st] stomach to allow it that title before, for he was a sad fello[w] to be sure, had one Child, *bastard,* and did his indeavour to get many more as it seems by *Lady Davers,* and his own confession two—but I dont know—I have a poor judgme[n]t of my own." Burr was less sure of her own judgement than Eliza Lucas, and she asked Prince's opinion: "I wish you would be so good as to let me ha[ve] your thoughts on this affair, and I should be glad if it is not two much trouble on the whole History." Burr did not want to censure the work so harshly, but the plot compelled her to criticism. She then added a personal remark which lets us see a touching picture of her as she reads. Burr wrote Prince: "you need not wonder if I write a little up the scrawl for I have Sally in my Lap." Burr, in her own personal life, was at almost the same stage that the fictional Pamela was in her life. Pamela has just experienced the birth of Billy, her first child, and Burr read the book while she tended to the business of raising her first child, Sally.

Burr objected primarily to the author's blatant materialism, his direct equation of virtue and money. "In my humble opinion *Riches,* and *honour,*" she wrote, "are set up two much—can Money reward virtue? And besides Mr *Bs* being a *libertine* he was a *dreadfull high-spirited Man, impatient of contradiction* as he says of himself—*Pamela* had a task of it, with all Mr *Bs* good qualities. She was as much affraid of him as of a Lyon—if the author had [le]ft it to me to have intitled the Books, I think I should hav[e] chose *Virtue tryed,* instead of *rewarded.*" At this point in the novel, Pamela's match hardly seems like a good one. Pamela must attend to her domestic responsibilities of maintaining their home and raising their child while she constantly worries about Mr. B's possible infidelity with the Countess.

Burr read about the eventual outcome between the Countess and Mr. B a few days later and wrote: "Well—*Pamelas* virtue is *rewarded* at last, Mr. *B.* is become a good Man. I confess I had waited for this *reward* 'till I was quite discouraged, and after that *black* affair of the Countess I wholy dispared of a *reward* in this World—but I want to find a little fault for all—Might not Mr *Fielding* as well have spared himself the pains of this last tryal? Was not her virtue thoroughly tryed before?" Burr's comment suggests one way she may have interpreted the meaning of the book's title. Since she had read *Clarissa* first, she appears to have expected a similar denouement. She had anticipated that the title meant that Pamela's virtue—like Clarissa's—would be rewarded in heaven, not on earth. Part of her disappointment with Pamela Andrews had to do with the fact that she was not as strong-willed as Clarissa Harlowe. Burr's complex and ambiguous attitudes toward the book faded after she finished the final volume. Her ultimate pleasure in the book is a little disappointing: "Well I have finnished *Pamela*. Tis realy a ve[ry] good thing for all my ill nature about it."

It is difficult to compare Lucas's reaction to the book with Burr's. After all, Lucas recorded her comments after she had finished reading all four volumes. Burr's comments were made while she was reading the book. Still, the two women agreed on several things. Both felt that the author provided many important comments concerning female virtue. In her comments, Eliza Lucas wrote that she esteemed the author "much for the regard he pays to virtue and religion throughout the whole piece"; and Burr wrote, "There is sertainly many excellent observations and rules laid down [so] that I shall never regret my pains."[12] The two remarks suggest that the rules of conduct which *Pamela* presented could be detached from the work as a whole. Indeed, Richardson's remarks concerning virtuous behavior *were* extracted from the novel. A work entitled *Paths of Virtue Delineated,* an anthology of passages selected from *Pamela, Clarissa,* and *Sir Charles Grandison,* was a popular item at the *Virginia Gazette* office.[13] Even if readers found the plot distasteful, they nevertheless could read many worthwhile comments about virtuous feminine behavior. While Lucas and Burr both objected to aspects of the book—Lucas to Pamela's immodesty, Burr to Mr. B's licentiousness—both also found much to admire.

Abigail Adams also mentioned *Pamela* in her correspondence, but she commented on the work during the 1780s, long after she first read *Pamela* and Richardson's other works. Her remarks about the book survive in a letter she wrote from London to her niece, Lucy Cranch; her tone differs from that of Lucas and Burr, who made their comments in letters to close friends. Both Lucas and Burr seem to say, "This is what I think about the book. What do you think?" Adams, on other hand, seems to say, "This is what you should think." She begins her discussion of Richardson with a reference to his *Letters Written to and for Particular Friends on the Most Important Occasions* (1741): "I believe Richardson has done more towards embellishing the present age, and teaching them the talent of letter-writing, than any other modern I can name. You know I am passionately fond of all his works, even to his 'Pamela.'" Adams's approval of *Pamela* seems somewhat qualified. In other words, she is saying, "I like all of Richardson's works, even *Pamela.*" Adams's experiences in London helped make Richardson's degenerate characters, such as Mr. B, all the more believable: "In the simplicity of our manners, we judge that many of his descriptions and some of his characters are beyond real life; but those, who have been conversant in these old corrupted countries, will be soon convinced that Richardson painted only the truth in his abandoned characters; and nothing beyond what human nature is capable of attaining, and frequently has risen to, in his amiable portraits." Adams applauded Richardson's elevation of virtue and condemnation of vice: "He never loses sight of religion, but points his characters to a future state of restitution as the sure ground of safety to the virtuous, and excludes not hope from the wretched penitent." She continued: "The oftener I have read his books, and the more I reflect upon his great variety of characters, perfectly well supported, the more I am led to love and admire the author. . . . He may have his faults, but they are so few, that they ought not to be named in the brilliant clusters of beauties which ornament his works."[14] Adams's comment suggests that she has read *Pamela* as well as Richardson's other works numerous times, and each time her approval had grown. Upon first reading, in other words, she did not like *Pamela* as well as she did upon second or third reading. Adams's comments therefore are similar to those of Burr *after* finishing the book. Once Burr and Adams had finished the work and knew how things would turn out, then the book became much more comfortable and more acceptable. Reading the book for a second time was much less disconcerting, because the reader already knew how the protagonist's virtue would be rewarded.

Although their reactions to the book and its characters differed markedly, both Eliza Lucas and Esther Edwards Burr ultimately felt ambivalent about the book and its title character. Abigail Adams's approval was less qualified, but her remarks hinted that she had preferred Richardson's other works to *Pamela*. To what extent can we generalize from Burr's, Lucas', and Adams's experiences reading *Pamela*? Did other colonial American women react similarly to these women? While I located no other women's comments about *Pamela*, I found several comments by colonial American men. Overall, these comments were much like each other but different from those of Burr and Lucas. Sending his sister Mary the third and fourth volumes of *Pamela*, New York barrister Elisha Parker recommended:

> They are books that have been generally well esteemed of and read by your part of the world especially. I think 'em by far the most proper book of any I ever saw for the youth of both, but especially of your sex. Virtue is there painted in such lively and amiable colours with such great rewards attending it and the bad and its consequences of a vicious course of life so well described that it can't but deeply fix in the mind of an unprejudiced reader a lasting love of the one and utter abhorance of the other. I have too good an opinion of you to think the assistance of books is wanted. However, the more virtuously inclined the mind of any person is, the more will it delight in hearing of virtue praised and this with the advantage that it will be got by reading a stile so beautiful and natural as the stile of *Pamela*.[15]

When Mrs. William Allen acquired a copy of *Pamela* during the winter of 1741–42, her husband read the work and found it "a most agreeable fund of discourse and reflections of the finest sort." Pennsylvania provincial secretary and cleric Richard Peters wrote, "To be sure no book ever yet penned in my opinion come up to Pamela, the model and envy of her sex."[16] When Rev. Ebenezer Parkman's daughter Molly borrowed *Pamela* from a neighbor, he read it, too. Parkman recorded in his diary, "Finish'd the second Volume of Pamela. See some Remarks I would draw up, on this Latter Piece."[17] Jonathan Edwards wrote in a manuscript notebook: "Pamela in Monthly Review of Decem. 1752 p. 470 Speaks of Pamela as an *Interesting original* worthy to be *spoken of in terms of high Respect which has afforded entertainment to Readers of all*

Ranks."[18] In his "Progress of Dulness," John Trumbull humorously suggested that young American women modeled themselves after Pamela:

> Thus *Harriet* reads, and reading really
> Believes herself a young Pamela,
> The high-wrought whim, the tender strain
> Elate her mind and turn her brain.
> Before her glass, with smiling grace
> She views the wonders of her face;
> There stands in admiration moveless
> And hopes a Grandison, or Lovelace.

These various comments from early American men clarify the difference between the contemporary male response and the contemporary female response. The male attitudes were straightforward; quite simply, Pamela was a paragon of virtue. The female attitudes, however, remained complex, disparaging, and ambiguous.

Pamela's enormous popularity prompted many similar works. These together formed an emerging literary genre which, to be most accurate, should be called didactic fictional discourse, but which became known as the novel. From the 1740s until beyond the colonial period, instructive novels with exemplary female protagonists were written, published, and imported into the colonies. Their instructive aspects and their similarities to Richardson's works were publicized to help sell the books. Bookseller James Rivington, for example, advertised Rousseau's *La Nouvelle Héloïse* with the following comment: "The New Eloisa, written by the ingenious Rousseau. This is the favorite novel; every one who hears of it, reads and admires it. Elocution, Sensibility, Refinement and Humor constitute its principal Ornaments, and it is the only Novel that has been equally well received with the celebrated Clarissa Harlowe, to which it bears some Resemblance, only the New Eloisa is allowed to be a more masterly and instructive Performance."[19] Everyone knew these types of books were pleasurable to read; the key selling point was that they were simultaneously instructive.

Works by Eliza Haywood, Frances Sheridan, Frances Moore Brooke, Sarah Fielding, and Charlotte Ramsay Lennox were delightfully instructive and widely read. The colonial woman read Haywood's *History of Miss Betsy Thoughtless, History of Jemmy and Jenny Jessamy,* and *Hus-*

band and Wife; Sheridan's *Memoirs of Miss Sydney Bidulph*; Brooke's *Julia Mandeville*; and Sarah Fielding's *Governess, or the Little Female Academy*, perhaps the most heavily didactic of these works. Fielding's *Governess* tells the story of Mrs. Teachum and her nine pupils. The work is basically a program for girls' education, thinly disguised as fiction.[20]

Charlotte Ramsay Lennox deserves special attention. She was, after all, born in New York and lived there until she was around fifteen, and her *Life of Harriot Stuart*, a work known from Massachusetts to South Carolina, contains descriptions of colonial New York.[21] But Lennox's *The Female Quixote* really established her reputation. *The Female Quixote* tells the story of one Arabella, a young woman with a passion for novel-reading which causes her to have a somewhat unrealistic view of the world. She sees the men she encounters as being much like the men in her books. Imagining every man to have designs on her leads her into all kinds of confusion and trouble. Arabella's misconceptions bring her near death, but eventually she recovers and marries sensibly.

The impact Lennox's *The Female Quixote* had in colonial America becomes obvious in a letter Eliza Huger wrote to Eliza Lucas Pinckney in 1774:

> I have returned you "The Earl of Salisbury" as the servant told me you had not yet finish'd it. When you are inclin'd for a very high diversion I will send you the "Female Quixote," which, tho' not quite so well wrote as the Don of that name, will afford you a good deal of entertainment from the absurdities she commits. When you have read it I shall be oblig'd for your opinion, whether it is not a very proper Book for young Folks, to shew them the consiquence of being too fond of those books which all girls would rather read than things of more consequence.[22]

To be sure, Eliza Huger's remarks contained much irony. The "Earl of Salisbury" was Thomas Leland's historical novel, *Longsword, Earl of Salisbury*. In other words, as she returned one novel and recommended another, Huger asserted that young women should be cautioned against too much novel reading.

Writing her *Memoir* in the early nineteenth century, Hannah Adams described growing up during the colonial period and portrayed her teenage fondness for reading novels as very similar to that of the misguided Arabella. Adams recalled: "I read with avidity a variety of books, previously to my mind's being sufficiently matured, and strengthened to make a proper selection. I was passionately fond of novels; and, as I lived in a state of seclusion, I acquired false ideas of life."[23] The elderly Hannah Adams, looking back at her own girlish reading, saw her young self as a kind of Arabella who let novel reading cloud her understanding of the real world. Later in the *Memoir*, Adams tried to explain another problem with novel reading: "Reading much religious controversy must be extremely trying to a female, whose mind, instead of being strengthened by those studies which exercise the judgment, and give stability to the character, is debilitated by reading romances and novels, which are addressed to the fancy and imagination, and are calculated to heighten the feelings."[24] While Adams criticizes her youthful reading from the perspective of a half-century beyond, she never is quite able to conceal the pleasure she received from novel reading during her teenage years.

Hannah Adams's remarks attest to the prejudice against novels which lingered well into the nineteenth century. For those who wanted romance and adventure but preferred not to read fiction, travel books provided suitable reading. In *The Female Spectator*, Eliza Haywood recommended reading "travels" for several reasons. Perilous voyages, she wrote, "raise in us the most lively ideas of the power and goodness of divine providence." Furthermore, reading about the exploits of both men-of-war and merchant ships was one way women could express their gratitude to the sailors who essentially protected and enhanced the British way of life. She explained: "To the royal navy we are indebted for the preservation of every thing the world calls dear;—they are the bulwark of our laws, our liberties, our religion, our estates, and very lives:—by them we sleep securely, undreading all incursions and foreign depredations." Merchant sailors, on the other hand, risked their lives to import exotic spices and fruit and elegant clothing and furniture from all parts of the world. Haywood concluded that stories of both naval exploits and merchant sailor adventures were well worth reading: "The least we can do, therefore, is to commiserate their sufferings, and rejoice in their escapes from those imminent dangers with which they are continually surrounded, even in those voyages which have the most prosperous event."[25]

The travel book most likely to be found on the colonial woman's bookshelf during the first half of the eighteenth century was George Anson's *Voyage Round the World*. Not surprisingly, Esther Edwards Burr knew the work. After Sarah Prince had invited Burr to visit Boston,

Burr responded that her family—daughter Sally was around a year old—made it impossible to take such an extended trip.[26] Besides, they would soon be moving to Princeton when the college was relocated there, and she would be expecting another child, Aaron Burr, Jr., the following year. Burr wrote to her friend: "I find I was not settled till I had a Child, and now I am effectually settled, a journey seems a Vast thing. I am to go to Princeton soon, which seems like Ansons voyage almost."[27] The editors of Burr's *Journal* mistranscribed *Ansor* for *Anson* and consequently did not identify the reference, but Burr clearly was alluding to the well-known travel writer. Anson's travels once had taken him to the southern coast of colonial America. A Carolina woman who had met Anson found him "handsome, good-natured, polite, well bred, generous, and humane; passionately fond of music, and so old-fashioned as to make some profession of religion." In his 1762 sale catalog, bookseller James Rivington emphasized the book's sentimental appeal, and in the catalog for Mein's Circulating Library in Boston, Anson's *Voyages* was listed among numerous other works which appealed to women readers.[28]

Nearly all the reasons for reading travels that Eliza Haywood listed in *The Female Spectator* apply to Anson's *Voyages*, but the work attracted female readers for other reasons as well. First published at a time when the novel was making a significant impact on the literary marketplace, Anson's work provided its readers with a nonfiction alternative to the novel which contained as much action and pathos as any novel. It brought the war between England and Spain alive, set it on a world stage, and gave readers an insider's view of the strategies involved in sea battles. Importantly, the work exposed its female readers to life aboard a man-of-war in His Majesty's Service, a life which was completely beyond the realm of their experience. Anson's stories of death, privation, suffering, and perseverance were touching. Finally, the book's appearance in the late 1740s coincided with a time when women were being encouraged to read geography and learn how to use a globe.[29] Anson's frequent references to latitudes and out-of-the-way places allowed readers to follow his route as he circumnavigated the globe.

Abigail Adams enjoyed reading travels and comparing other lands to her own. After reading Patrick Brydone's *Tour through Sicily and Malta,* she noticed similar climatic effects during a New England spring: "I sit down to write tho I feel very Languid; the approach of Spring unstrings my nerves, and the South winds have the same Effect upon me which Brydon says the Siroce winds have upon the inhabitants of Sicily.

It gives the vapours, blows away all their gaiety and spirits and gives a degree of Lassitude both to the Body and mind, which renders them absolutely incapable of performing their usual functions."[30] Travel books provided colonial readers with excellent opportunities to compare their own land and culture with those of others.

One of colonial America's most enthusiastic readers of travel literature was Abigail Adams's younger sister, Elizabeth Smith. Elizabeth (or Betsy, as the family called her) was seventeen when Isaac Smith, Jr., her cousin and a student at Harvard, visited her and recommended some books. After she had finished the books he lent her, she returned them with a long letter. The letter is important for her comments on travel writing, but it is perhaps more important for her rhetorical stance. Since the letters of Eliza Lucas and Esther Edwards Burr, discussed above, were written to female correspondents, their contents are more forthright than they would have been had the two women been writing to male correspondents. Though the frankness of both women reveals their genuine attitudes toward *Pamela*, their letters reveal more about their true feelings than letters written to men would have. Within colonial society, women seldom were able to express themselves in the way Lucas and Burr do in the letters to their friends Mary Bartlett and Sarah Prince. Betsy Smith's letter to her cousin Isaac, a letter written by an articulate, intelligent colonial woman to a male correspondent, more accurately reflects how the colonial woman presented herself within her restricted social context.

Betsy Smith began the letter with thanks and then expressed a desire for Isaac to supply her with further similar books: "If at any time when you have Books that you think would be eddifying or instructive, I shall look upon it as a peculiar favour, if you will oblige me with the reading of them."[31] The works Isaac had lent her included *Travels through France and Italy* (1766), Tobias Smollett's satirical—if not caustic—travelogue of the journey he and his wife had taken from Boulogne, France, through Paris and Lyons, and eventually to Nice. From Nice, the Smolletts traveled to Italy, seeing Pisa, Florence, and Rome. Betsy Smith remarked: "There a[re] many mortifying pictures in human nature, which if exhibited to our veiw, are enough to humble the proudest mortals. Some Nations are remarkable for their hypocricy, some for their avirice, inhospitallity, and a revengeful temper [and for?] the contrary. But in many Countrys Idleness, and Dirtiness seems to be the prevailing evil."

Betsy Smith then commented on Smollett's depiction of the French: "What a shocking and ridiculous character does Smollet give of the French." But she added, "He does not exceed the discriptions I have met with else where." Clearly, Betsy Smith felt she had something to prove to her cousin. Her comments display her wide reading and show that she could compare Smollett's text with other works she knew. All in all, Smollett had encountered few people or places to admire, and Betsy refused to believe his almost universally deprecating remarks: "I think it very strange, and greatly to be lamented, that in all those places which he travelled through, Pisa was the only one, of which he could give a good character, and he speaks of it as something very extraordinary that here he found some good company, and even a few men of taste and learning." Betsy Smith then felt the need to express her overall impression of Smollett's works: "Perhaps he did not exercise so unprejudiced and impartial a Temper, as he hoped would ever distinguish his writings. But all must allow that he has an excellent faculty of dressing up a story in a very humoursome manner." She next generalized from her reading: "We are too apt to form a general character of a people, by a few, that we are acquainted with in a Place. Sometimes Persons meet with extraordinary kindness, and perhaps, as often, with very ill treatment: and this may so prejudice him in favour of, or against a Family, Town, or Country, that he is not capable of that impartiallity which is an essential Qualification of an Historiographer." Betsy Smith's comment shows that she had read enough histories and travels that she already had acquired important criteria for judging subsequent literary works which came to her attention.

She then criticized another work Isaac had loaned her, *A Compendium of the Most Approved Modern Travels* (1757). This four-volume anthology of recent travel literature contained materials from Erik Pontippidan's *Natural History of Norway*, Richard Pococke's *Description of the East*, Alexander Drummond's *Travels in Europe and Asia*, Alexander Russel's *Natural History of Aleppo*, and Jonas Hanway's *Historical Account of the British Trade over the Caspian Sea, with a Journal of Travels from London through Russia.* Betsy remarked, "In the Modern Travels, according to Pontippidans account, Norway seems to demand our respect, more than any other Country that is described. I think he has given the inhabitants, a much more amiable character, than Pococke, Drummond, Russel, Hanway, or Smollet, has, of any of those various places, which they travelled through." Betsy Smith's reference to the various authors from the collection proves to her cousin that she had thoroughly read the four-volume work.

She set her letter aside before finishing it, but she resumed it six days later, on her eighteenth birthday. Instead of continuing her literary critique, she gave her muse free reign: "'Tis the funeral of the former year, and I feel as great solemnity on my mind, as if I was actually attending the funeral of some near relation, or taking a farewell of some Dear Friend. This Day compleats eighteen suns, that have [had] their anual circuit, since I first drew the breath of life, and every year seems shorter than the former." Striving for literary effect, she continued, "Moment flies on moment—Hours on hours. 'Tomorrow and tomorrow creeps on.' Months suceed months. Time hurries on, with a resistless unrelenting hand. The present moment is all that we can call our own. Eighteen years seem att first veiw to be but as so many months; yet by more closely attending, and taking a retrospect of all those transactions within my remembrance, time seems to lengthen while I reflect upon them." Her deliberate striving for literary effect seems to suggest that she still was trying to "prove" herself to her older and better educated cousin.

Betsy then felt the need to apologize for her bookish comments in the first part of the letter: "Pardon me my Cousin for so freely remarking upon those Books you lent me, it was not because I thought you had not made much better observations yourself, but it is what you encouraged when you was here, and now you ought certainly to excuse me." She realized that, even if her comments seemed silly to him, they were important to her: "There is one advantage will accrue at lest, and that is, I shall more deeply impress upon my memory what I have read." Reading compelled Betsy Smith to writing, and writing reinforced the importance of her reading.

The volume of travels read most widely by women during the last decade of the colonial period was Lady Mary Wortley Montagu's *Letters . . . Written, During Her Travels in Europe, Asia and Africa* (1763). Printer Sarah Goddard of Rhode Island reprinted Montagu's *Letters* in 1766.[32] Malcolm Adams, a Baltimore general store proprietor, made an inventory on 29 August 1767 indicating that he had five copies of Montagu's *Letters* for sale.[33] Philadelphia printer Robert Bell published an *Additional Volume to the Letters of Montagu with Poems, and Her Defence of Marriage* (1768).

Montagu's *Letters* appealed to its female readers for many reasons.

She wrote the letters to several different correspondents and specifically shaped her prose to each correspondent. Many of the people she wrote to were women. Juxtaposing Montagu's letters to women with those to men fascinatingly reveals how her experiences changed in the telling. The letters to female friends provide intimate glimpses into the women's world of Eastern Europe and the Middle East. One of Montagu's most exotic descriptions is of the Turkish baths, a place where women could loiter with one another without shame, discomfort, or fear, as a man, if caught on the premises, instantly was put to death. In another letter, Montagu describes the veils the Muslim women had to wear. Rather than seeing the veil as dehumanizing, Montagu sees it as liberating. The veil lets the woman pass through the community anonymously and thus allows her to engage in intrigues without fear of being caught.

Anne Grant read Montagu's *Letters* but found it uninformed, at least concerning one point of fact. She wrote in her *Memoirs*:

> Lady Mary Montague ludicrously says, that the court of Vienna was the paradise of old women; and that there is no other place in the world where a woman past fifty excites the least interest. Had her travels extended to the interior of North America, she would have seen another instance of this inversion of the common mode of thinking. Here a woman never was of consequence, till she had a son old enough to fight the battles of his country; from that date she held a superior rank in society; was allowed to live at ease, and even called to consultations on national affairs.[34]

Grant's comment shows that she saw Lady Montagu as an intellectual model—but not as an unreachable, infallible one. Her comment also reflects pride in her birthplace and an interest in women's relationship to society. Another widely-read work that specifically addressed the place of women in other cultures as well as her own, was *Hymen; or, An Accurate Description of the Ceremonies Used in Marriage, by Every Nation in the Known World*. John Mein's Circulating Library in Boston had a copy of the work, and it also could be found on sale at the *Georgia Gazette* office.[35]

The American woman wanted to read exciting books written by or about women, but her burgeoning pride of place created an interest in reading American books and therefore prompted a Mary Rowlandson revival during the early 1770s. Rowlandson's *Soveraignty and Goodness of God* first had appeared in 1682, and it had been reprinted in 1720; but it had been neglected during the next five decades.[36] In 1770, however, it was reprinted in Boston, under the title *A Narrative of the Captivity*. Other Boston editions appeared in 1771 and 1773; and a New London, Connecticut, edition was published in 1773. Rowlandson's captivity narrative made an ideal read. Not only could it be perused as an exciting, if frightening, travel narrative, but also Rowlandson's unshakable faith made the work appropriate closet reading.

While both the novels and travel books attracted readers for their tales of romantic adventure, the two kinds of works shared another characteristic. The women novelists, their heroines, and the female travel writers provided colonial women with intellectual role models. Taken as a whole, these various works prepared the way for the numerous American women novelists who were to emerge after the colonial period.

CHAPTER 6

Science Books

South Carolinian Martha Laurens learned to read by the time she was three and, in the next half-dozen years, mastered English and French grammar. As her husband David Ramsay later described her early learning: "She was indefatigable in cultivating an acquaintance with books; and, by means of abridging, transcribing, and committing to memory, was very successful in retaining much of what she read."[1] Shortly before her tenth birthday in 1769, her father, Henry Laurens, boasted that his daughter "is forward in her learning, she reads well & begins to write prettily, is not dull in the french Grammar, & plays a little on the Harpsichord, but better than all, she handles her needles in all the useful branches & some of the most refined parts of Womens work & promises me to learn to make minced Pies & to dress a Beef Steak."[2] While Laurens was proud of his daughter's book learning, her domestic promise made him prouder still.

After her mother's death, Martha, eleven at the time, remained in South Carolina with her aunt and uncle, Mary and James Laurens, while her father took her brothers abroad to be educated. Henry Laurens believed that his sons needed the educational opportunities England had to offer, but Martha could better pursue her proper education by staying in her aunt's household. Still, Henry Laurens's correspondence shows that he helped direct her education from across the ocean. Writing to his brother James shortly after Martha's twelfth birthday, Henry approved James's plan to provide Martha with a drawing teacher, expressed curiosity about her progress in arithmetic, and recommended that she read Catharine Macaulay's *History of England*, but he ended by stating: "And amidst all these finer Branches of a Carolina Ladies Education, I hope She will learn to cut out and make up a Piece of Linnen, and even a Piece of white or blue Woolen for her Negroes, to administer family Medicine, and be able by and by, to direct her Maids with Judgement and understanding, in such and many other essential Duties in Domestic Life, which She has now an Opportunity of learning from her Dear Aunt."[3] When she was fourteen, Martha wrote to her father, still in England, asking him to send her a globe, and he agreed to do so. He wrote back telling her that he was sending: two eighteen-inch globes, an earthly globe along with a celestial one; a guidebook for the two globes; various scientific instruments; and a dozen pencils monographed with her initials. He concluded, "When you are measuring the surface of this world, remember you are to act a part on it, and think of a plumb pudding and other domestic duties."[4] Willing to encourage his daughter's interest in science, Henry Laurens was unwilling to let that interest take precedence over the traditional feminine domestic responsibilities. His several remarks to his daughter suggest the uneasy relationship between learning and domesticity near the end of the colonial period.

Since the beginning of the colonial era, as the books on housewifery, physick, and midwifery have shown, certain areas of science had been women's special province. With the rise of modern science during the seventeenth century, however, domestic sciences diminished in importance, while the experimental, theoretical sciences increased.[5] Through much of the seventeenth century, women retained control of the traditional feminine sciences, but they were discouraged from pursuing modern science. In the late seventeenth and early eighteenth centuries, however, it became acceptable for women to learn modern science. At first they were encouraged to pursue natural history, which, after all, was closely related to the process of gathering herbs for home remedies. Later they were encouraged to pursue natural philosophy, which generally meant astronomy, geography, and Newtonian optics.

The life of Maria Taylor Byrd, William Byrd II's second wife, helps illustrate how the early eighteenth-century colonial woman might have taken an interest in science. Maria Taylor was born and raised in England; from an upper-middle-class family, she received an excellent education, learning French and Greek. After her marriage to William Byrd in 1724, she moved to Virginia with her husband. During her first six years of marriage, Maria Byrd gave birth to four children—three girls and a boy. The day-to-day responsibilities of raising a family and directing a large household put her in close touch with the traditional domestic sciences, but, surviving evidence indicates, her scientific curiosity extended beyond the confines of the nursery and the pantry. Like other women of the period, Maria took an interest in collecting curiosities of natural history. One time, for example, she asked a friend to get her some conch shells from Barbados.[6] Maria was interested in local natural history, too. When John Bartram visited the Byrd's Westover home during the fall of 1738, he was taken by the ornate wrought iron which decorated the Westover gate; Maria took an interest in his botanical observations. Bartram recalled: "Col. Byrd's Lady persuaded me mightily to draw plants. She saw me draw the iron flourishes on the top of their garden gates which pleased her so well that she said she was sure I could draw plants if I could but try."[7] Maria Byrd, it appears, instrumentally encouraged the work of colonial America's foremost botanist.

After her husband's death, Maria took over responsibility for her son's education. She considered sending William Byrd III to England to complete his schooling and even began planning the trip, but she eventually decided against it. She wrote to a correspondent, "I thought again he woud certainly get the Small-Pox, which is most terrible fatal to those who are born in America, and that I shoud be accessory to his Death." Though he remained in Virginia, William Byrd III apparently did not take intellectual advantage of the excellent book collection his father had assembled. Instead, he considered selling the library for ready cash. It was largely through Maria's efforts (and later, the efforts of William Byrd III's wife, Mary Willing Byrd) that the splendid Byrd library remained intact until her son's death.[8]

Maria Taylor Byrd's scientific curiosity, while noteworthy, was by no means unique. Many other colonial women became interested in natural history during the period. Elizabeth Teackle owned a copy of Francis Bacon's *Sylva Sylvarum; or, A Natural Historie.*[9] South Carolinian Mary Stafford remembered the encouragement of her English kinsman, the natural historian James Petiver, as upon emigrating to America in 1711, she first explored the Carolina backwoods.[10] Another South Carolinian, Martha Daniell Logan, corresponded with John Bartram and wrote a "Gardener's Kalendar."[11] Bostonian Sarah Noyes owned a Greek and Latin edition of Aelian's *Variae Historiae* (Geneva, 1630), which she inscribed "Sarah noyes her booke."[12]

In the mid-eighteenth century, New Yorker Jane Colden became colonial America's most important woman of science. When Jane first began to show an interest in botany, her father, Cadwallader Colden, wrote to his friend Peter Collinson, "As it is not usual for woemen to take pleasure in Botany as a Science I shall do what I can to incourage her in this amusement which fills up her idle hours to much better purpose tha[n] the usual amusements eagerly pursued by others of her sex."[13] Colden's words reflect a contemporary commonplace. Increasing amounts of leisure time, especially among the well-to-do, had given eighteenth-century women greater opportunity for recreational pursuits. The science books directed specifically to female readers emphasized that studying science was a much loftier pursuit than the more frivolous ways in which women spent their time. One author of an introductory science book urged women to "detach some of their happy Leisure from being lost by Sports, Play, or worse Avocations, and to dedicate it to the Improvement of their Minds."[14]

Cadwallader Colden taught Jane the Linnean system of classification and bought her some botanical books to aid her studies. He wrote Collinson, "As she cannot have the opportunity of seeing plants in a Botanical Garden I think the next best is to see the best cuts or pictures of them for which purpose I would buy for her Tourneforts Institutes & Morison's Historia plantarum, or if you know any better books for this purpose as you are a better judge than I am I will be obliged to you in making the choice."[15] The works her father specifically requested were Joseph Pitton Tournefort's *Institutiones rei herbariae* (Paris, 1719) and Robert Morison's *Plantarum historiae universalis,* both of which contained engravings of numerous plant species. The engravings influenced Jane's own botanical drawings. Equipped with knowledge of the Linnaean system and some key books, Jane delved into botanic research at Coldengham, the family's home in rural New York. She also began corresponding with the day's most prominent naturalists. To one of her queries, John Bartram responded: "The viney plant thee so well discribes I take to be the dioscoria of hill & Gronovius tho I never searched the characters of the flower so curiously as I find thee hath done but pray search them books."[16] Bartram's offhand references to the botanical works of John Hill and Gronovius suggest that Jane was familiar with them and could readily check the references. Jane Colden eventually contributed to the Edinburgh Philosophical Society and compiled a lengthy descriptive catalog of New York flora.[17]

Her scientific curiosity also showed in her domestic pursuits. In 1756, she kept an accurate log of her cheese-making activities. Far different from the usual manuscript recipe compilations, Jane Colden's "Cheese Book" provided a detailed record of her various experiments with both ingredients and cheese-making techniques. It was less a recipe book and more a scientist's experimental record. At the end of the surviving document, she proudly recorded having produced 348 pounds of cheese, which she had sold for £12/13/3.[18]

Visitors to Coldengham recognized Jane's intelligence. Walter Rutherford, for example, found her "a Florist and Botanist" and stated, "She has discovered a great number of Plants never before described and has given their Properties and Virtues, many of which are found useful in Medicine, and she draws and colors them with great beauty. Dr. Whyte, of Edinburg, is in the number of her correspondents." Rutherford concluded: "N.B. She makes the best cheese I ever ate in America."[19] While it is pleasing to read a testimonial which shows that Jane Colden's meticulous cheese-making experiments resulted in an excellent product, Rutherford's comments are ultimately disappointing, for he elevated her domestic skills above her scientific pursuits. He viewed her cheese-making abilities and the medicinal usefulness of her newly-discovered plants as more noteworthy than her contributions to scientific knowledge.

From the mid-eighteenth century on, the growing popularity of novel reading—or, more precisely, the fear of too much novel reading—increased the opportunities women had to read science books. Demarville, the author of a mid-eighteenth-century work, *The Young Lady's Geography,* suggested: "Every endeavour to entice from the hands of the Fair, obscene and ridiculous novels, (which serve only to vitiate their morals, inflame their passions, and eradicate the very seeds of virtue) by persuading them to the study of a science both useful and amusing, and without some knowledge of which they cannot read even a public paper of intelligence with pleasure or advantage."[20] Demarville's forward-looking stance suggests that learning the basics of science was seen as more than just another recreational pursuit; rather, it provided important information which women could use in their daily lives.

The seventeenth-century science book read most by colonial women was Bernard Le Bovier de Fontenelle's introduction to Cartesian thought, *Entretiens sur la pluralité des mondes,* commonly known as *The Plurality of Worlds.* This work, consisting of dialogues on the Copernican system, could be found throughout colonial America in the original French or in one of three different English versions, including the earliest, Aphra Behn's translation.[21] The dialogues, between a Cartesian philosopher and a charming, inquisitive Marquise, took place in her ornately landscaped garden. The male figure played the part of teacher and the female the part of eager though naïve pupil. As Erica Harth explains in her sophisticated treatment of the subject, it is important to note that Fontenelle did not write the work specifically for women readers. He wrote it for anyone curious about science who had no prior scientific training. The Marquise, therefore, serves as a rhetorical device, a stand-in for the reader, a way to make scientific discourse more easily comprehensible and more pleasurable to read.[22] The format also enhanced the work's readability. The dialogue—a prose genre with which the colonial woman had been familiar since her catechism—made print discourse seem less like reading and more like talking. Thus it permitted her, through reading, to participate vicariously in intellectual conversation—often the only way she could participate in scientific discourse.

The Marquise's voice, much like the feminine voices within some of the cookery books, made the work appeal to women readers. Indeed, the work's female voice is what initially prompted Aphra Behn to translate it. Behn, however, found inconsistencies in the Marquise's words. Fontenelle, she remarked, "makes her say a great many very silly things, tho' sometimes she makes Observations so learned, that the greatest Philosophers in *Europe* could make no better."[23] Though women were not Fontenelle's only readers, they did form the ideal audience for the new scientific discourse, because, unlike the more traditionally educated men, they did not carry the burden of a traditional classical education, with all its prejudices and preconceptions.[24] They could assimilate the new theories without the interference of prior knowledge.

Understandably, Fontenelle's work greatly influenced subsequent introductory science texts for women. During the first half of the eighteenth century, numerous volumes consisting of dialogues between knowledgeable male figures and inquisitive female protagonists were published. In John Harris's *Astronomical Dialogues Between a Gentleman and a Lady* (1719), a copy of which could be found at the Library Company of Philadelphia,[25] the literary debt is obvious. In the first dialogue, it quickly became apparent that Harris designed his work to be a kind of primer for Fontenelle's. The female speaker told her mentor, who had given her a copy of Fontenelle: "I find there are many things previously necessary to the understanding of it, which you must oblige me with explaining."[26] The male speaker then proceeded to explain the use of globes and the elements of astronomy and geography. Like Fontenelle, Harris attempted to make his work as pleasurable as possible. To that end, he liberally included digressions, reflections, poetry, and witticisms.[27]

The most important work influenced by Fontenelle's *Plurality of Worlds* was Francesco Algarotti's *Sir Isaac Newton's Philosophy Explain'd for the Use of the Ladies,* widely known in Elizabeth Carter's English translation. Both William Byrd and Robert Carter of Nomony Hall acquired copies for their daughters, and the work was advertised in the *South Carolina Gazette* during the 1750s.[28] Dedicating his book to Fontenelle, Algarotti wrote: "Your *Plurality of Worlds* first softened the savage Nature of Philosophy, and called it from the solitary Closets and Libraries of the Learned, to introduce it into the Circles and Toilets of Ladies."[29] To make *Sir Isaac Newton's Philosophy Explain'd for the Use of the Ladies* as intriguing as possible, Algarotti built a kind of plot into the book. He explained in his preface: "I have made a sort of Change or Catastrophe in the Philosophy of my Marchioness, who is at first a *Cartesian,* afterwards a Proselyte to *Malebranche,* and at last obliged to embrace the [Newtonian] System."[30]

From the mid-eighteenth century on, works by Benjamin Martin and James Ferguson became widely known. Martin's *Young Gentleman and Lady's Philosophy* was advertised from New York to the Carolinas, and Ferguson's *Easy Introduction to Astronomy, for Young Gentlemen and Ladies* could be found at the Library Company of Philadelphia. James Rivington had copies for sale in Philadelphia and New York.[31] Both works used the same device: a college-educated brother returned home to teach science to his inquisitive sister. By making the teacher a college student and a brother, Martin and Ferguson made teacher and student more like equals than is usual. Both were close in age and shared a common upbringing. The brother-sister combination also allowed for familiarity without intimacy, avoiding the flirtatious overtones which had been prominent in both Fontenelle's *Plurality of Worlds* and Algarotti's *Sir Isaac Newton's Philosophy Explain'd for the Use of the Ladies.*

Martin presented *Young Gentleman and Lady's Philosophy* as a dialogue between Cleonicus and his sister Euphrosine. The two discussed astronomy, the use of globes, pneumatics, optics, sound, hydrostatics, and hydraulics. Early in the work, Cleonicus called natural philosophy "a peculiar grace in the fair sex. . . . it is now growing into a fashion for the ladies to study philosophy; and I am very glad to see a sister of mine so well inclined to promote a thing so laudable and honourable in her sex." Euphrosine is relieved to hear his words. She responds: "I often wish it did not look quite so masculine for a woman to talk of philosophy in company; I have often sat silent, and wanted resolution to ask a question for fear of being thought assuming or impertinent. I should be glad to see your assertions verified; how happy will be the age when the ladies may modestly pretend to knowledge, and appear learned without singularity and affectation!"[32]

While most young colonial women got their first taste of science from these dialogues, scientific discourse did not always have to be simplified and made pleasing by adding clever tropes and witty repartee, so that women might understand the new concepts. Theophilus Grew's *Description and Use of the Globes, Celestial and Terrestrial* (Germantown, Pennsylvania, 1753), one of the earliest homegrown science textbooks, was "chiefly designed for the instruction of the young gentlemen at the Academy of Philadelphia" and was a fairly sophisticated treatment of its subject, filled with calculations, equations, technical diagrams—the kinds of things deliberately excluded from Fontenelle's and other works. But one surviving copy indicates that young gentlewomen also made up part of the book's readership. The back flyleaf of the Clements copy is inscribed "Miss Eliza. W. Ewing."

Eliza Ewing's scientific aptitude notwithstanding, there is no denying the attractiveness of the scientific dialogues. An additional reason for their popularity among colonial women may have been that the relationship between an older, knowing male and a naïve but inquisitive young woman had its counterpart in the real lives of many young colonial women. Surviving letters indicate that such mentoring often took place between men—uncles, brothers, suitors, cousins—and young women eager to become more learned. The letter of John Bartram to Jane Colden shows him playing Cleonicus to Jane's Euphrosine. Well before he began courting Eliza Lucas, Charles Pinckney encouraged her to read and recommended several books.[33]

The surviving letters of James Iredell indicate that he similarly encouraged Hannah Johnston (his future wife) to read and develop her mind. After Iredell learned that she was reading Thomas Burnet's *Theory of the Earth*, a work somewhat outdated in its cosmology but one which continued to provide interesting speculative reading well into the nineteenth century, he was thrilled, and his fondness for her blossomed. In a letter to her, he praised her newfound intellectual concerns. His epistle ably articulates male attitudes toward women's reading late in the colonial period:

What a dignified Readiness of Mind do you not show in your choice of Books, many of which you select for useful Instruction, instead of constantly reading those of frothy Entertainment. What a Happiness to have a Mind capable of even exalted Studies! What Goodness, and Command of Attention, to apply them! Indeed, my dear Hannah, you cannot conceive the Joy I felt when your Sister told me you was reading Burnet's Theory. What Brutes are those who would deny your Sex any degree of literary attainment! For my own Part, I know of no Character more pleasing than a sensible Woman who has read elegantly and judiciously, who is fond of this honorable Exercise of her mental Powers, but is unassuming of any particular distinction on that account.[34]

The remarks echo the feminine ideal voiced in James Fordyce's *Sermons to Young Women,* a work which Iredell had read the preceding year with an eye to comparing his bride-to-be with Fordyce's recommended feminine behavior. Iredell's reaction to Fordyce shows how powerfully Fordyce had captured the prevailing notions of femininity during the second half of the eighteenth century. There was, however, no place for the learned lady in Fordyce's notion of femininity.

Fordyce was against women's learning science for its own sake. He explained that "war, commerce, exercises of strength and dexterity, abstract philosophy, and all the abstruser sciences, are most properly the province of men. I am sure those masculine women, that would plead for your sharing any part of this province equally with us, do not understand your true interests."[35] Fordyce's derogatory tone emphasized the incongruity of his oxymoron, "masculine women." Benjamin Martin's *Euphrosine* could discourse on science without fear of looking masculine; but, to Fordyce, masculinity and femininity were categories which could not overlap. A few pages later, however, he did admit that studying astronomy was an acceptable pastime for women, but only because it helped confirm their belief in the Almighty. According to Fordyce, the principal facts of astronomy:

> open and enlarge the mind; they delight and humanize the heart; they remind us that we are citizens of the universe; they show us how small a part that we fill in the immense orb of being. Amidst the amplitude of such contemplations, superfluous trifles shrink away; wealth and grandeur "hide their diminished heads"; a generous ambition rises in the thoughtful mind, to approve itself to the all-inspecting eye of Him to

whom none of his works are indifferent, but to whom those only can be acceptable, that, under the uncertainty and imperfection of sublunary things, seek their security, happiness, and glory, in doing well.[36]

The Plurality of Worlds had been a largely secular work. For Fontenelle, learning science was important for enlightening the mind. In Fordyce's scheme, however, astronomy for women seems little more than an extension of the religious sublime. Studying the stars, he implies, heightens woman's awe of the Almighty.

Both James Fordyce's *Sermons to Young Women* and James Gregory's *A Father's Legacy to His Daughters,* published less than ten years after Fordyce's work, propounded a feminine ideal which excluded learning in any depth. As James Gregory wrote, men generally looked "with a jealous and malignant eye on a woman of great parts, and a cultivated understanding."[37] While the introductory science books for women implied that learning science heightened their moral virtue, these later conduct books argued that the sciences detracted from, rather than enhanced, a woman's virtue. Basically, Fordyce and Gregory advanced what Londa Schiebinger has called the theory of complementarity—the idea that men and women were not physical and moral equals, but rather were complementary opposites.[38] The only way for men and women to achieve equality, therefore, was for each sex to cultivate its distinctive faculties. Erudite learning was a male faculty, homemaking a female faculty. The theory of complementarity helped to shape the domestic or woman's sphere and to distinguish it from the public, male sphere. While the notion of the domestic sphere as woman's would not be defined completely until after the colonial period, Fordyce and Gregory anticipated attitudes toward women, science, and domesticity dominant in the late eighteenth and early nineteenth centuries. As these two authors' works were published, the interrelationships among women, science, and domesticity remained in a state of flux. Women read science at the same time they read Fordyce's and Gregory's cautions against learning science. Many continued to believe that women could learn both housewifery and natural philosophy. Like Henry Laurens, some colonial parents encouraged their daughters' interest in learning, while simultaneously admonishing them not to neglect their domestic responsibilities.

The prevailing attitudes toward women, books, and learning are evident in a poem which appeared in the *Pennsylvania Magazine* during the mid-1770s. The anonymously published "A Letter From Miss ***** to Her

God-Mother" was written as a verse epistle from a young woman to an older woman who had acted as her mentor.[39] The speaker of the poem begins by making fun of man's (explicitly mankind's, but implicitly the male's) insatiable curiosity:

> Dear Madam, you need not be told
> That—whether they be young or old,
> Rich, poor, lame, lazy, sick or well,
> Since Adam and his help-mate fell,
> Mankind incessantly pursue
> The chase of something strange or new.

Using the phrase "his help-mate" instead of naming Eve, the poet suggests that a woman's identity traditionally depended upon that of her husband. The word "help-mate," which first came into use during the seventeenth century and frequently appeared in both the conduct and housewifery books, associates Eve with the colonial woman. The remainder of the initial verse paragraph lists many outrageous occurrences: dolphins "flounce aloft among the trees" and sheep for "pasture plunge into the deep." The bizarre catalog prepares the reader for an even greater curiosity described in the second verse paragraph:

> Since novelty and wonder, then,
> Can thus delight the sons of men,
> O what a pleasure must it be,
> To read a letter writ by me!

Writing apparently was a skill formerly not possessed, or at least seldom practiced, by the poem's speaker.

She vaguely describes her recent personal history in the third verse paragraph, which begins:

> 'Tis not a quarter of a year,
> Since first I came, a stranger, here;
> Who, all my life before, had been
> Secluded from this busy scene.

Since the poem appeared in the *Pennsylvania Magazine,* the word *here* may refer to Philadelphia. The lines thus give the impression that the poem is being recited by a young woman who had been raised in the country and recently had moved to the city. To read the poem in this way, however, is to assume that it was autobiographical. The following lines cannot be interpreted so literally:

> Debarr'd all commerce with mankind,
> And in a narrow cell confin'd,
> Where never sun nor moon appear'd,
> Nor human voice was ever heard.

Clearly, these lines describe a state of mind, not any particular geographical location. Figuratively, she had been in the dark. In that quarter of a year since she left her darkness and entered the "busy scene," her knowledge has improved remarkably.

The next two verse paragraphs detailed the wide range of her recent accomplishments: "Untaught in languages, I speak / Italian, Latin, French, or Greek, / As glibly as my mother-tongue!" All this in less than a quarter of a year? Clearly, at this point the poem reveals itself as a fantasy. Rather than telling the writer's autobiography, the poem is speaking through a fictive persona. The speaker has acquired her learning rapidly, upon being transported from her dark, narrow cell. The poem thus becomes the story of a woman's personal enlightenment. It is important to note the careful word choice. Though the speaker states that she was "untaught," she shows that she was not *unlearned*. In other words, she states that, even though no one had taught her these languages, she had learned them anyway. The passage stresses the limited opportunities the colonial woman had to attend school but asserts that women would not let such limitations bar them from learning. A woman could learn by herself or with other women. Books, the speaker implies, provided a way for young women to educate themselves.

In the next verse paragraph, she compares her own learning with that of the nearby college boys:

> In arts and sciences my knowledge
> Might shame the lads of Princeton college.
> I can explain the globes and maps,
> As readily as pin my caps;
> Mechanics too, and hydrostatics,
> Astronomy and mathematics,

Discoveries by sea and land;
I know them all—and understand
The works of Newton, Boyle, and Locke,
As well as—how to make a smock,
Or fix a tucker to my frock!

While the tetrameter couplets are reminiscent of Samuel Butler's *Hudibras* and the catalog of knowledge is not dissimilar to the catalog of mock learning attributed to Sir Hudibras, the context of the poem forces the reader to take these lines seriously. Although the speaker's rapid acquisition of multiple languages in the previous verse paragraph reveals the poem's fantasy, the deliberate reference to Princeton helps bring it back to reality. It might have been hyperbolic to suggest that anyone could learn four languages in a quarter of a year, but it was no exaggeration to suggest that a woman could master the same scientific concepts that the boys learned at college. Each field of science mentioned could have been learned from such basic scientific texts as Benjamin Martin's *Young Gentleman and Lady's Philosophy*. Furthermore, the poet's knowledge of discoveries showed that she had studied geography and read travel literature. She could have learned mechanics and hydrostatics from reading and experimenting with scientific instruments. Martin's scientific text emphasized that women could and should be able to use such instruments. Expressing her knowledge of both fields, she reveals her understanding of the scientific method.

The learned triumvirate cited by the poet—Newton, Boyle, and Locke—differs from the Enlightenment's usual trinity: Newton, Bacon, and Locke. Thomas Jefferson called these latter "the three greatest men that have ever lived, without any exception," who together had "laid the foundation of those superstructures which have been raised in the Physical & Moral sciences."[40] In one sense, the author had no need to mention Bacon. Her knowledge of scientific experimentation—revealed by the reference to mechanics and hydrostatics—shows that she understood the value of Baconian empiricism. Substituting Boyle for Bacon, the poet conveys her respect for scientific experimentation while continuing to maintain the importance of religion. Boyle's devotional works had been recommended reading at least since George Hickes's English translation of Fénelon's *Instructions for the Education of a Daughter*.[41] Furthermore, several of Boyle's scientific works sought to reconcile religious beliefs with modern science.

In addition to understanding various disciplines of natural philosophy, the speaker possesses domestic knowledge. In the triplet closing the verse paragraph, the poet ironically rhymes *Locke* with two terms commonly used in dressmaking, *smock* and *frock*. Far from demoting Locke, the triplet serves to elevate traditional womanly domestic pursuits. The lines deliberately refutes the emergent theory of complementarity. Not only could women learn as well as—or even better than—men, but they could master such scientific knowledge without neglecting their domestic responsibilities.

In the final verse paragraph, the writer abandons her persona—the woman of superior learning—and speaks from a humbler stance, perhaps the poet's own voice or that of yet another persona. She thanks her godmother for her help and encouragement and also thanks her godmother's "associates," apparently a close group of female friends who had helped to foster the young woman's learning:

And here, O let me not forget
A far, far more endearing debt!
A triple debt, dear Madam, due
To your associates and to you,
The guardians of my tender youth,
The vouchers for my faith and truth,
Whose solemn promise has been given
In my behalf, and heard in heav'n!

"A Letter From Miss * * * * * to Her God-Mother" clarifies how educational opportunities available to men and to women differed at the end of the colonial period. While men had greater opportunities to be taught, colonial women still could learn, if they took advantage of the books available to them. Having a small but carefully chosen group of books on her bookshelf gave the colonial woman the chance to reach a level of knowledge which just might "shame the lads of Princeton college."

Notes

Abbreviations

ARLCP	*Annual Report of the Library Company of Philadelphia*
BLC	*British Library General Catalogue of Printed Books to 1975.* London: Clive Bingley, 1979.
Bristol	Bristol, Roger P. *Supplement to Charles Evans' American Bibliography.* Charlottesville: Univ. Press of Virginia, 1970.
DNB	*Dictionary of National Biography.* Ed. Leslie Stephen and Sidney Lee. London, 1885–1900.
Evans	Evans, Charles. *American Bibliography.* 12 vols. Chicago: for the Author, 1903–1934.
Guerra	Guerra, Francisco. *American Medical Bibliography 1639–1783.* New York: Lathrop C. Harper, 1962.
Halkett and Laing	Kennedy, James, W. A. Smith, and A. F. Johnson, *Dictionary of Anonymous and Pseudonymous English Literature (Samuel Halkett and John Laing).* Edinburgh and London: Oliver and Boyd, 1926–1934.
MiU-C	Clements Library, Univ. of Michigan, Ann Arbor
MWA	American Antiquarian Society, Worcester, Mass.
NUC	*National Union Catalog: Pre-1956 Imprints.* London: Mansell, 1968–1981. 754 vols.
PAAS	*Proceedings of the American Antiquarian Society*
PBSA	*Papers of the Bibliographical Society of America*
PMHB	*Pennsylvania Magazine of History and Biography*
Sabin	Sabin, Joseph, Wilberforce Eames, and R. W. G. Vail. *Bibliotheca Americana.* New York: for the Bibliographical Society of America, 1868–1936. 29 vols.

Shipton and Mooney   Shipton, Clifford K. and James E. Mooney. *National Index of American Imprints through 1800: The Short-Title Evans.* Worcester: American Antiquarian Society and Barre Publishers, 1969.

VMHB   *Virginia Magazine of History and Biography*

WMQ   *William and Mary Quarterly*

Chapter 1. Reading Women

1. Mar. 1774; Philip Vickers Fithian, *Journal & Letters of Philip Vickers Fithian 1773–1774: A Plantation Tutor of the Old Dominion,* new edition, ed. Hunter Dickinson Farish (Williamsburg, Va.: Colonial Williamsburg, 1965), 83. For a good overview of Robert Carter's library and his bookish interests, see John R. Barden, "Reflections of a Singular Mind: The Library of Robert Carter of Nomony Hall," *VMHB* 96 (1988):83–94.

2. Dr. Alexander Hamilton, *The History of the Ancient and Honorable Tuesday Club,* ed. Robert Micklus (Chapel Hill: Univ. of North Carolina Press, 1990), 1:144.

3. Richard Allestree, *The Lady's Calling* (London, 1673), sigs. b3r, b2v.

4. Mary Astell, *A Serious Proposal to the Ladies* (1701; rpt. New York: Source Book Press, 1970), 18–19. The Custis copy of Astell is inscribed, "E Libris Joannis Custis, 1716. Pretium 3 sh." This dated inscription indicates, curiously enough, that John Custis acquired the volume the year *after* his wife, Frances Parke Custis, died. The copy eventually descended to George Washington through his wife, Martha Custis. See W. W. Abbot, ed., *The Papers of George Washington: Colonial Series* (Charlottesville: Univ. Press of Virginia, 1988), 6:298. The marriage of John and Frances Custis was a rocky one, by all accounts, and it is interesting to see among the Custis books a copy of Francisco Manuel de Mello's *Government of a Wife; Or, Wholesom and Pleasant Advice for Married Men* (London, 1697); Abbot, *Papers of George Washington: Colonial Series,* 6:290.

5. Fithian, *Journal & Letters,* 6.

6. Lucia Bergamasco, "Female Education and Spiritual Life: The Case of Ministers' Daughters," *Current Issues in Women's History,* ed. Arina Angerman, Geerte Binnema, Annemieke Keunen, Vefie Poels, Jacqueline Zirkzee, and Judy de Ville (New York: Routledge, 1989), 41.

7. Julius Herbert Tuttle, "The Libraries of the Mathers," *PAAS* 20 (1910):326; Henry Joel Cadbury, "Harvard College Library and the Li-

braries of the Mathers," *PAAS* 50 (1940):41, 43; Thomas H. Johnson, "Jonathan Edwards's Background of Reading," *Transactions, The Colonial Society of Massachusetts, 1930–1933* 28 (1935):194.

8. Eliza Haywood, *The Female Spectator: Being Selections from Mrs. Eliza Heywood's Periodical,* ed. Mary Priestley (London: John Lane, The Bodley Head, 1929), 57, 60. For the intellectual background of the idea that the soul has no sex, see Eleanor Commo McLaughlin, "Equality of Souls, Inequality of Sexes: Woman in Medieval Theology," in *Religion and Sexism: Images of Woman in the Jewish and Christian Traditions,* ed. Rosemary Radford Ruether (New York: Simon and Schuster, 1974), 213–66; and Londa Schiebinger, *The Mind Has No Sex?: Women in the Origins of Modern Science* (Cambridge: Harvard Univ. Press, 1989), 168–70.

9. The two best recent studies are: Cathy N. Davidson, *Revolution and the Word: The Rise of the Novel in America* (New York: Oxford Univ. Press, 1986), and Linda K. Kerber, *Women of the Republic: Intellect and Ideology in Revolutionary America* (Chapel Hill: Univ. of North Carolina Press, 1980), 189–264. Both derive nearly all of their evidence from the post-1776 period.

10. Thomas James Holmes, *Cotton Mather: A Bibliography of His Works* (Cambridge: Harvard Univ. Press, 1940), no. 21.

11. For a brief survey of manuscript culture in early America, see David S. Shields, "The Manuscript in the British American World of Print," *PAAS* 102 (1992):403–16.

12. E. Jennifer Monaghan, "Literacy Instruction and Gender in Colonial New England," *Reading In America: Literature and Social History,* ed. Cathy N. Davidson (Baltimore: Johns Hopkins Univ. Press, 1989), 70; David D. Hall, "The Uses of Literacy in New England, 1600–1850." *Printing and Society in Early America,* ed. William L. Joyce, David D. Hall, Richard D. Brown, and John B. Hench (Worcester: American Antiquarian Society, 1983), 24–25. For other treatments of women's literacy, see Linda Auwers, "Reading the Marks of the Past: Exploring Female Literacy in Colonial Windsor, Connecticut," *Historical Methods* 13 (Fall 1980):204–14; Joel Perlmann and Dennis Shirley, "When Did New England Women Acquire Literacy?" *WMQ* 3d ser. 48 (1991):50–67.

13. David D. Hall, *Worlds of Wonder, Days of Judgment: Popular Religious Belief in Early New England* (Cambridge: Harvard Univ. Press, 1990), 32.

14. William Byrd, *The London Diary (1717–1721) and Other Writings,* ed. Louis B. Wright, and Marion Tinling (New York: Oxford Univ. Press,

1958), 469. For a further discussion of this episode, see Kevin J. Hayes, *The Library of William Byrd of Westover* (Madison, Wisconsin and Philadelphia: Madison House and The Library Company of Philadelphia, 1996). For a good discussion of similar uses of books, see David Cressy, "Books as Totems in Seventeenth-Century England and New England," *Journal of Library History* 21 (1986):92–106.

15. For the most thorough treatment of the subject, see Marylynn Salmon, *Women and the Law of Property in Early America* (Chapel Hill: Univ. of North Carolina Press, 1986).

16. William Nelson, ed., *Calendar of New Jersey Wills, Vol. 1. 1670–1730,* vol. 23 of *Documents Relating to the Colonial History of the State of New Jersey* (Paterson: New Jersey Historical Society, 1901), 452–53.

17. "Books in Colonial Virginia," *VMHB* 10 (1903):389–405.

18. Louis B. Wright, *The First Gentlemen of Virginia: Intellectual Qualities of the Early Colonial Ruling Class* (San Marino, Calif.: Huntington Library, 1940), 237; Philip Alexander Bruce, *Institutional History of Virginia in the Seventeenth Century* (New York: G. P. Putnam's Sons, 1910), 408, 409.

19. Anne Floyd Upshur and Ralph T. Whitelaw, "Library of the Rev. Thomas Teackle," *WMQ* 2d ser. 23 (1943):301–3; Jon Butler, "Thomas Teackle's 333 Books: A Great Library on Virginia's Eastern Shore, 1697," *WMQ* 3d. ser. 59 (1992):449–91. Butler carefully identifies the Teackle books, but the titles Elizabeth and Catharine Teackle received are more easily accessible using the earlier study. For more on the Teackle library, see Jon Butler, "Magic, Astrology, and the Early American Religious Heritage, 1600–1760," *American Historical Review* 84 (1979):327–30; and Kevin J. Hayes, "Libraries and Learned Societies," *Encyclopedia of the North American Colonies,* ed. Jacob Ernest Cooke (New York: Charles Scribners' Sons, 1993), 126.

20. William S. Pelletreau, ed., *Abstracts of Wills on File in the Surrogate's Office, City of New York . . . 1730–1744,* vol. 27 of *Collections of the New-York Historical Society* (New York, 1895), 186–87, 353, 411, 417; Nelson, *Calendar of New Jersey Wills, Vol. 1. 1670–1730,* 430; William S. Pelletreau, ed., *Abstracts of Wills on File in the Surrogate's Office, City of New York . . . 1744–1753,* vol. 28 of *Collections of the New-York Historical Society* (New York, 1896), 136.

21. "Letter-Book of Samuel Sewall," *Massachusetts Historical Society Collections,* 6th ser., 1 (1886):189. Hezekiah Usher's will is worth quoting at length, if for no other reason than as a document in the history of mi-

sogyny: "And unto my dear wife, whom I may count very dear by her Love to what I had but not a real Love to me, which should accounted it more worth than any other outward Enjoyment; and for her covetousness & over-reaching & cunning Impression that has almost ruinated me by a gentle behavior, having only words but as sharp swords to me, whose Cunning is like those to be as an Angel of Light to others but wanting Love and Charity for me. . . . And therefore I do cut her off from the benefit of all my Estate, & do not bestow anything upon her but what the law doth allow."

22. The copies of Baxter, Lawson, and Russel survive at MWA. The copies of Chalkley, Colman, Cooper, Edwards, Foxcroft, Stoddard, and Walter survive at MiU-C.

23. Samuel Sewall records sending a copy of Loring's work to the Reverend Moody on 16 Aug. 1728; Samuel Sewall, *The Diary of Samuel Sewall 1674–1729,* ed. M. Halsey Thomas (New York: Farrar, Straus, 1973), 1062. While courting Madame Winthrop, Sewall gave her a copy of John Preston's *The Churches Marriage* (1638). He recorded in his diary: "She commended the book I gave her, Dr. Preston, the Church's Marriage; quoted him saying 'twas inconvenient keeping out of a Fashion commonly used"; Samuel Sewall, *Diary,* 964–65.

24. MWA copy.

25. Landon Carter, *The Diary of Colonel Landon Carter of Sabine Hall, 1752–1778,* ed. Jack P. Greene (Richmond: Virginia Historical Society, 1987), 786–87. For the attribution of *Sentimental Fables* to Thomas Marryat, see *DNB,* 12:1089. For more information on Newbery's children's books, see S. John Roscoe, *Newbery and His Successors 1740–1814: A Bibliography* (Wormley, England: Five Owls Press, 1973).

26. The Dodsley volume survives at MiU-C; the Goldsmith, Marrow, and Gessner volumes survive at MWA. Elizabeth DeLancey to Cadwallader Colden, 2 October 1751: "Please Sir to take the trouble to send to Parkers for a litle Book Sister Jane recommends, call'd the Economy of human life"; *The Letters and Papers of Cadwallader Colden* (New York: New York Historical Society, 1921), 4:302. For a note on the popularity of Marrow's work in Boston during 1744, see, Dr. Alexander Hamilton, *Gentleman's Progress: The Itinerarium of Dr. Alexander Hamilton,* ed. Carl Bridenbaugh (Chapel Hill: Univ. of North Carolina Press, 1948), 112.

27. Maxine L. Margolis, *Mothers and Such: Views of American Women and Why They Changed* (Berkeley: Univ. of California Press, 1984), 19.

28. Louis C. Karpinski, *Bibliography of Mathematical Works Printed in America Through 1850* (Ann Arbor: Univ. of Michigan Press, 1940), 37–38; [Lawrence C. Wroth,] "The Colonial Scene—1602–1800," *PAAS* 60 (1950):131–32.

29. Edwin Wolf, 2d, "More Books from the Library of the Byrds of Westover," *PAAS* 88 (1978), no. S6.

30. Louis B. Wright and Marion Tinling, eds., *The Secret Diary of William Byrd of Westover 1709–1712* (Richmond: Dietz Press, 1941), 461.

31. Maude H. Woodfin and Marion Tinling, eds., *Another Secret Diary of William Byrd of Westover* (Richmond: Dietz Press, 1942), 386–87; Marion Tinling, ed., *The Correspondence of the Three William Byrds of Westover, Virginia 1684–1776* (Charlottesville: Univ. Press of Virginia, 1977), 348.

32. Edwin Wolf 2d, "The Dispersal of the Library of William Byrd of Westover." *PAAS* 68 (1958), no. 73; Wolf, "More Books from the Library of the Byrds of Westover," no. S22. When Wolf located Maria Byrd's copy of Cowley's *Works*, the volume was privately owned. It has since been acquired by the Alderman Library, Univ. of Virginia, Charlottesville. For more on Maria Taylor Byrd, see chap. 6.

33. Hayes, *The Library of William Byrd, passim.*

34. Edwin Wolf 2d, *The Library of James Logan of Philadelphia 1674–1751* (Philadelphia: The Library Company of Philadelphia, 1974), nos. 762, 739, 1163; Edwin Wolf 2d, *Book Culture of a Colonial American City,* 197; Frederick B. Tolles, *Meeting House and Counting House: The Quaker Merchants of Colonial Philadelphia 1682–1763* (1948; New York: Norton, 1963), 152; Frederick B. Tolles, *James Logan and the Culture of Provincial America* (Boston: Little, Brown, 1957), 191.

35. Benjamin Franklin, *The Papers of Benjamin Franklin,* ed. Leonard Labaree, et al. (New Haven: Yale Univ. Press, 1959–), 2: 130; C. William Miller, *Benjamin Franklin's Philadelphia Printing 1728–1766: A Descriptive Bibliography* (Philadelphia: American Philosophical Society, 1974), no. 99.

36. The MiU-C copy of William Penn's *Some Fruits of Solitude, in Reflections and Maxims Relating to the Conduct of Life* (1706) is inscribed "Hannah Storrs Fry." During the colonial period, *Old Mr. Dod's Sayings; Or, Posies Gathered Out of Mr. Dod's Garden* was reprinted at Cambridge (1673), Boston (1731), Philadelphia (1768). and New London, Connecticut. The New London edition is undated, but the MWA copy is inscribed "Bridget Noyes her book 1774."

37. Benjamin Franklin, *Benjamin Franklin's Autobiography: A Norton Critical Edition,* ed. J. A. Leo Lemay and P. M. Zall (New York: Norton, 1986), 57; Library Company of Philadelphia, *A Catalogue of Books Belonging to the Library Company of Philadelphia: A Facsimile of the Edition of 1741 Printed by Benjamin Franklin,* ed. Edwin Wolf 2d (Philadelphia: The Library Company, 1956), 38, 46, 50, 52.

38. Edwin Wolf 2d, review of David Kaser, *A Book for a Sixpence: The Circulating Library in America, PMHB* 104 (1980):384.

39. Austin Baxter Keep, *History of the New York Society Library* (1908; rpt. Boston: Gregg, 1972), 188.

40. New York Society Library, *The Charter, and Bye-Laws, of the New-York Society Library; With a Catalogue of the Books Belonging to the Said Library* (New York: H. Gaine, 1773), *passim.*

41. Chester T. Hallenback, "A Colonial Reading List," *PMHB* 56 (1932):289–340, *passim.*

42. Ruth Robinson Ross, *Union Library Company of Hatborough: An Account of the First Two Hundred Years Done Out of the Original Records* (Hatboro, Pa.: Union Library Company, 1955), 31.

43. Hallenback, "Colonial Reading List," 320–21.

44. Each of these writers will be discussed in greater detail in subsequent chapters.

45. Joseph Towne Wheeler, "Booksellers and Circulating Libraries in Colonial Maryland," *Maryland Historical Magazine* 34 (1939):114–16.

46. Hennig Cohen, *The South Carolina Gazette, 1732–1755* (Columbia: Univ. of South Carolina Press, 1953), 147.

47. Quoted in David Kaser, *A Book for a Sixpence: The Circulating Library in America* (Pittsburgh: Beta Phi Mu, 1980), 27.

48. Quoted in ibid., 30.

49. Hennig Cohen, *South Carolina Gazette,* 154.

50. Wheeler, "Booksellers and Circulating Libraries," 118.

51. John Mein, *A Catalogue of Mein's Circulating Library* (Boston: [McAlpine and Fleeming], 1765). 36.

52. Kaser, *A Book for a Sixpence,* 36; Robert Winans, *A Descriptive Checklist of Book Catalogues Separately Printed in America 1693–1800* (Worcester: American Antiquarian Society, 1981), no. 82; *Maryland Gazette,* 8 July 1773; quoted in Wheeler, "Booksellers and Circulating Libraries," 117.

53. John Eliot Alden, "John Mein, Publisher: An Essay in Bibliographic Detection," *PBSA* 36 (1942):211–12.

54. Wheeler, "Booksellers and Circulating Libraries," 124.

55. A. J. Wall, "Samuel Loudon (1727–1813) (Merchant, Printer and Patriot)" *New York Historical Society Quarterly Bulletin* 6 (1922):77; Kaser, *A Book for a Sixpence,* 37.

56. Isaiah Thomas, *The History of Printing in America,* ed. Marcus A. McCorison (New York: Weathervane Books, 1970) 211; Edward Cox and Edward Berry, *A Catalogue of a Very Large Assortment of . . . Books . . . Which Are to Be Sold by Cox & Berry at Their Store in King-Street, Boston* ([Boston, 1772?]), 3.

57. The *Virginia Gazette Daybooks* are conveniently available on microfilm. See Paul P. Hoffman, ed., *Virginia Gazette Daybooks 1750–1752 & 1764–1766* (Univ. of Virginia Library: Microfilm Publications, 1967). The microfilm indexes the *Virginia Gazette* office patrons but not the books purchased. "Daybook," 1750–52, fols. 25, 33; "Daybook," 1764–66, fols. 8, 25, 41, 140. For additional information from the "Daybooks," see Cynthia Z. Stiverson and Gregory A. Stiverson, "The Colonial Retail Book Trade: Availability of Reading Material in Mid-Eighteenth-Century Virginia," *Printing and Society in Early America*, eds. William L. Joyce, David D. Hall, Richard D. Brown, and John B. Hench (Worcester: American Antiquarian Society) 132–73; and James Southall Wilson, "Best-Sellers in Jefferson's Day," *Virginia Quarterly Review* 36 (1960):222–37. The Stiversons' study provides the statistical-economic background; Wilson's essay is impressionistic, but more useful on the literary taste which the daybooks reflect.

58. John Harvard Ellis, Introduction to *The Works of Anne Bradstreet* (1867; rpt., New York: Peter Smith, 1932), xliii.

59. Ibid., xliii, xlix.

60. Anne Bradstreet, *The Complete Works of Anne Bradstreet,* ed. Joseph R. McElrath, Jr. and Allan P. Robb (Boston: Twayne, 1981), *passim.*

61. William John Potts, "Bathsheba Bowers," *PMHB* 3 (1879):110–12; Benjamin Franklin, *Autobiography,* 12, 28; *Pennsylvania Gazette,* 15 Dec. 1757, contains a poem "By a Female Hand," entitled, "On the Author of that excellent Book, entitled, The Way to Health, long Life and Happiness." See J. A. Leo Lemay, *A Calendar of American Poetry in the Colonial Newspapers and Magazines and in the Major English Magazines through 1765* (Worcester: American Antiquarian Society, 1972), no. 1393.

62. Esther Edwards Burr, *The Journal of Esther Edwards Burr 1754–1757,*

ed. Carol F. Karlsen and Laurie Crumpacker (New Haven: Yale Univ. Press, 1984), 14.

63. Burr, *Journal*, 62–63. For a thorough discussion of the idea of female friendship within the Burr-Prince correspondence, see Lucia Bergamasco, "Amité, amour et spiritualité dans la Nouvelle-Angleterre du XVIIIe siècle: L'experience d'Esther Burr et de Sarah Prince" *Annales économies sociétés civilisations* 41 (1986):295–323.

64. Burr, *Journal*, 64.

65. Ibid., 94.

66. Quoted in Robert Middlekauff, *Ancients and Axioms: Secondary Education in Eighteenth-Century New England* (New Haven: Yale Univ. Press, 1963), 106.

67. Lucas to Mrs. Boddicott, 2 May 1740, *The Letterbook of Eliza Lucas Pinckney 1739–1762,* ed. Elise Pinckney (Chapel Hill: Univ. of North Carolina Press, 1972), 7.

68 Eliza Lucas to Mrs. Pinckney, ca. 1741, in Eliza Lucas Pinckney *Letterbook,* 19.

69. Eliza Lucas to Miss Bartlett, ca. Apr. 1742, in Eliza Lucas Pinckney, *Letterbook,* 35.

70. Eliza Lucas to Miss Bartlett, c. Mar.–Apr. 1742, in Eliza Lucas Pinckney, *Letterbook,* 33–34.

71. William Franklin to Elizabeth Graeme, 24 October 1758, in Simon Gratz, ed., "Some Material for a Biography of Mrs. Elizabeth Fergusson, née Graeme," *PMHB* 39 (1915):267.

72. Eliza Stedman to Elizabeth Graeme, 7 August 1762, in Gratz, "Some Material for a Biography," 268–69.

73. Ann Graeme to Elizabeth Graeme, n.d., in Gratz, "Some Material for a Biography," 270.

74. Hannah Griffitts to Elizabeth Graeme, 4 Dec. 1775, in Gratz, "Some Material for a Biography," 287. For clarity, I have punctuated and capitalized the passage to conform to modern usage.

75. Edwin Wolf, 2d, "Report of the Librarian," *ARLCP for 1962* (Philadelphia: The Library Company of Philadelphia, 1963), 43. For more on Elizabeth Graeme Ferguson, see Edwin Wolf 2d, "Report of the Librarian," *ARLCP for the Year 1978* (Philadelphia: The Library Company of Philadelphia, 1979), 41–44; Martha C. Slotten, "Elizabeth Graeme Ferguson: A Poet in 'The Athens of North America,'" *PMHB* 108 (1984):259–88; John C. Van Horne, "Report of the Librarian," *ARLCP*

for the Year 1985 (Philadelphia: The Library Company of Philadelphia, 1986), 15–19.

76. Abigail Adams to Mary Smith Cranch, 15 July 1766, in *Adams Family Correspondence,* ed. L. H. Butterfield et al. (Cambridge: Belknap Press of Harvard Univ. Press, 1963), 1:54.

77. Abigail Adams to John Adams, 21 Apr. 1776, in *Adams Family Correspondence,* 1:389.

78. John Adams to Abigail Adams, 12 Apr. 1776, in *Adams Family Correspondence,* 1:376.

79. Abigail Adams to John Adams, 21 Apr. 1776, in *Adams Family Correspondence,* 1:389.

80. Abigail Adams to John Adams, 21 Sept. 1777, in *Adams Family Correspondence,* 2:347–348.

81. Abigail Adams to John Adams, 19 Aug. 1774, in *Adams Family Correspondence,* 1:143.

82. Mercy Otis Warren to Abigail Adams, 25 July 1773, in *Adams Family Correspondence,* 1:86.

83. Hannah Adams, *A Memoir of Miss Hannah Adams, Written by Herself* (Boston: Gray and Bowen, 1832), 3.

84. Ibid., 7.

85. Anne Grant, *Memoirs of an American Lady, with Sketches of Manners and Scenes in America as They Existed Previous to the Revolution,* ed. James Grant Wilson (New York: Dodd, Mead, 1903), pt. 1, p. 144.

86. Ibid., pt. 2, pp. 69–70.

87. *Reliquiae Turellae, et Lachrymae Paternae: The Father's Tears over his Daughter's Remains* (Boston: S. Kneeland & T. Green for J. Edwards and H. Foster, 1735), 78–79. Colman's library was auctioned 7 July 1748, but apparently no record of its contents remain. See George L. McKay, *American Book Auction Catalogues 1713–1934: A Union List* (New York: New York Public Library, 1937), no. 9693.

88. [Thomas Walter], "An Account of Mrs. Katharin Mather by Another Hand," in *Victorina: A Sermon Preached on the Decease and at the Desire of Mrs. Katharin Mather,* by Cotton Mather (Boston: B. Green for Daniel Henchman, 1717); Holmes, *Cotton Mather,* no. 427. For a biographical sketch of Katherine Mather, see Kate M. Cone, "Cotton Mather's Daughter," pt. 1, *Outlook* 81 (7 Oct. 1905):324–29; and pt. 2, *Outlook* 81 (14 Oct. 1905):372–75.

89. Thomas Prince, *The Sovereign God Acknowledged and Blessed, Both in*

Giving and Taking Away: A Sermon Occasioned by the Decease of Mrs. Deborah Prince (Boston: Rogers and Fowle for T. Rand, 1744), 21.

90. Eva Eve Jones, "Extracts from the Journal of Miss Sarah Eve," *PMHB* 5 (1881):21. For additional examples, see Laurel Thatcher Ulrich, "Vertuous Women Found: New England Ministerial Literature, 1668–1735," *American Quarterly* 28 (1976):24.

91. Elizabeth H. Jervey, "Marriage and Death Notices from the Carolina Gazette," *South Carolina Historical and Genealogical Magazine* 36 (1935):137.

92. Wayne Craven, *Colonial American Portraiture: The Economic, Religious, Social, Cultural, Philosophical, Scientific, and Aesthetic Foundations* (New York: Cambridge Univ. Press, 1986), 175–76.

Chapter 2. Devotional Books

1. Henry Heywood, *Two Catechisms by Way of Question and Answer* (Charles-Town, South Carolina: P. Timothy, 1749); quoted in A. S. W. Rosenbach, *Early American Children's Books* (1933; rpt. New York: Kraus, 1966), no. 33.

2. Though Brewster's name does not appear on the imprint, James Rendel Harris and Stephen K. Jones, *The Pilgrim Press* (Cambridge, England: W. Heffer and Sons, 1922), 73–74, attribute the work to his press.

3. Wilberforce Eames, *Early New England Catechisms* (1898; rpt. New York: Burt Franklin, n.d.); Edmund S. Morgan, *The Puritan Family: Religion and Domestic Relations in Seventeenth-Century New England* (New York: Harper and Row, 1966), 98–99; Worthington Chauncey Ford, *The Boston Book Market, 1679–1700* (Boston: Club of Odd Volumes, 1917), 101, 155, 159; C. William Miller, *Benjamin Franklin's Philadelphia Printing 1728–1766: A Descriptive Bibliography* (Philadelphia: American Philosophical Society, 1974), nos. 51, 81, 188, 309–10, 341, 371, 434, 464–65.

4. Cotton Mather, *Addresses to Old Men, and Young Men, and Little Children* (Boston: R. Pierce, for Nicholas Buttolph, 1690), 111.

5. James Janeway, *A Token for Children* (Boston, 1700), x.

6. *Scripture-Instruction* (Ephratra, Pa., 1754), 2. Rhoda Garretson's copy survives at MWA.

7. Joseph Sewall and Thomas Prince, Preface to *Compleat Body of Divinity* (Boston, 1726), i. Thanks to Jerome E. Anderson for calling my attention to the Willard subscription list.

8. Charles E. Hambrick-Stowe, *The Practice of Piety: Puritan Devotional*

Disciplines in Seventeenth-Century New England (Chapel Hill: Univ. of North Carolina Press, 1982), 140–41. I am indebted to Hambrick-Stowe's excellent discussion of Puritan devotional practice.

9. Janeway, *Token for Children,* xii.
10. Quoted in N. H. Keeble, *The Literary Culture of Nonconformity in Later Seventeenth-Century England* (Athens: Univ. of Georgia Press, 1987), 159.
11. Keeble, *Literary Culture of Nonconformity,* 132–33.
12. Michael Warner, *The Letters of the Republic: Publication and the Public Sphere in Eighteenth-Century America* (Cambridge: Harvard Univ. Press, 1990), 22.
13. Ibid., 20.
14. Isaac Watts, *Psalms of David* (Philadelphia: B. F[ranklin] and H. M[eredith] for Thomas Godfrey, 1729), iv–v.
15. Janeway, *Token for Children,* xii.
16. Thomas White, *A Little Book for Little Children* (Boston, 1702), 19.
17. John Flavel, *Husbandry Spiritualized* (London, 1669); Cotton Mather, *Diary of Cotton Mather,* ed. Worthington Chauncey Ford (1911; rpt. New York: Frederick Ungar, n. d.) 2:242.
18. Isaac Watts, *Divine Songs* (Philadelphia: Franklin and Hall, 1750), iv.
19. Crouch was also known as "R. B.," "Richard Burton," and "Robert Burton." His works were ubiquitous in early America. The best-known colonial reader of Crouch's historical works was Benjamin Franklin; see *Benjamin Franklin's Autobiography: A Norton Critical Edition,* eds. J. A. Leo Lemay and P. M. Zall (New York: Norton, 1986), 9.
20. Rosenbach, *Early American Children's Books,* xxxv, no. 8.
21. MWA copy. See also Rosenbach, *Early American Children's Books,* no. 34. For the fullest bibliography of *The History of the Holy Jesus,* see Sabin, 21:98.
22. Shipton and Mooney, 968–70. Selma L. Bishop, *Isaac Watts's* Hymns and Spiritual Songs *(1707): A Publishing History and A Bibliography* (Ann Arbor: Pierian Press, 1974), lists several American reprintings of Watts inscribed by women. The MiU-C copy of a 1771 Boston edition of *Hymns* bound with a copy of Watt's *Psalms of David* is inscribed, "Mrs. Susanna Coker's Book" (Bishop, *Isaac Watts's* Hymns, no. 61). The Connecticut Historical Society copy of another 1771 Boston edition is inscribed, "Barbary Noyes Her Book / A. D. 1776" (Bishop, *Isaac Watts's* Hymns, no. 63). The Speer Theological Library at Princeton, N.J. owns a copy of the 1772 Philadelphia edition which is inscribed, "Sarah Moulder /

Her Book Given by her Mother" (Bishop, *Isaac Watts's* Hymns, no. 79);
The Union Theological Seminary copy of a 1772 Boston edition is inscribed, "Frances Greenleaf / Boston, 1722 [*sic*]" (Bishop, *Isaac Watts's*
Hymns, no. 80). The MWA copy of the 1772 Philadelphia edition is inscribed, "Eliza Porter" (Bishop, *Isaac Watts's* Hymns, no. 81). The MiU-
C copy of Isaac Watts' *Hymns and Spiritual Songs* (Boston, 1769) is inscribed: "Sarah Lewis" (not located by Bishop).

23. Quoted in F. J. Harvey Darton, *Children's Books in England: Five Centu-*
    ries of Social Life (Cambridge: Cambridge Univ. Press, 1958), 108.

24. Watts, *Divine Songs, 9.*

25. Ibid., 10.

26. Laurel Thatcher Ulrich, *Good Wives: Image and Reality in the Lives of*
    Women in Northern New England 1650–1750 (1982; New York: Vin-
    tage Books, 1991), 108–9, 117.

27. Quoted in Ellis Paxson Oberholtzer, *The Literary History of Philadelphia*
    (1906; rpt. Detroit: Gale, 1969), 79–80.

28. C. William Miller, *Benjamin Franklin's Philadelphia Printing,* nos. 2,
    227; Shipton and Mooney, 969–71.

29. Senex [pseud.], "Female Education in the Last Century," *American An-*
    nals of Education 1 (1831):522.

30. Benjamin Franklin, "Apology for Printers," in *Benjamin Franklin: Writ-*
    ings, ed. J. A. Leo Lemay (New York: Library of America, 1987), 173.
    For my term "steady seller," I follow David D. Hall, who has defined a
    steady seller as a book which went through five or more editions in a pe-
    riod of at least fifty years. See "The Uses of Literacy in New England,
    1600–1850," *Printing and Society in Early America,* eds. William L.
    Joyce, David D. Hall, Richard D. Brown, and John B. Hench (Worcester:
    American Antiquarian Society, 1983), 29.

31. Martha Brewster, "A Funeral Poem, on the Death of the Reverend Isaac
    Watts, D.D." in Pattie Cowell, ed., *Women Poets in Pre-Revolutionary*
    America 1650–1775: An Anthology (Troy, New York: Whitston, 1981),
    118.

32. Louis B. Wright, *The First Gentlemen of Virginia: Intellectual Qualities*
    of the Early Colonial Ruling Class (San Marino: Huntington Library,
    1940), 135, argues that Cowley was one of the most widely read poets in
    colonial Virginia; for Maria Taylor Byrd's copy, see above, chap. 1, n. 32.
    To his English translation of François de Salignac de la Mothe Fénelon,
    Traité de l'education des filles, entitled *Instructions for the Education of a*
    Daughter (London: for Jonah Bowyer, 1707), George Hickes added a

postscript in which he recommended what books a woman should read; Cowley is the only poet mentioned. For additional discussion of Hickes's recommendations, see chap. 3. For a further discussion of Cowley and the other poets mentioned here, see David S. Shields, "The Religious Sublime and New England Poets of the 1720s," *Early American Literature* 19 (1984–85):231–48.

33. Phillis Wheatley was perhaps colonial America's most notable female reader of Milton. When she traveled to London, the Earl of Dartmouth gave Phillis Wheatley five guineas to purchase books; among her purchases was a copy of *Paradise Lost* which survives at the Houghton Library, Harvard Univ., Cambridge, Mass.; *The Poems of Phillis Wheatley: Revised and Enlarged Edition,* ed. Julian D. Mason, Jr. (Chapel Hill: Univ. of North Carolina Press, 1989), 197. Robert Feke painted Boston woman Mrs. Charles Apthorp with a copy of *Paradise Lost;* Henry Wilder Foote, *Robert Feke: Colonial Portrait Painter* (Cambridge: Harvard Univ. Press, 1930), 123–24.

34. Jane Colman Turell was probably Blackmore's most enthusiastic colonial reader. After she sent her verse tribute, "On the Poems of Sir Richard Blackmore," to her father, Benjamin Colman responded with pleasure and called Blackmore "the *Christian Poet,* and after the Reverend Dr. *Watts* the *Laureat* in the Church of Christ"; *Reliquiae Turellae, et Lachrymae Paternae. The Father's Tears over his Daughter's Remains* (Boston: S. Kneeland & T. Green for J. Edwards and H. Foster, 1735), 82. Jane's poem alludes to each of Blackmore's popular epic poems, *King Arthur* (1697), *Eliza* (1705), and *Alfred* (1723). Since Blackmore's poetry was not collected during her lifetime, she was obviously familiar with the three separate works. If she didn't own them herself, either her father or her husband, Ebenezer Turell, probably did.

35. References to Elizabeth Singer Rowe are numerous. For example, Mein's circulating library in Boston had a copy of *Miscellaneous Works in Prose and Verse of Mrs. Elizabeth Rowe* (1756); John Mein, *A Catalogue of Mein's Circulating Library* (Boston, 1765), 38. Philadelphian William Logan gave a copy of Rowe's *Miscellaneous Works* to his daughter Sarah; Edwin Wolf 2d, "Report of the Librarian," *ARLCP for 1963* (Philadelphia: The Library Company of Philadelphia, 1964), 40. Ebenezer Parkman found Rowe's writings "incomparable," and probably recommended them to his daughter Molly; Clifford K. Shipton, *New England Life in the 18th Century: Representative Biographies from* Sibley's

Harvard Graduates (Cambridge: The Belknap Press of Harvard Univ. Press, 1963), 184.

36. Cowell, *Women Poets,* 47; David B. Morris, *The Religious Sublime: Christian Poetry and Critical Tradition in 18th-Century England* (Lexington: Univ. Press of Kentucky, 1972), 142, 148; Shields, "Religious Sublime," 231–48, *passim.*

37. Hannah Adams, *A Memoir of Miss Hannah Adams, Written by Herself* (Boston: Gray and Bowen, 1832), 10.

38. Ibid., 4–5.

39. *Adams Family Correspondence,* ed. L. H. Butterfield et al. (Cambridge: Belknap Press of Harvard Univ. Press, 1963), 1:85, 390.

40. Thomas Foxcroft, *A Sermon Preach'd at Cambridge, After the Funeral of Mrs. Elizabeth Foxcroft* (Boston: B. Green, for Samuel Gerrish, 1721), 46.

41. Benjamin Colman to Jane Colman, 10 August 1725, in *Reliquiae Turellae,* 69–70. Cotton Mather, *Awakening Thoughts on the Sleep of Death* (Boston, 1712); quoted in Thomas James Holmes, *Cotton Mather: A Bibliography of His Works* (Cambridge: Harvard Univ. Press, 1940), no. 21. Hannah Hill, *A Legacy for Children* (Philadelphia: Andrew Bradford, 1717), 32.

42. Increase Mather is quoted in David D. Hall, *Worlds of Wonder, Days of Judgment: Popular Religious Belief in Early New England* (Cambridge: Harvard Univ. Press, 1990), 50; Worthington Chauncy Ford, *Boston Book Market,* 86, 127; Cotton Mather, *Addresses to Old Men,* 108; Philip Alexander Bruce, *Institutional History of Virginia in the Seventeenth Century* (New York: G. P. Putnam's Sons, 1910), 408.

43. Quoted in Harry Escott, *Isaac Watts: Hymnographer* (London: Independent Press, 1962), 206.

44. As C. John Sommerville has noticed, "The most noteworthy feature of these stories is the status they accord to children. . . . these stories showed that life could be lived fully, within its moral and spiritual dimensions, before the end of childhood"; *The Discovery of Childhood in Puritan England* (Athens: Univ. of Georgia Press, 1992), 31.

45. Holmes, *Cotton Mather,* no. 403-E.

46. Quoted in Darton, *Children's Books in England,* 55.

47. Sarah Rede, *A Token for Youth* (Boston, 1766), 13–14.

48. Rosenbach, *Early American Children's Books,* no. 10.

49. Earlier editions of Hannah Hill, *Legacy for Children,* appeared in 1714

and 1715, but apparently none survives; Rosenbach, *Early American Children's Books,* no. 13; Shipton & Mooney, 354.

50. Holmes, *Cotton Mather,* 285; Samuel Sewall, *The Diary of Samuel Sewall 1674–1729,* ed. M. Thomas Halsey (New York: Farrar, Straus, 1973), 927.

51. MiU-C copy; Richard Beale Davis, *Intellectual Life in the Colonial South 1585–1763* (Knoxville: Univ. of Tennessee Press, 1978), 2:787.

52. C. John Sommerville, *Popular Religion in Restoration England* (Gainesville: Univ. Presses of Florida, 1977), 35.

53. William S. Powell, "Books in the Virginia Colony Before 1624," *WMQ* 3d ser. 5 (1948):177; Bruce, *Institutional History,* 421; Ellis Lawrence Raesly, *Portrait of New Netherland* (New York: Columbia Univ. Press, 1945), 258; Ford, *Boston Book Market,* 156; Shipton and Mooney, 67.

54. *Meditations and Prayers for Household Piety* (Boston, 1728); not in Evans, not in Bristol.

55. Hoffman, *Virginia Gazette Daybook,* 3 Dec. 1764, fol. 125. In New England, Taylor was known as the author of *Contemplations of the State of Man* (Boston, 1723). Though this is a spurious work now excluded from the Taylor canon, it shows that the New England community did not refuse to read the Anglican divines if they could teach them something. Robert Gathorne-Hardy and William Proctor Williams, *A Bibliography of the Writings of Jeremy Taylor to 1700* (Dekalb: Northern Illinois Univ. Press, 1971), no. T3.

56. Paul Elmen, "Richard Allestree and *The Whole Duty of Man,*" *The Library* 5th ser. 6 (1951):19.

57. Worthington Chauncey Ford, *Boston Book Market,* 142, 167; Walter B. Edgar, "Some Popular Books in Colonial South Carolina," *South Carolina Historical Magazine* 72 (July 1971):174; Elizabeth Cometti, "Some Early Best Sellers in Piedmont North Carolina," *Journal of Southern History* 16 (1950):325; "The Degge Family," *WMQ* 1st ser. 21 (1912–13):195; Evans, no. 5888; George A. Aiken, "Steele's 'Ladies' Library,'" *Athenaeum,* no. 2958 (5 July 1884):16.

58. While I have located no surviving volumes of the American edition of *Pilgrim's Progress,* the MWA copy of a copycat work, John Dunton's *Hue and Cry after Conscience; or, the Pilgrims Progress by Candle-Light* (Boston, 1720) is inscribed "Hannah Storer's, Jan'y 1754."

59. Hugh Amory, "Under the Exchange: The Unprofitable Business of Michael Perry, a Seventeenth-Century Boston Bookseller," *PAAS* 103 (1993):53.

60. Elizabeth Ashbridge, "Some Account of the Fore Part of the Life of Elizabeth Ashbridge," ed. Daniel B. Shea, *Journeys in New Worlds: Early American Women's Narratives,* ed. William L. Andrews (Madison: Univ. of Wisconsin Press, 1990), 158–59.
61. Ibid., 147.
62. Ibid., 151.
63. Ibid., 152.
64. Ibid., 154.
65. Ibid., 157.
66. Ibid.
67. Ibid., 159.
68. Tillotson's name frequently appears in book inventories of the period. In a survey of selected colonial South Carolina library inventories, e.g., Walter B. Edgar found fifteen copies of Tillotson's *Sermons*; Edgar, "Some Popular Books," 174. For an excellent discussion of Tillotson's influence, see Norman Fiering, "The First American Enlightenment: Tillotson, Leverett, and Philosophical Anglicanism," *New England Quarterly* 54 (1981): 307–44.
69. Moses Coit Tyler, *A History of American Literature* (New York: G. P. Putnam's, 1878), 171–75; Perry Miller, *The New England Mind: From Colony to Province* (1953; rpt. Boston: Beacon Press, 1966), 269; Teresa Toulouse, "'Syllabical Idolatry': Benjamin Colman and the Rhetoric of Balance," *Early American Literature* 18 (1983–84):263–64.
70. The MiU-C copy of Colman's *Some of the Glories* (1728) is inscribed: "Mary Hubbard." While I am hesitant to ascribe London imprints to colonial American provenance, there is an *errata* leaf mounted inside the back cover. According to Sabin, no. 14525, the *errata* leaf was printed in Boston.
71. Benjamin Colman, *Government and Improvement of Mirth* (Boston, 1707), 11.
72. William Law, *Serious Call to a Devout and Holy Life,* ed. Paul G. Stanwood (New York: Paulist Press, 1978), 105–6, 116.
73. Quoted in Fiering, "The First American Enlightenment," 308.
74. George Whitefield, . . . *Shewing . . . Errors of . . . The Whole Duty of Man* (Charleston, 1740; Philadelphia, 1740).
75. Thomas Prince, *The Sovereign God Acknowledged and Blessed, Both in Giving and Taking Away: A Sermon Occasioned by the Decease of Mrs. Deborah Prince* (Boston: Rogers and Fowle for T. Rand, 1744), 22–23. Also see the anonymous poem by a "Gentlewoman," *A Poem in Honour*

*of the Reverend Mr. Whitefield: Composed upon Hearing Him Preach
with So Much Flame the Truths of the Blessed Gospel of the Son of God.
Boston, Nov 28th 1744* ([Boston?: 1745?]); not in Evans, not in Bristol.

76. Morris, *Religious Sublime,* 156.

77. For good general overviews of Hervey, see W. E. M. Brown, *The Polished
Shaft: Studies in the Purpose and Influence of the Christian Writer in the
Eighteenth Century* (London: Society for the Propagation of Christian
Knowledge, 1950); and Flora McLaughlin Kearney, *James Hervey and
Eighteenth-Century Taste* (Muncie, Indiana: Ball State Univ., 1969).

78. James Hervey, *Meditations and Contemplations,* was reprinted in Boston
and Philadelphia in 1750; Shipton and Mooney, 353. Virginia bookseller
William Hunter had a hundred copies of the work in stock in 1751;
Cynthia Z. Stiverson and Gregory A. Stiverson, "The Colonial Retail
Book Trade: Availability of Reading Material in Mid-Eighteenth-Century
Virginia," *Printing and Society in Early America,* eds. William L. Joyce,
David D. Hall, Richard D. Brown, and John B. Hench (Worcester: American Antiquarian Society, 1983), 156. "On Reading Mr. Hervey's Medita-
tions, in the West-Indies" appeared in the *London Magazine* 23 (January
1754), 39–40; J. A. Leo Lemay, *A Calendar of American Poetry in the
Colonial Newspapers and Magazines and in the Major English Magazines
through 1765* (Worcester: American Antiquarian Society, 1972), no.
1173. At one point in 1767, Baltimore shopkeeper Malcolm Adams had
six copies of *Meditations,* three copies of *Dialogues,* and four copies of
Hervey's *Sermons;* Joseph Towne Wheeler, "Booksellers and Circulating
Libraries in Colonial Maryland," *Maryland Historical Magazine* 34
(1939), 131. In a survey of selected colonial South Carolina library inventories, Walter B. Edgar found twenty-one copies of *Meditations and Contemplations;* Edgar, "Some Popular Books," 174. William Byrd's daughters knew Hervey's *Meditations and Contemplations;* Kevin J. Hayes, *The
Library of William Byrd of Westover* (Madison, WI and Philadelphia:
Madison House and The Library Company of Philadelphia, 1996), case
11, fifth shelf. *Georgia Gazette,* 10 November 1763, advertised Hervey's
"Meditations," "Dialogues," and "Letters."

79. Hervey, *Meditations and Contemplations* (Philadelphia, 1750), x–xi.

80. Burr, *Journal,* 114. Burr mentioned Hervey elsewhere in her journal. On
10 June 1755, she described attending a recitation at the Philadelphia
Academy: ". . . we dressd and went to the Accademy to see the young
gentlemen deliver of pieces, some out of plays, some out of Mr Hervys
meditations, and one of Popes Pastorals" (120–21). On 15 June 1755, she

wrote, "There is somthing very solemn in the sound of Thunder—Elihus poetical discription of it 37 chapter of Job is extreamly Natureal, and striking. I dont think it is half so elegantly painted by any poet as that just mentioned, tho Mr Hervy has done it extreamly well" (125).

81. MWA copy.

82. Cynthia Z. Stiverson, and Greogory A. Stiverson, "Books Both Useful and Entertaining: A Study of Book Purchasing by Virginians in the Mid-Eighteenth Century," unpublished research report, 1976, Colonial Williamsburg, Williamsburg, Va., 72.

83. Abigail Adams to James Lovell, 13 February 1780, in *Adams Family Correspondence,* 3:273.

84. Penelope Dawson to Samuel Johnston, ca. 1773, in James Iredell, *The Papers of James Iredell*, ed. Don Higginbotham (Raleigh: Division of Archives and History Department of Cultural Resources, 1976), 143. Perhaps Sterne's greatest colonial American enthusiast was another North Carolinian, Dr. John Eustace, who once sent Sterne a walking stick in appreciation. See Laurence Sterne, *Letters of Laurence Sterne,* ed. Lewis Perry Curtis (Oxford: Clarendon Press, 1935), 403–4, 411; see also Lodwick Hartley, "The Dying Soldier and the Love-lorn Virgin: Notes on Sterne's Early Reception in America," *The Winged Skull: Papers from the Laurence Sterne Bicentenary Conference,* ed. Arthur H. Cash and John M. Stedmond (Kent, Ohio: Kent State Univ. Press, 1971), 159. After Eustace's death in 1769, Margaret Eustace inherited her husband's copy of *Tristam Shandy*; J. Bryan Grimes, ed. *North Carolina Wills and Inventories* (1912; rpt. Baltimore: Genealogical Publishing Company, 1967), 491.

85. Benjamin Franklin, *The Papers of Benjamin Franklin,* eds. Leonard W. Labaree et al. (New Haven: Yale Univ. Press, 1959–), 10: 212.

86. Benjamin Franklin, *Writings,* 13.

87. James Rivington and Samuel Brown, *A Catalogue of Books, Sold by Rivington and Brown* (Philadelphia?, 1762), no. 717.

88. James Iredell, *Papers,* 47. The editor of the Iredell *Papers* cites Sterne's *Sentimental Journey* as Macartney's source, but it is more likely she was echoing "Yorick's Sermons."

89. Amory, "Under the Exchange," 53; Shipton and Mooney, 271.

90. Donald F. Bond, ed., *The Spectator* (Oxford: The Clarendon Press, 1965), 1:155.

91. Cynthia Z. Stiverson and Gregory A. Stiverson, "Books Both Useful and

Entertaining," 72; Edgar, "Some Popular Books," 174; *Georgia Gazette,* 10 November 1763.

92. Fithian, *Journal and Letters,* 223–29; Charleston Library Society member Douglas Campbell's copy of *The Ladys Religion* was mentioned in an advertisement in *South Carolina Gazette*(3 February 1757); Hennig Cohen, *South Carolina Gazette,* 142.

93. *A Lady's Religion* (London: for W. Owen, 1748), iii–iv.

Chapter 3. Conduct Books

1. Mrs. Gordon B. Ambler, ed., "Diary of M. Ambler, 1770," *VMHB* 45 (1937):158.

2. Ibid., 170.

3. Paul Elmen, "Richard Allestree and *The Whole Duty of Man,*" *The Library* 5th ser. 6 (1951):19; J. Paul Hunter, *Before Novels: The Cultural Contexts of Eighteenth-Century English Fiction* (New York: W. W. Norton, 1990), 264.

4. Worthington Chauncey Ford, *The Boston Book Market 1679–1700* (Boston: Club of Odd Volumes, 1917), 172; Hugh Amory, "Under the Exchange: The Unprofitable Business of Michael Perry, a Seventeenth-Century Boston Bookseller," *PAAS* 103 (1993):54; "The Degge Family," *WMQ* 1st ser. 21 (1912–13):193–98; Joseph Towne Wheeler, "Reading and Other Recreations of Marylanders, 1700–1776," *Maryland Historical Magazine* 38 (1943):52; Edward C. Papenfuse, Alan F. Day, David W. Jordan, and Gregory A. Stiverson, *A Biographical Dictionary of the Maryland Legislature, 1635–1789* (Baltimore: Johns Hopkins Univ. Press, 1979), 284–85.

5. Kathryn Shevelow, "Fathers and Daughters: Women as Readers of the *Tatler,*" in *Gender and Reading: Essays on Readers, Texts, and Contexts,* ed. Elizabeth A. Flynn and Patrocinio P. Schweickart (Baltimore, Md.: Johns Hopkins Univ. Press, 1986), 111; Alison Adburgham, *Women in Print: Writing Women and Women's Magazines from the Restoration to the Accession of Victoria* (London: Allen and Unwin, 1972), 33–35.

6. George Savile, First Marquess of Halifax, "The Lady's New-Year's-Gift," in *The Complete Works of George Savile First Marquess of Halifax,* ed. Walter Raleigh (Oxford: Clarendon Press, 1912), 7.

7. "The Life and Character of Mrs. Mary Lloyd," in Mary Lloyd, *Meditations on Divine Subjects* (New York: J. Parker, 1750), 22. For more on this idea, see Laurel Thatcher Ulrich, "Vertuous Women Found: New England Ministerial Literature, 1668–1735," *American Quarterly* 28 (1976):20–40.

8. Howard Mumford Jones, "The Importation of French Literature in New York City, 1750–1800" *Studies in Philology* 28 (1931):770–72; Howard Mumford Jones, "The Importation of French Books in Philadelphia, 1750–1800" *Modern Philology* 32 (1934):160; Richard Beale Davis, *A Colonial Southern Bookshelf: Reading in the Eighteenth Century* (Athens: Univ. of Georgia Press, 1979), 54–55; Edwin Wolf 2d, *The Book Culture of a Colonial American City: Philadelphia Books, Bookmen, and Booksellers* (Oxford: Clarendon Press, 1988), 53–54.

9. Edward Cox and Edward Berry, *A Catalogue of a Very Large Assortment of . . . Books . . . Which Are to Be Sold by Cox & Berry at Their Store in King-Street, Boston* ([Boston, 1772?]); *A Catalogue of Books, Sold by Rivington and Brown* (Philadelphia?, 1762), no. 467.

10. Edwin Wolf 2d, "Report of the Librarian," *ARLCP for the Year 1962* (Philadelphia, 1963), 39; Ellis Paxson Oberholtzer, *The Literary History of Philadelphia* (1906; rpt. Detroit: Gale, 1969), 82.

11. Carolyn C. Lougee, "*Noblesse*, Domesticity, and Social Reform: The Education of Girls by Fénelon and Saint-Cyr," *History of Education Quarterly* 14 (1974):88; Pattie Cowell, "Early New England Women Poets: Writing as Vocation," *Early American Literature* 29 (1994):103.

12. Fénelon, "Fenelon on the Education of Girls (1687)," trans. Kate Lupton, in Sol Cohen, ed. *Education in the United States: A Documentary History* (New York: Random House, 1973), 87.

13. Fénelon, *Instructions for the Education of a Daughter* (London: for Jonah Bowyer, 1707), 294.

14. Martha Laurens to Elizabeth Brailsford, n.d. [ca. mid-1770s], in Martha Laurens Ramsay, *Memoirs of the Life of Martha Laurens Ramsay*, ed. David Ramsay (Philadelphia: James Maxwell, 1811), 259.

15. Edwin Wolf 2d, "Report of the Librarian," *ARLCP for 1963* (Philadelphia, 1964), 41.

16. The MWA copy of the Germantown edition survives with the inscription, "Rhoda Hughes."

17. Thomas James Holmes, *Cotton Mather: A Bibliography of His Works* (Cambridge: Harvard Univ. Press, 1940), no. 83.

18. Pattie Cowell, Introduction to *Ornaments for the Daughters of Zion*, by Cotton Mather (Delmar, N.Y.: Scholar's Facsimiles & Reprints, 1978), xxii, notes both Whitefield's enthusiasm for the work and the fact that Whitefield recommended the work "to all, especially the Boston ladies," but Cowell does not make the obvious conclusion—that Whitefield was largely responsible for its reprinting.

19. Cotton Mather, *Ornaments for the Daughters of Zion,* 82.

20. Ibid., 83–84.

21. E. Jennifer Monaghan, "Literacy Instruction and Gender in Colonial New England," *Reading in America: Literature and Social History,* ed. Cathy N. Davidson (Baltimore: Johns Hopkins Univ. Press, 1989), 61. The best study of arithmetical knowledge in colonial America is Patricia Cline Cohen, *A Calculating People: The Spread of Numeracy in Early America* (Chicago: Univ. of Chicago Press, 1982).

22. George A. Aiken, "Steele's 'Ladies' Library,'" *Athenaeum* no. 2958 (5 July 1884):16–17; Stephen Parks, "George Berkeley, Sir Richard Steele, and *The Ladies Library,"* *Scriblerian* 8 (Autumn 1980):1–2; E. J. Furlong, and D. Berman, "George Berkeley and *The Ladies Library,"* *Berkeley Newsletter,* no. 4 (1980):4–7.

23. Mary Sumner Benson, *Women in Eighteenth-Century America: A Study of Opinion and Social Usage* (New York: Columbia Univ. Press, 1935), n. 22, cites advertisements from the 1730s through the 1760s in the *Pennsylvania Gazette, New York Gazette, and Connecticut Courant.* The *Ladies Library* was also advertised in the *South Carolina Gazette* during the 1750s; Hennig Cohen, *The South Carolina Gazette 1732–1775* (Columbia: Univ. of South Carolina Press, 1953), 138, 143. The *New York Mercury* advertised the work in the 1760s; Paul Leicester Ford, ed., *The Journals of Hugh Gaine Printer* (New York: Dodd, Mead, 1902), 1:194. Arthur Miller of Kent County, Md., owned a copy of the *Ladies Library* in 1734; Joseph Towne Wheeler, "Books Owned by Marylanders, 1700–1776," *Maryland Historical Magazine* 35 (1940):344. The Library Company of Philadelphia had a copy; Library Company of Philadelphia, *The Charter, Laws, and Catalogue of Books, of the Library Company of Philadelphia* (Philadelphia: Joseph Crukshank, 1770), no. L131. Boston booksellers Edward Cox and Edward Berry's 1772 sale catalogue lists *Lady's Library; A Catalogue of a Very Large Assortment of . . . Books.* Walter B. Edgar, "Some Popular Books in Colonial South Carolina," *South Carolina Historical Magazine* 72 (July 1971):177. Benjamin Franklin to Deborah Franklin, 19 February 1758, in *The Papers of Benjamin Franklin,* ed. Leonard W. Labaree et al., (New Haven: Yale Univ. Press, 1959–), 3:383–84.

24. P. G. Stanwood, "General Introduction," *Holy Living and Holy Dying,* by Jeremy Taylor (Oxford: Clarendon Press, 1989), 1:lv; Aiken, "Steele's 'Ladies' Library,'" 16; Hunter, *Before Novels,* 257.

25. Jonathan Edwards once wrote, ". . . let there be much Compliance with

the *readers* weakness and according to the Rules in the Ladies library Vol. p. 340 &seq."; Thomas H. Johnson, "Jonathan Edwards's Background of Reading," *Transactions, The Colonial Society of Massachusetts, 1930–1933* 28 (1935):198. Thomas Siegel, "Harvard College Library and Its Users," a paper presented at the Conference on Volume One of the Collaborative History of the Book, American Antiquarian Society, 19 September 1992.

26. [George Berkeley, comp.], *The Ladies Library* (London: for Jacob Tonson, 1714), 2. Kenneth A. Lockridge, *On the Sources of Patriarchal Rage: The Commonplace Books of William Byrd and Thomas Jefferson and the Gendering of Power in the Eighteenth Century* (New York: New York Univ. Press, 1992), 47–73, argues that Thomas Jefferson's misogynistic quotations from literature are exceptional. Many of the quotations Jefferson enters into his commonplace book, however, are the same as those cited in [Berkeley], *Ladies Library*. The popularity of *The Ladies Library* means that these very quotations were also widely known.

27. [Berkeley,] *Ladies Library*, 6.

28. *Poetry and Prose of Alexander Pope*. ed. Aubrey Williams (Boston: Houghton Mifflin, 1969), 317.

29. W. W. Abbot, ed., *The Papers of George Washington: Colonial Series* (Charlottesville: Univ. Press of Virginia, 1988), 6: 295, dates the Custis copy 1707. The unique copy printed by Boston printer Thomas Fleet "at the Heart and Crown in Cornhill" which survives at MWA (not in Evans; not in Bristol) is undated, but was printed some time between 1731 and 1758, the years Fleet's Cornhill press was active. See Jeanne M. Malloy, "American Secular Prose Dialogues before 1790," Ph.D dissertation (Univ. of Delaware, 1991).

30. Ned Ward, *Female Grievances Debated* ([Boston:] T. Fleet, n.d.), 17–18.

31. Chester T. Hallenback, "A Colonial Reading List," *Pennsylvania Magazine of History and Biography* 56 (1932):335; Library Company of Philadelphia, *The Charter, Laws, and Catalogue of Books, of the Library Company of Philadelphia* (1770), nos. N247, N259. *New York Mercury*, to cite only one example, advertised it in 1760; Ford, ed., *Journals of Hugh Gaine*, 1:194. Shipton and Mooney, 959.

32. After Elizabeth Timothy had taken over her husband's printing and bookselling business, she advertised *Reflections on Courtship and Marriage* for sale on 18 Oct. 1746 in the *South Carolina Gazette*; Hennig Cohen, *The South Carolina Gazette*, 133. C. William Miller, *Benjamin Franklin's Philadelphia Printing 1728–1766: A Descriptive Bibliography*

(Philadelphia: American Philosophical Society, 1974), no. 408, mentions that Franklin sent copies to his New York associate James Parker and to Jonas Green in Annapolis. While Miller does not record Franklin sending copies to Elizabeth Timothy, Franklin occasionally sent her other books to sell. The work she advertised was surely Franklin's edition.

33. Benjamin Franklin, *Papers,* 3:74. Though the editors of the Franklin *Papers* assert that Franklin was not the author, some continue to attribute the work to him. See Sarah Emily Newton, "An Ornament to Her Sex: Rhetorics of Persuasion in Early American Conduct Literature for Women and the Eighteenth-Century American Seduction Novel," Ph.D. dissertation (Univ. of California, Davis, 1976), 57; Vern L. Bullough, Brenda Shelton, and Sarah Slavin, *The Subordinated Sex: A History of Attitudes Toward Women,* rev. ed. (Athens: Univ. of Georgia Press, 1988), 273.

34. *Reflections on Courtship and Marriage* (Philadelphia: B. Franklin, 1746), 21–22.

35. Benson, *Women in Eighteenth-Century America,* 130.

36. Eliza Haywood, *The Female Spectator,* was available throughout colonial America. *Pennsylvania Gazette* advertised it for sale on 6 Feb. 1750. *New York Mercury* on 4 June 1753; Paul Leicester Ford, *The Journals of Hugh Gaine Printer,* 1:190. Advertisements appeared in the *South-Carolina Gazette* on 12 June 1753 and 24 April 1755; Hennig Cohen, *South Carolina Gazette,* 138, 140. Philadelphia bookseller David Hall had it for sale in 1762; Philadelphia's Amicable Library acquired a copy in 1765, and the Bradfords had the work on sale at their Philadelphia shop in 1767; Wolf, *Book Culture of a Colonial American City,* 185–87. Georgia bookseller James Johnston advertised a copy for sale in the *Georgia Gazette,* 10 Nov. 1763. *Connecticut Courant* advertised it on 10 August 1767; Benson, *Women in Eighteenth-Century America,* 41. North Carolinian Margaret Eustace owned a copy in 1769; J. Bryan Grimes, ed., *North Carolina Wills and Inventories* (1912; rpt. Baltimore: Genealogical Publishing Company, 1967), 491. The Library Company of Philadelphia also owned a copy; Library Company of Philadelphia, *The Charter, Laws, and Catalogue of Books, of the Library Company of Philadelphia* (1770). For the best critical discussion, see Helene Koon, "Eliza Haywood and the *Female Spectator,*" *Huntington Library Quarterly* 42 (1978), 43–55.

37. Eliza Haywood, *The Female Spectator* (London: A. Millar, W. Law, & R. Cater, 1775), 2:38.

38. Worthington Chauncy Ford, *Boston Book Market,* 172. After the original

London 1753 edition, William Kenrick's *The Whole Duty of a Woman* was frequently reprinted in America; Shipton and Mooney, 398. See also Edwin Wolf 2d, "Report of the Librarian," *ARLCP for the Year 1982* (Philadelphia: The Library Company of Philadelphia, 1983), 20.

39. Kenrick, *Whole Duty of a Woman* (1788), 6.

40. Ibid., 16.

41. "Advice to the Fair Sex," *Boston Gazette,* 21 August 1753; Lemay, *Calendar,* no. 1149.

42. MiU-C copy.

43. William Byrd's daughters may have read Edmund Moore's *Fables for the Female Sex.* The title of this work is listed on a supplemental manuscript page pasted into the manuscript catalogue of William Byrd's library which survives at the Library Company of Philadelphia; Kevin J. Hayes, *The Library of William Byrd of Westover* (Madison, Wisconsin and Philadelphia: Madison House and The Library Company of Philadelphia, 1996). The estate inventory of Rhode Island architect Peter Harrison lists a copy; Carl Bridenbaugh, *Peter Harrison: First American Architect* (Chapel Hill: Univ. of North Carolina Press, 1949), 164–67. In 1770, the Library Company of Philadelphia owned a copy of the third edition (1749); Library Company of Philadelphia, *The Charter, Laws, and Catalogue of Books, of the Library Company of Philadelphia* (1770), no. F655. Mein's Circulating Library in Boston had a copy; John Mein, *Catalogue of Mein's Circulating Library* (Boston, 1765), 14. The 1762 Philadelphia reprint (not in Evans, not in Bristol) was located by Edwin Wolf 2d, "Report of the Librarian," *ARLCP for the Year 1966* (Philadelphia: The Library Company of Philadelphia, 1967), 46.

44. *New York Mercury* advertised *The Accomplish'd Woman* on 9 Apr. 1759; Paul Leicester Ford, *Journals of Hugh Gaine,* 1:192. Boston booksellers Cox and Berry for sale in their 1772 *Catalogue of a Very Large Assortment,* 3, advertised the *Accomplish'd Woman.*

45. Abigail Adams to Mercy Otis Warren, 16 July 1773, in *Adams Family Correspondence,* ed. L. H. Butterfield et al. (Cambridge: Belknap Press of Harvard Univ. Press, 1963–), 1:84–85.

46. Advertised in the *New York Mercury* on 23 June 1760; Paul Leicester Ford, *Journals of Hugh Gaine,* 1:194.

47. Library Company of Philadelphia, *Charter, Laws, and Catalogue of Books, of the Library Company of Philadelphia* (1770), no. G411; John E. Mason, *Gentlefolk in the Making: Studies in the History of English*

Courtesy Literature and Related Topics from 1531 to 1774 (1935; rpt. New York: Octagon Books, 1971), 199.

48. Not in Evans; not in Bristol.

49. Library Company of Philadelphia, *Charter, Laws, and Catalogue of Books, of the Library Company of Philadelphia* (1770), no. F549.

50. Julius Herbert Tuttle, "The Libraries of the Mathers," *PAAS* 20 (1910):330.

51. Several copies of Anne Thérèse de Marguenat de Courcelles, Marquise de Lambert, *Polite Lady,* were sold at the *Virginia Gazette* office in 1764–66; Hoffman, *Virginia Gazette Daybooks,* 19 March 1764, fol. 25; Cynthia Z. Stiverson, and Gregory A. Stiverson, "Books Both Useful and Entertaining: A Study of Book Purchasing by Virginians in the Mid-Eighteenth Century," Unpublished research report, Colonial Williamsburg, 1976, 105.

52. North Carolinian James Milner's estate inventory (17 Dec. 1773) lists a copy; Grimes, *North Carolina Wills and Inventories,* 517.

53. Perhaps the most well-known colonial reader of the work was Martha Washington; see Abbot, *Papers of George Washington: Colonial Series,* 6:291.

54. Hallenbeck, "A Colonial Reading List," 324.

55. *Biographium Foemineum: The Female Worthies* (London: for S. Crowdes [etc.], 1766), v–vi.

56. Mein, *Catalogue of Mein's Circulating Library,* 36; Edward Cox and Edward Berry, *A Catalogue of a Very Large Assortment of . . . Books . . . Which Are to Be Sold by Cox & Berry at Their Store in King-Street, Boston* ([Boston, 1772?]), 3. Hoffman, *Virginia Gazette Daybooks,* "Daybook," 1764–66, fol. 41, shows that Armistead Lightfoot purchased a copy for Sally Grimes. Also in Virginia, Priscilla Carter and her sisters knew the work. Philip Vickers Fithian, *Journal and Letters of Philip Vickers Fithian 1773–1774: A Plantation Tutor of the Old Dominion,* new ed., ed. Hunter Dickinson Farish (Williamsburg: Colonial Williamsburg, 1965), 223–29, lists it in the inventory of their father's library.

57. Sidney A. Kimber, "The 'Relation of a Late Expedition to St. Augustine,' With Biographical and Bibliographical Notes on Isaac and Edward Kimber," *PBSA* 28 (1934):81–96, reprints a list of Edward Kimber's works which survive in a manuscript notebook in his hand. In a follow-up study Frank Gees Black, "Edward Kimber: Anonymous Novelist of the Mid-Eighteenth Century" *Harvard Studies and Notes in Philology and*

Literature 17 (1935):27–42, specifically identifies and attributes to Kimber the novels from the manuscript list and also mentioned Kimber's authorship of *The Ladies Complete Letter-Writer*. While the standard bibliographical references—*NUC,* Halkett and Laing—have since attributed to Kimber the novels Black mentions, they have not attributed *The Ladies Complete Letter-Writer* to him. Another piece of evidence I have located provides supplemental proof of Kimber's authorship. On the title page of *The Ladies Complete Letter-Writer* are the following lines:

> What's Female Beauty, but an Air Divine,
> Through which the Soul's unsully'd Graces shine?
> That, like a Sun, irradiates all between;
> The Body charms, because the Mind is seen.
>
> Incert. Auct.

Edward Kimber, discussing Maryland women in a travel narrative, "Itinerant Observations in America," *London Magazine* 15 (July 1746):329, quotes exactly the same lines, also attributing them to the same "Incert. Auct."

58. [Edward Kimber], *The Ladies Complete Letter-Writer* (London: for the editor, and sold by T. Lownds, 1763), i–ii.
59. Ibid., ii.
60. Ibid., 1.
61. Ibid., 2–3.
62. Ibid., 3.
63. Edward Kimber, "Fidenia," *London Magazine* 13 (March 1744):147–48.
64. [Edward Kimber], *Ladies Complete Letter-Writer,* 2–3.
65. Ibid., 15.
66. Ibid., 16.
67. This notion is taken up in greater detail in chap. 5.
68. James Fordyce, *Sermons to Young Women* (Boston, 1767), iii.
69. At his death in 1768, Boston bookseller Jeremy Condy had the work in stock; Elizabeth Carroll Reilly, "The Wages of Piety: The Boston Book Trade of Jeremy Condy," *Printing and Society in Early America*, eds. William L. Joyce, David D. Hall, Richard D. Brown, and John B. Hench (Worcester: American Antiquarian Society, 1983), 128. Herbert A. Johnson, *Imported Eighteenth-Century Law Treatises on American Libraries 1700–1799* (Knoxville: Univ. of Tennessee Press, 1978), 67. North Carolinian James Reed's (26 Nov 1777) estate inventory shows a copy of Fordyce; Grimes, ed., *North Carolina Wills and Inventories,* 539.

New-York Society Library, *The Charter, and Bye-Laws, of the New-York Society Library; With a Catalogue of the Book Belonging to the Said Library* (New York: H. Gaine, 1773). The Library Company of Philadelphia owned two copies of Fordyce's *Sermons*; Library Company of Philadelphia, *The Charter, Laws, and Catalogue of Books, of the Library Company of Philadelphia* (1770), nos. F404, F405. The Hatboro (Pa.) Union Library copy was frequently checked out; Hallenbeck, "A Colonial Reading List," *passim.*

70. Strahan's letter to Hall has been reprinted twice. In the *PMHB* 13 (1889):484–85, and again in J. E. Pomfret, ed., "Some Further Letters of William Strahan, Printer," *PMHB* 60 (1936):461–62. The 1889 reprint says the letter is undated, and Pomfret dates it "July 1751"—clearly an error since it refers to Fordyce's *Sermons.*

71. The work was advertised for sale in the *South Carolina Gazette* during the 1760s; Hennig Cohen, *South Carolina Gazette,* 150, 151; Mein, *Catalogue of Mein's Circulating Library*; the Phillips / Foxcroft / Huntington copy of Fordyce survives at MWA.

72. Benson, *Women in Eighteenth-Century America,* 59.

73. Abigail Adams to Mary Smith Cranch, 31 Jan. 1767, in *Adams Family Correspondence,* 1:61.

74. James Iredell, *The Papers of James Iredell,* ed. Don Higginbotham (Raleigh: Division of Archives and History Department of Cultural Resources, 1976), 203. Higginbotham does not identify "Fordyce's Sermons," but the context of the journal entry makes clear that Iredell was reading Fordyce's *Sermons to Young Women.*

75. James Fordyce, *Sermons to Young Women* (Philadelphia: for Thomas Dobson, 1787), 139.

76. Ibid., 138.

77. Joseph Towne Wheeler, "Booksellers and Circulating Libraries in Colonial Maryland," *Maryland Historical Magazine* 34 (1939):120.

78. Ibid., 124.

79. John Gregory, *A Father's Legacy to His Daughters* (Philadelphia, 1775), 5.

80. Ibid., 16.

81. Rpt. in Pattie Cowell, ed., *Women Poets in Pre-Revolutionary America 1650–1775: An Anthology* (Troy, New York: Whitston, 1981), 312.

Chapter 4. Housewifery, Physick, Midwifery

1. Captain John Smith, *The Complete Works of Captain John Smith (1580–*

1631), ed. Philip L. Barbour (Chapel Hill: Univ. of North Carolina Press, 1986), 2:184, 191; Richard Beale Davis, "The Literary Climate of Jamestown Under the Virginia Company, 1607–1624," *Toward a New American Literary History,* eds. Louis J. Budd, Edwin H. Cady, and Carl L. Anderson, 36–53 (Durham, N. C.: Duke Univ. Press, 1980); William S. Powell, "Books in the Virginia Colony Before 1624," *William and Mary Quarterly* 3d ser. 5 (1948):179.

2. F. N. L. Poynter, *A Bibliography of Gervase Markham 1568?–1637* (Oxford: The Oxford Bibliographical Society, 1962), 128–31. The 1657 inventory of John Mottrom of Northumberland County, Va., lists a copy of Markham's *English-Housewife;* "Books in Colonial Virginia," *VMHB* 10 (1903):402. A London bookseller sent multiple copies of Markham's *A Way to Get Wealth* to Boston in 1684; Worthington Chauncey Ford, *The Boston Book Market 1679–1700* (Boston: Club of Odd Volumes, 1917), 133. At his death in 1690, Virginian John Carter II owned a copy of *A Way to Get Wealth;* Louis B. Wright, "The 'Gentleman's Library' in Early Virginia: The Literary Interests of the First Carters," *Huntington Library Quarterly* 1 (1937–38):42. Edwin Wolf 2d, "A Parcel of Books for the Province in 1700," *PMHB* 89 (1965):443, notes that a London bookseller sent three copies of Markham's *Way to Get Wealth* and two copies of Markham's *Master-Piece* in 1700, both of which contained much of the same material as his *English-Housewife.* James Logan owned Markham's *English Housewife* and *A Way to Get Wealth;* Edwin Wolf 2d, *The Library of James Logan of Philadelphia 1674–1751* (Philadelphia: The Library Company of Philadelphia, 1974), no. 1313; John C. Van Horne, "Report of the Librarian," *ARLCP for the Year 1986* (Philadelphia: The Library Company of Philadelphia, 1987), 21. George E. Gifford, Jr., "Botanic Remedies in Colonial Massachusetts, 1620–1820," *Medicine in Colonial Massachusetts 1620–1820,* Publications of the Colonial Society of Massachusetts 57 (1980), 275.

3. Quoted in Suzanne W. Hull, *Chaste Silent & Obedient: English Books for Women 1475–1640* (San Marino: Huntington Library, 1982), 45.

4. Gervase Markham, *The English Housewife,* ed. Michael R. Best (Kingston and Montreal: McGill-Queen's Univ. Press, 1986), 8.

5. Quoted in Leonard N. Beck, "Two 'Loaf-givers': Or a Tour through the Gastronomic Libraries of Katherine Golden Bitting and Elizabeth Robins Pennell," *Quarterly Journal of the Library of Congress* 38 (1981):81.

6. Beck, "Two 'Loaf-givers,'" 85; William Rabisha, *The Whole Body of Cookery Dissected* (London: R. W. for Giles Calvert, 1661), sig. A4r. A

copy is listed in the 1701 inventory of Virginian Ralph Wormeley II of Rosegill; "Libraries in Colonial Virginia," *WMQ* 1st ser. 11 (1894):169–74. Wormeley had a reputation for good drink and good board, and he owned other domestic works, William y-Worth's *New Art of Making Wines* (1691) and a work inventoried as "the art of brewing" which may have been Thomas Tryon's *New Art of Brewing Beer, Ale, and Other Sorts of Liquors* (1690) or William y-Worth's *New and True Art of Brewing* (1692). It is unknown how the domestic responsibilities were distributed in the Wormeley household, but I suspect Wormeley himself oversaw the brewing and wine making while his wife took charge of cooking. Wormeley had a reputation among Rosegill visitors for both his hospitality and the potency of his libations. Huguenot traveller Durand wrote that dining with Wormeley and the Virginia governor at Rosegill, he had "wine from Portugal, cider & beer. As it was now nearly five months that I had drunk nothing but water, I found these wines so strong that I asked leave to dilute them with an equal quantity of water. The Governor & Monsieur Wormeley laughed at me." Gilbert Chinard, ed. and trans., *A Huguenot Exile in Virginia* (New York: Press of the Pioneers, 1934), 147.

7. Worthington Chauncy Ford, *Boston Book Market,* 94, 103. For the best discussion of Hannah Wolley, see Elaine Hobby, *Virtue of Necessity: English Women's Writings 1649–1688* (Ann Arbor: Univ. of Michigan Press, 1989), 166-77.

8. Quoted in Hobby, *Virtue of Necessity,* 168.

9. Ibid., 170.

10. C. Malcolm Watkins, *The Cultural History of Marlborough, Virginia* (Washington: Smithsonian Institution Press, 1968), 201; Kevin J. Hayes, *The Library of William Byrd of Westover* (Madison and Philadelphia: Madison House and The Library Company of Philadelphia, 1996), case 10, lowest shelf; Thomas Woody, *A History of Women's Education in the United States* (1929; rpt. New York: Octagon Books, 1966), 230–31.

11. Richard Bradley, *Country Housewife and Lady's Director* (1727), vii–viii.

12. Eleanor Lowenstein, *Bibliography of American Cookery Books 1742–1860* (Worcester: American Antiquarian Society, 1972), no. 1, lists Parks's edition of *The Compleat Housewife* as the earliest cookery book printed in colonial America, but recipes were printed earlier in William Bradford's edition of *Young Secretary's Guide* (Philadelphia, 1737); see John C. Van Horne, "Report of the Librarian," *ARLCP for the Year 1986,* 21.

13. *New York Mercury,* 20 July 1761; Guerra, no. a-326; John T. Winterich, *Early American Books and Printing* (Boston: Houghton Mifflin, 1935), 100. To cite only a few examples from booksellers' advertisements and library inventories: David Hall advertised *Compleat Housewife* in a broadside advertisement, *Imported in the Last Ships from London* [1754?]. *New York Mercury* advertised the work during the 1750s and 1760s; Paul Leicester Ford, ed., *The Journals of Hugh Gaine* (New York: Dodd, Mead, 1902), 1:192, 198. James Rivington had copies for sale in New York and Philadelphia; Rivington and Samuel Brown, *A Catalogue of Books, Sold by Rivington and Brown* (Philadelphia?, 1762), no. 664; The *South Carolina Gazette* advertised it several times during the 1760s; Hennig Cohen, *The South Carolina Gazette 1732–1775* (Columbia: Univ. of South Carolina Press, 1953), 145, 148, 152. Both *Maryland Gazette* (4 December 1751) and *Georgia Gazette* (10 November 1763) advertised the work for sale. The North Carolina inventories of Richard Eagles (29 March 1769) and Dr. John Eustace (8 April 1769) both show copies of the "Compleat house Wife"; J. Bryan Grimes, ed., *North Carolina Wills and Inventories* (1912; rpt. Baltimore: Genealogical Publishing Company, 1967), 488, 491. Martha Washington owned a copy; W.W. Abbot, ed., *The Papers of George Washington: Colonial Series* (Charlottesville: Univ. Press of Virginia, 1988), 6:291. Walter B. Edgar located six copies in colonial South Carolina libraries; "Some Popular Books in Colonial South Carolina," *South Carolina Historical Magazine* 72 (July 1971):177.

14. *NUC,* no. S0628143.

15. Rivington and Brown, *Catalogue of Books,* no. 779.

16. Hannah Glasse, *The Art of Cookery Made Plain and Easy* (1796; rpt. Hamden, CT: Archon, 1971), iii–vi.

17. Cynthia Z. Stiverson and Gregory A. Stiverson, "Books Both Useful and Entertaining: A Study of Book Purchasing by Virginians in the Mid-Eighteenth Century," unpublished research report, 1976, Colonial Williamsburg, Williamsburg, Va., 107.

18. Hoffman, *Virginia Gazette Daybooks,* 28 April 1764, fol. 41; James Southall Wilson, "Best-Sellers in Jefferson's Day," *Virginia Quarterly Review* 36 (1960):230–31; *Georgia Gazette,* 10 November 1763; Hennig Cohen, *The South Carolina Gazette,* 152; Joseph Towne Wheeler, "Booksellers and Circulating Libraries in Colonial Maryland," *Maryland Historical Magazine* 34 (1939):132–33; John Mein, *A Catalogue of Mein's Circulating Library* (Boston, 1765), 23.

19. Cynthia Z. Stiverson and Gregory A. Stiverson, "Books Both Useful and

Entertaining," 107. New York Printer Hugh Gaine advertised a new edition in *New York Mercury,* 19 Oct. 1761 and 9 Nov. 1761, but Guerra, no. a-318, surmises that Gaine refers to the London edition, not to a separately printed New York edition. Mein, *A Catalogue of Mein's Circulating Library,* 34.

20. Mein, *A Catalogue of Mein's Circulating Library,* 34. Copies of "Johnson's Cookery" were also sold in Virginia; see *Virginia Gazette Daybooks,* 28 Mar. 1764, fol. 28. Theophilus Grew, *Virginia Almanack, for . . . 1754* (Williamsburg: William Hunter, [1753]) reprinted a medicinal recipe from the work, "Mrs. Johnson's cure for a Cancer"; Guerra, no. b-90.

21. The same advertisement also appears in Cox and Berry's edition of William Cadogan's *Essay Upon Nursing* (Boston, 1772).

22. Karen Hess, *Martha Washington's Booke of Cookery* (New York: Columbia Univ. Press, 1981).

23. Richard J. Hooker, ed., *A Colonial Plantation Cookbook: The Receipt Book of Harriott Pinckney Horry, 1770* (Columbia: Univ. of South Carolina Press, 1984), 52, 58.

24. The copy of the sixth edition of "Harrison's Cookery" which I describe has been filmed as part of the microfilm series, *The Eigteenth Century* (Woodbridge, CT: Research Publications International, 1984–), reel 4124. Surviving copies of Martha Bradley's *British Housewife* (1760?) and Glasse, *Art of Cookery,* contain similar manuscript notes. See R. C. Alston, *Books with Manuscript: A Short Title Catalogue of Books with Manuscript Notes in the British Library* (London: The British Library, 1994), 65, 317.

25. The earliest known American almanac which contained the man of signs was John Foster's Boston *Almanack for . . . 1678* (Boston: J. Foster, for John Usher, 1678); Guerra, no. b-4.

26. Guerra, nos. b-4, b-11. The years used to describe the almanacs are the years which they were designated, not necessarily the years they were printed.

27. Quoted in Guerra, no. b-18.

28. Guerra, nos. b-17, b-36, b-51, b-58, b-62.

29. Gifford, "Botanic Remedies," 269.

30. Guerra, nos. b-63, b-65, b-175.

31. *South Carolina & Georgia Almanack for . . . 1765,* sig. C4v.

32. Cotton Mather, *The Angel of Bethesda,* ed. Gordon W. Jones (Barre, Mass.: American Antiquarian Society and Barre Publishers, 1972), 107.

Mather's text incidentally provides the earliest known use of African-slave English: "I have since mett with a Considerable Number of these *Africans*, who all agree in one Story; That in their Country *grandy-many* dy of the *Small-Pox*: But now they Learn This Way: People take Juice of *Small-Pox*; and cutty-skin, and putt in a Drop; then by'nd by a little *sicky, sicky*: then very few little things like *Small-Pox*; and no body dy of it; and no body have *Small-Pox* any more."

33. Guerra, nos. b-87, b-104, b-114.

34. Gifford, "Botanic Remedies," 269.

35. Benjamin Franklin, *The Papers of Benjamin Franklin,* ed. Leonard W. Labaree et al. (New Haven: Yale Univ. Press, 1959–) 2:155–56.

36. *Virginia Gazette,* 20 Mar. 1752 and 29 May 1752; *Virginia Almanack for 1753* (Williamsburg, 1752).

37. Londa Schiebinger, *The Mind Has No Sex?: Women in the Origins of Modern Science* (Cambridge: Harvard Univ. Press, 1989), 115.

38. C. William Miller, *Benjamin Franklin's Philadelphia Printing 1728–1766: A Descriptive Bibliography* (Philadelphia: American Philosophical Society, 1974), nos. 84, 120, 131.

39. Ibid., no. 439. *BLC* and Evans attribute authorship of *The Young Man's Best Companion* to a "Mrs. Slack," and A. S. W. Rosenbach suggests that George Fisher may have been a pseudonym. On the other hand, Cathy N. Davidson, *Revolution and the Word: The Rise of the Novel in America* (New York: Oxford Univ. Press, 1986), 6, finds the work so obviously masculine that she never considers female authorship. Guerra, no. a-226, ably clarifies that the author was George Fisher, not Mrs Ann [Fisher] Slack (1719–78), who wrote under her maiden name of A. Fisher.

40. Grimes, *North Carolina Wills and Inventories,* 491. The Eustace collection was one of the finest private libraries in colonial North Carolina; it deserves to be reconstructed.

41. Mary Morris, "Every One Their Own Physician," in *House-Keeper's Pocket-Book, and Compleat Family Cook,* by Sarah Harrison, 6th ed. (London, 1755), 1.

42. Cynthia Z. Stiverson and Gregory A. Stiverson, "Books Both Useful and Entertaining," 107.

43. Worthington Chancey Ford, *Boston Book Market,* 131, 146.

44. David L. Cowen, "The Boston Editions of Nicholas Culpeper," *Journal of the History of Medicine and Allied Sciences* 11 (April 1956):157.

45. William Nelson, ed., *Calendar of New Jersey Wills, Vol. 1. 1670–1730,*

vol. 23 of *Documents Relating to the Colonial History of the State of New Jersey* (Paterson: New Jersey Historical Society, 1901), 164.

46. Guerra, nos. b-92, b-51.

47. Gifford, "Botanic Remedies," 276; Patricia A. Watson, *The Angelical Conjunction: The Preacher-Physicians of Colonial New England* (Knoxville: Univ. of Tennessee Press, 1991), 78.

48. Cowen, "The Boston Editions of Nicholas Culpeper," 165.

49. While Bristol, no. B3330, lists the year 1771 as the first American edition of Buchan's work, Edwin Wolf 2d, "Report of the Librarian," *ARLCP for the Year 1972* (Philadelphia: The Library Company of Philadelphia, 1973), 25–26, shows convincingly that the first American edition appeared in 1772.

50. John Wesley, *Primitive Physick* (1764), vii, xi.

51. Abigail Adams to Mary Smith Cranch, 7 July 1784, in *Adams Family Correspondence,* ed. L. H. Butterfield et al. (Cambridge: The Belknap Press of Harvard Univ. Press, 1993), 5:363. A comment from Abigail Adams to her sister Elizabeth Smith Shaw, 14 December 1784, begins, "Let me read you a medical lesson from a favorite Author, Buckhan . . ."; in *Adams Family Correspondence, 6:29.*

52. Richard W. Wertz, and Dorothy C. Wertz, *Lying-In: A History of Childbirth in America* 2d ed. (New Haven: Yale Univ. Press, 1989), 1; Catherine M. Scholten, "'On the Importance of the Obstetrick Art': Changing Customs of Childbirth in America, 1760 to 1825," *WMQ* 3d ser. 34 (1977):427; Daniel Blake Smith, *Inside the Great House: Planter Family Life in Eighteenth-Century Chesapeake Society* (Ithaca: Cornell Univ. Press, 1980), 29; Carolyn Johnston, *Sexual Power: Feminism and the Family in America* (Tuscaloosa: Univ. of Alabama Press, 1992), 5–6. Although it falls beyond the chronological scope of the present work, the best treatment of midwifery in early America is Laurel Thatcher Ulrich, *A Midwife's Tale: The Life of Martha Ballard, Based on Her Diary, 1785–1812* (New York: Vintage, 1991).

53. Hugh Chamberlen, "The Translator to the Reader," *Diseases of Women with Child, and in Child-Bed,* by Francis Mauriceau (London: for Andrew Bell, 1710), xvi.

54. Vern L. Bullough, "An Early American Sex Manual, Or, Aristotle Who?" *Early American Literature* 7 1973):236–46; Otho T. Beall, Jr., *"Aristotle's Master Piece* in America: A Landmark in the Folklore of Medicine," *WMQ* 3d. ser. 20 (1963):207–22; R. W. G. Vail, "What a

Young Puritan Ought to Know," *PAAS* 49 (1939):259–66; Edwin Wolf 2d, "Report of the Librarian," *ARLCP for the Year 1984* (Philadelphia, 1985), 14–16; Worthington Chauncey Ford, *Boston Book Market,* 142; Shipton and Mooney, 33–34. Elizabeth Cometti, "Some Early Best Sellers in Piedmont North Carolina," *Journal of Southern History* 16 (1950):329, supplies a book inventory from a North Carolina general store which lists, "1/2 doz Aristotle." Cometti does not identify the work, but it was surely one of the pseudo-Aristotelian works. For the distinctions between the sexual theories of the real Aristotle from those set forth in the pseudo-Aristotelian works, see Maryanne Cline Horowitz, "The 'Science' of Embryology Before the Discovery of the Ovum," *Connecting Spheres: Women in the Western World, 1500 to the Present,* ed. Marilyn J. Boxer and Jean H. Quataert (New York: Oxford Univ. Press, 1987), 86–94.

55. Ralph Straus, *The Unspeakable Curll: Being Some Account of Edmund Curll, Bookseller; to Which is Added a Full List of His Books* (London: Chapman and Hall, 1928), 81–82, 106, 119; Roger Thompson, *Unfit for Modest Ears: A Study of Pornographic, Obscene and Bawdy Works Written or Published in England in the Second Half of the Seventeenth Century* (Totowa, N.J.: Rowman and Littlefield, 1979), 162–66.

56. Roger Thompson, *Sex in Middlesex: Popular Mores in a Massachusetts County, 1649–1699* (Amherst: Univ. of Massachusetts Press, 1986), 131.

57. Richard W. Wertz and Dorothy C. Wertz, *Lying-In,* 17.

58. Worthington Chauncey Ford, *Boston Book Market,* 146; *NUC,* nos. C0828674–C0828694.

59. Nicolas Culpeper, *Directory for Midwives* (London: Peter Cole, 1656), sigs. A4r–A4v.

60. Cotton Mather, *Diary of Cotton Mather,* ed. Worthington Chauncey Ford (1911; rpt. New York: Frederick Ungar, n. d.), 2:618. On 29 February 1723/4, Mather recorded, "Some near a Time of Travail, must have my *Elizabeth* putt into their hands" (2:700).

61. Cotton Mather, *Angel of Bethesda,* 248.

62. William R. LeFanu, *Notable Medical Books from the Lilly Library Indiana Univ.,* eds. S. O. Waife, Elizabeth McCain, Ruth Weber, and Charles E. Hammond (Indianapolis: Lilly Research Laboratories, 1976), 85.

63. The inventory of Massachusetts attorney and later state Supreme court justice Francis Dana lists a copy; Herbert A. Johnson, *Imported Eighteenth-Century Law Treatises on American Libraries 1700–1799* (Knoxville: Univ. of Tennessee Press, 1978), 66. At his death in 1768, Boston

bookseller Jeremy Condy had two copies in stock; Elizabeth Carroll Reilly, "The Wages of Piety: The Boston Book Trade of Jeremy Condy," *Printing and Society in Early America,* eds. William L. Joyce, David D. Hall, Richard D. Brown, and John B. Hench (Worcester: American Antiquarian Society, 1983), 128. Advertisements for the work can be found in *Father Abraham's Almanac . . . for . . . 1760;* Guerra, 310. The French edition of Mauriceau was advertised in the *South Carolina Gazette* (2 October 1762); Hennig Cohen, *The South Carolina Gazette,* 146.

64. Hugh Chamberlen, "The Translator to the Reader," in *The Diseases of Woman with Child,* by François Mauriceau (London: for Andrew Bell, 1710), xiii.

65. Ibid., xiv.

66. Dr. Alexander Hamilton, *Gentleman's Progress: The Itinerarium of Dr. Alexander Hamilton 1744,* ed. Carl Bridenbaugh (Chapel Hill: Univ. of North Carolina Press), 116.

67. Watkins, *Cultural History of Marlborough,* 201–2.

Chapter 5. Facts and Fictions

1. Ann Eliza Bleecker, "The History of Maria Kittle" was written in 1779, but it was first printed in Ann Eliza Bleecker, *The Posthumous Works of Ann Eliza Bleeker,* ed. Margaretta V. Faugeres (New York: T. and J. Swords, 1793), 19. The work was subsequently printed separately in 1797; Evans, no. 31837.

2. Cotton Mather, *Ornaments for the Daughters of Zion* (Boston, 1741), 82; Ebenezer Turell, *The Life and Character of the Reverend Benjamin Colman* (Boston: Rogers and Fowle, 1749), 212. For more on Abigail Colman, see Clayton Harding Chapman, "Benjamin Colman's Daughters," *New England Quarterly* 26 (1953):169–92.

3. C. William Miller, *Benjamin Franklin's Philadelphia Printing 1728–1766: A Descriptive Bibliography* (Philadelphia: American Philosophical Society, 1974), no. 293.

4. Hubertis Cummings, *Richard Peters: Provincial Secretary and Cleric 1704–1776* (Philadelphia: Univ. of Pennsylvania Press, 1944), 74.

5. Hennig Cohen, *The South Carolina Gazette 1732–1775* (Columbia: Univ. of South Carolina Press, 1953), 133.

6. Dr. Alexander Hamilton, *Gentleman's Progress: The Itinerarium of Dr. Alexander Hamilton 1744,* ed. Carl Bridenbaugh (Chapel Hill: Univ. of North Carolina Press, 1948), 112. Bridenbaugh does not specifically iden-

tify "Anti-Pamela," but Hamilton clearly refers to the work which has been attributed to Eliza Haywood.

7. T. C. Duncan Eaves, and Ben D. Kimpel, *Samuel Richardson: A Biography* (Oxford: Clarendon Press, 1971), 149.

8. Eliza Lucas to Mary Bartlett, c. 1742, in Eliza Lucas Punckney, *The Letterbook of Eliza Lucas Pinckney 1739–1762,* ed. Elise Pinckney (Chapel Hill: Univ. of North Carolina Press, 1972), 47–48. Subsequent references to Lucas' comments about *Pamela* are taken from this letter and will not be cited separately.

9. Eaves and Kimpel, *Samuel Richardson,* 122, discussing the early reception of *Pamela,* state, "No one seems to have minded the lavish and lengthy praises heaped on Pamela." Clearly, Eliza Lucas did. Lucas' comments suggest a significant difference between the English response and the American response to *Pamela,* a topic which deserves further study.

10. Cynthia Z. Stiverson, and Gregory A. Stiverson, "Books Both Useful and Entertaining: A Study of Book Purchasing by Virginians in the Mid-Eighteenth Century," unpublished research report, 1976, Colonial Williamsburg, Williamsburg, Va., 90; Thomas H. Johnson, "Jonathan Edwards and the 'Young Folks' Bible,'" *New England Quarterly 5* (1932):39–40.

11. Esther Edwards Burr, *The Journal of Esther Edwards Burr 1754–1757,* ed. Carol F. Karlsen and Laurie Crumpacker (New Haven: Yale Univ. Press, 1984), 98–108. Subsequent references to Burr's references to *Pamela* will not be cited separately.

12. Eliza Lucas Pinckney, *Letterbook,* 47; Burr, *Journal,* 107.

13. Cynthia Z. Stiverson and Greogory A. Stiverson, "Books Both Useful and Entertaining," 104. James Rivington had copies of the work on sale in New York and Philadelphia; see Rivington and Samuel Brown, *A Catalogue of Books, Sold by Rivington and Brown* (Philadelphia?, 1762), no. 134.

14. Abigail Adams to Lucy Cranch, 27 Aug. 1785, in *Adams Family Correspondence* (Cambridge: Belknap Press of Harvard Univ. Press, 1963–), 6:312–13.

15. Elisha Parker to Mary Parker, 29 June 1743, quoted in Esther Singleton, *Social New York Under the Georges 1714–1776* (1902; rpt. New York: Benjamin Blom, 1968), 340–41.

16. Cummings, *Richard Peters,* 74.

17. 22 July 1746, Ebenezer Parkman, *The Diary of Ebenezer Parkman 1703–1782,* ed. Francis G. Walett (Worcester: American Antiquarian Society,

1974), 139. It is not known what Parkman wrote about *Pamela*, but his comments about Richardson's subsequent book, *Clarissa* survive. Parkman wrote: "I think these sorts of Books are indeed to be read Sparingly; and others to be preferred far before them but yet Such as are bred in the Country & cant be afforded to live at Boarding schools, may by those Means come to some Taste of brilliant sense, when they cant be polishd by Conversation. But this indulgence had need be kept under a Strict Guard, & Caution." See Clifford K. Shipton, *New England Life in the 18th Century: Representative Biographies from* Sibley's Harvard Graduates (Cambridge: The Belknap Press of Harvard Univ. Press, 1963), 185.

18. Quoted in Johnson, "Jonathan Edwards and the "Young Folks' Bible," 40.

19. *Pennsylvania Gazette,* 2 Feb. 1762, quoted in Howard Mumford Jones, "The Importation of French Books in Philadelphia, 1750–1800," *Modern Philology* 32 (1934):166.

20. Edwin Wolf 2d, *The Book Culture of a Colonial American City: Philadelphia Books, Bookmen, and Booksellers* (Oxford: Clarendon Press, 1988), 189–91.

21. Mein's Circulating Library had a copy of *Hariot Stuart*; John Mein, *A Catalogue of Mein's Circulating Library* (Boston: [McAlpine and Fleeming,] 1765), 11. Hennig Cohen, *South Carolina Gazette*, 137. In Virginia, William Byrd's daughters may have read the work; it is one of a handful of titles listed in the Byrd library catalog added to the collection after Byrd's death; Kevin J. Hayes, *The Library of William Byrd of Westover* (Madison, Wisconsin and Philadelphia: Madison House and The Library Company of Philadelphia, 1996), case nine, sixth shelf.

22. Quoted in Harriot Horry Ravenel, *Eliza Pinckney* (New York: Charles Scribner's Sons, 1896), 254.

23. Hannah Adams, *A Memoir of Miss Hannah Adams, Written by Herself* (Boston: Gray and Bowen, 1832), 4.

24. Ibid., 14–15.

25. Eliza Haywood, *The Female Spectator* (London: for A. Millar, W. Law, and R. Carter, 1775), 3:147–49.

26. For a good discussion of the relationship between pregnancy, infancy, and travel, see Laurel Thatcher Ulrich, *Good Wives: Image and Reality in the Lives of Women in Northern New England 1650–1750* (1982; New York: Vintage Books, 1991), 138–44. For a good general treatment of

women and travel in early America, see Patricia Cline Cohen, "Safety and Danger: Women on American Public Transport, 1750–1850," *Gendered Domains: Rethinking Public and Private in Women's History,* ed. Dorothy O. Helly and Susan M. Reverby, 109–22 (Ithaca: Cornell Univ. Press, 1992).

27. Burr, *Journal,* 101–2.

28. *DNB*; Rivington and Samuel Brown, *Catalogue of Books*; Mein, *Catalogue of Mein's Circulating Library,* 11.

29. See chap. 6.

30. Abigail Adams to John Adams, 2 April 1777; in *Adams Family Correspondence,* ed. L. H. Butterfield et al. (Cambridge: Belknap Press of Harvard Univ. Press, 1963–), 2:193.

31. Elizabeth Smith to Isaac Smith, Jr., 13 April 1768, in *Adams Family Correspondence* 1:63–65. Subsequent quotations are from this letter and will not be documented separately.

32. Leona M. Hudak, *Early American Women Printers and Publishers 1639–1820* (Metuchen, N.J.: Scarecrow, 1978), no. 8-6.

33. Joseph Towne Wheeler, "Booksellers and Circulating Libraries in Colonial Maryland," *Maryland Historical Magazine* 34 (1939):131.

34. Anne Grant, *Memoirs of an American Lady with Sketches of Manners and Scenes in America as They Existed Previous to the Revolution,* ed. James Grant Wilson (New York: Dodd, Mead, 1903), pt. 1, p. 141.

35. Mein, *Catalogue of Mein's Circulating Library,* 36; *Georgia Gazette,* 10 Nov. 1763.

36. Evans, nos. 331–32, 2173, 11841, 12217, 12988, 13589; Bristol, no. 42165. Kathryn Zabelle Derounian-Stodola has twice discussed the reception of Mary Rowlandson's captivity narrative. See "The Publication, Promotion, and Distribution of Mary Rowlandson's Indian Captivity Narrative in the Seventeenth Century," *Early American Literature* 23 (1988):239–61; and Derounian-Stodola, "The Indians Captivity Narratives of Mary Rowlandson and Olive Oatman: Case Studies in the Continuity, Evolution, and Exploration of Literary Discourse," *Studies in the Literary Imagination* 27 (1994):33–46. While Derounian-Stodola's discussion of the seventeenth-century reception of the work is solid, she oversimplifies the later reception. In the second essay, she describes the republication of the work during the eighteenth century as "periodic" and "regular." One edition in 1720 and five editions during the early 1770s seems neither periodic nor regular.

Chapter 6. Science Books

1. Martha Laurens Ramsay, *Memoirs of the Life of Martha Laurens Ramsay,* ed. David Ramsay (Philadelphia: James Maxwell, 1811), 13.

2. Henry Laurens to George Appleby, 26 September 1769, in Henry Laurens, *The Papers of Henry Laurens,* ed. Philip M. Hamer, et al. (Columbia: Univ. of South Carolina Press, 1968–), 7:150.

3. Henry Laurens to James Laurens, 12 December 1771, in Henry Laurens, *Papers,* 8:91.

4. Henry Laurens to Martha Laurens, 18 May 1774, in Henry Laurens, *Papers,* 9:457–58.

5. Londa Schiebinger, *The Mind Has No Sex?: Women in the Origins of Modern Science* (Cambridge: Harvard Univ. Press, 1989), 103.

6. William Mayo to a "Gentleman in Barbadoes," August 27, 1731: "The last time I was at Colo. Byrds his Lady desired me to send to Barbados for some Shells for her as Conk Shells Wilks and such Variety as may be got, let me beg the favour of you to get a small barrel full (enough may be had about Oistins and below Rock) and send them to Colo. William Byrd at Westover in James River and place the Charge to my Account"; "Old Letters," *Virginia Historical Register and Literary Notebook* 4 (1851):86; For women's collections of natural history in France, see Schiebinger, *The Mind Has No Sex?,* 37.

7. Undated fragment, John Bartram, *The Correspondence of John Bartram 1734–1777,* ed. Edmund Berkeley and Dorothy Smith Berkeley (Gainesville: Univ. Press of Florida, 1992), 151. The quotation has been modernized.

8. Kevin J. Hayes, *The Library of William Byrd of Westover* (Madison, Wisconsin and Philadelphia: Madison House and The Library Company of Philadelphia, 1996).

9. Jon Butler, "Thomas Teackle's 333 Books: A Great Library on Virginia' Eastern Shore, 1697," *William and Mary Quarterly* 3d. ser. 59 (1992):464, no. 13.

10. St. Julien R. Childs, "A Letter Written in 1711 by Mary Stafford to Her Kinswoman in England," *South Carolina Historical Magazine* 81 (1980):4.

11. Mary Barbot Prior, "Letters of Martha Logan to John Bartram, 1760–1763," *South Carolina Historical Magazine* 59 (1958):38–46. Logan's letters to Bartram are reprinted in *The Correspondence of John Bartram 1734–1777.*

12. Samuel Eliot Morison, "Old School and College Books in the Prince Li-

brary," *More Books: The Bulletin of the Boston Public Library* 11 (1936):84.

13. Cadwallader Colden to Peter Collinson, Oct. 1755?, *The Letters and Papers of Cadwallader Colden* (New York: New York Historical Society, 1918–37), 5:37.

14. John Harris, *Astronomical Dialogues between a Gentleman and a Lady* (London: T. Wood, for Benj. Cowse, 1719), iv.

15. Cadwallader Colden to Peter Collinson, October 1755?, in Cadwallader Colden, *The Letters and Papers of Cadwallader Colden,* 5:37.

16. Bartram to Jane Colden, 24 January 1757, in Bartram, *Correspondence,* 414–15.

17. James Britten, "Jane Colden and the Flora of New York," *Journal of Botany, British and Foreign* 33 (1895):12–15; Anna Murray Vail, "Jane Colden, an Early New York Botanist," *Contributions from the New York Botanical Garden* 4 (1966–67):21–34; Brooke Hindle, "A Colonial Governor's Family: The Coldens of Coldengham," *New-York Historical Society Quarterly* 45 (1961):233–50; Brooke Hindle, "Colden, Jane," *Notable American Women 1607–1950,* ed. Edward T. James, Janet Wilson James, and Paul S. Boyer (Cambridge: The Belknap Press of Harvard Univ. Press, 1971), 1:357–58; Jane Colden, *Botanic Manuscript of Jane Colden,* ed. H. W. Rickett and Elizabeth C. Hall (New York: The Garden Club of Orange and Dutchess Counties, 1963).

18. Jane Colden, "Jane Colden's Cheese Book," in Cadwallader Colden, *Letters and Papers,* 5:55–63.

19. Quoted in Vail, "Jane Colden," 32.

20. Demarville, *The Young Lady's Geography* (London: for R. Baldwin, 1765), sigs. A2r–A2v. Demarville (first name unknown) also wrote *Young Lady's Introduction to Natural History; Containing an Account of the Atmosphere, Light and Gravity of the Terraqueous Globe* (London, 1766). Both works were advertised in Edward Cox and Edward Berry, *A Catalogue of a Very Large Assortment of . . . Books . . . Which Are to Be Sold by Cox & Berry at their store in King-Street, Boston* [Boston, 1772?].

21. Patricia Phillips, *The Scientific Lady: A Social History of Women's Scientific Interests 1520–1918* (London: Weidenfeld and Nicolson, 1990), 85. Margaret Rees, for example, borrowed a copy from the Hatboro (Pa.) Union Library; see Chester T. Hallenbeck, "A Colonial Reading List," *Pennsylvania Magazine of History and Biography* 56 (1932):320–21. Hugh Gaine advertised the work for sale in the *New York Mercury,* 13

November 1752. See also, Howard Mumford Jones, "The Importation of French Books in Philadelphia, 1750–1800" *Modern Philology* 32 (1934):770; and Howard Mumford Jones, "The Importation of French Literature in New York City, 1750–1800," *Studies in Philology* 28 (1931):767–83.

22. Erica Harth, *Cartesian Women: Versions and Subversions of Rational Discourse in the Old Regime* (Ithaca: Cornell Univ. Press, 1992), 130.

23. Quoted in Harth, *Cartesian Women,* 129.

24. Phillips, *Scientific Lady,* 85.

25. Library Company of Philadelphia, *The Charter, Laws, and Catalogue of Books, of the Library Company of Philadelphia* (Philadelphia: Joseph Crukshank, 1770), no. A399.

26. John Harris, *Astronomical Dialogues,* 1.

27. Ibid., v.

28. Hayes, *Library of William Byrd;* Fithian's catalogue of Robert Carter's library lists a copy; Philip Vickers Fithian, *Journal and Letters of Philip Vickers Fithian 1773–1774: A Plantation Tutor of the Old Dominion,* new ed., ed. Hunter Dickinson Farish (Williamsburg: Colonial Williamsburg, 1965), 229. On 10 August 1752, The *South Carolina Gazette* advertised the work; Hennig Cohen, *The South Carolina Gazette 1732–1775* (Columbia: Univ. of South Carolina Press, 1953), 135.

29. Francesco Algarotti, *Sir Isaac Newton's Philosophy Explain'd for the Use of the Ladies in Six Dialogues on Light and Colours* (London: E. Cave, 1739), ii.

30. Ibid., viii.

31. *New York Mercury* (4 June 1753) advertised Martin's *Young Gentleman and Lady's Philosophy;* see Paul Leicester Ford, ed. *The Journals of Hugh Gaine Printer* (New York: Dodd, Mead, 1902), 190. The *South Carolina Gazette* advertised it on 21 January 1773; Hennig Cohen, *The South Carolina Gazette,* 155. In Virginia, Landon Carter ordered several books for his grandchildren in the 1770s including the second volume of *The Young Gentleman and Lady's Philosophy; The Diary of Colonel Landon Carter of Sabine Hall, 1752–1778,* ed. Jack P. Greene (Richmond: Virginia Historical Society, 1987), 786–87. Franklin bought a copy of James Ferguson's *Easy Introduction to Astronomy, for Young Gentlemen and Ladies* for the Library Company of Philadelphia in 1774; Edwin Wolf 2d, "Report of the Librarian," *ARLCP for 1964* (Philadelphia: The Library Company of Philadelphia, 1965), 34. James Rivington and Samuel

Brown, *A Catalogue of Books, Sold by Rivington and Brown* (Philadelphia?, 1762), no. 342.

32. Quoted in John R. Millburn, *Benjamin Martin: Author, Instrument-Maker, and "Country Showman"* (Leyden: Noordhoff. 1976), 73. For additional information concerning Martin, see Millburn, *Benjamin Martin: Author, Instrument-Maker and "Country Showman": Supplement* (London: Vade-Mecum Press, 1986); and John R. Millburn, *Retailer of the Science: Benjamin Martin's Scientific Instrument Catalogues, 1756–1782* (London: Vade-Mecum Press, 1986).

33. Eliza Lucas to Mrs. Pinckney, n.d., in Eliza Lucas Pinckney, *The Letterbook of Eliza Lucas Pinckney,* ed. Elise Pinckney (Chapel Hill: University of North Carolina Press, 1972), 19.

34. James Iredell to Hannah Johnston, c. April 1773, in James Iredell, *The Papers of James Iredell,* ed. Don Higginbotham (Raleigh: Division of Archives and History Department of Cultural Resources, 1976), 1:149. Iredell's editor glosses "Burnet's Theory" as Gilbert Burnet, *An Exposition of the Thirty-nine Articles of the Church of England* (1689), but the reference surely means Thomas Burnet's *Theory of the Earth.*

35. James Fordyce, *Sermons to Young Women* (Philadelphia: Dobson, 1787), 137–38.

36. Ibid., 140.

37. Quoted in Sarah Emily Newton, "An Ornament to Her Sex: Rhetorics of Persuasion in Early American Conduct Literature for Women and the Eighteenth-Century American Seduction Novel," Ph.D. dissertation (Univ. of California, Davis, 1976), 94.

38. Schiebinger, *The Mind Has No Sex?,* 217.

39. "A Letters from Mis ***** to Her God-Mother," *Pennsylvania Magazine* 1 (August 1775):374; rpt. in Cowell, ed., *Women Poets in Pre-Revolutionary America 1650–1775: An Anthology* (Troy, New York: Whitston, 1981) 314–15.

40. Jefferson to John Trumbull, 15 February 1789, in Thomas Jefferson, *Thomas Jefferson: Writings,* ed. Merrill D. Peterson (New York: Library of America, 1984), 939–40.

41. See chap. 2.

Sources

Abbot, W. W., ed. *The Papers of George Washington: Colonial Series.* 9 vols. to date. Charlottesville: Univ. Press of Virginia, 1983–.

Adams Family Correspondence. Ed. L. H. Butterfield et al. 6 vols. to date. Cambridge, Mass.: Harvard Univ. Press, Belknap Press, 1963–.

Adams, Hannah. *A Memoir of Miss Hannah Adams, Written by Herself.* Boston: Gray and Bowen, 1832.

Adburgham, Alison. *Women in Print: Writing Women and Women's Magazines from the Restoration to the Accession of Victoria.* London: Allen and Unwin, 1972.

Aiken, George A. "Steele's 'Ladies' Library.'" *Athenaeum* no. 2958 (5 July 1884): 16–17.

Alden, John Eliot. "John Mein, Publisher: An Essay in Bibliographic Detection." *Papers of the Bibliographical Society of America* 36 (1942): 199–214.

Alston, R. C. *Books with Manuscript: A Short Title Catalogue of Books with Manuscript Notes in the British Library.* London: British Library, 1994.

Ambler, Mrs. Gordon B., ed. "Diary of M. Ambler, 1770." *Virginia Magazine of History and Biography* 45 (1937): 152–70.

Amory, Hugh. "Under the Exchange: The Unprofitable Business of Michael Perry, a Seventeenth-Century Boston Bookseller." *Proceedings of the American Antiquarian Society* 103 (1993): 31–60.

Ashbridge, Elizabeth. "Some Account of the Fore Part of the Life of Elizabeth Ashbridge," ed. Daniel B. Shea. In *Journey in New Worlds: Early American Women's Narratives.* Ed. William L. Andrews. 117–80. Madison: Univ. of Wisconsin Press, 1990.

Auwers, Linda. "Reading the Marks of the Past: Exploring Female Literacy in Colonial Windsor, Connecticut." *Historical Methods* 13 (Fall 1980): 204–14.

Ballard, George. *Memoirs of Several Ladies of Great Britain.* Ed. Ruth Perry. Detroit, Mich.: Wayne State Univ. Press, 1985.

Barden, John R. "Reflections of a Singular Mind: The Library of Robert Carter of Nomony Hall." *Virginia Magazine of History and Biography* 96 (1988): 83–94.

Bartram, John. *The Correspondence of John Bartram, 1734–1777.* Ed. Edmund Berkeley and Dorothy Smith Berkeley. Gainesville: Univ. Press of Florida, 1992.

Beall, Otho T., Jr. "*Aristotle's Master Piece* in America: A Landmark in the Folklore of Medicine." *William and Mary Quarterly,* 3d. ser., 20 (1963): 207–22.

Beall, Otho T., Jr., and Richard H. Shryock. *Cotton Mather: First Significant Figure in American Medicine.* Baltimore, Md.: Johns Hopkins Univ. Press, 1954.

Beck, Leonard N. "Two 'Loaf-givers': Or a Tour through the Gastronomic Libraries of Katherine Golden Bitting and Elizabeth Robins Pennell." *Quarterly Journal of the Library of Congress* 38 (1981): 79–107.

Benson, Mary Sumner. *Women in Eighteenth-Century America: A Study of Opinion and Social Usage.* New York: Columbia Univ. Press, 1935.

Bergamasco, Lucia. "Amité, amour et spiritualité dans la Nouvelle-Angleterre du XVIIIe siècle: L'experience d'Esther Burr et de Sarah Prince." *Annales économies sociétés civilisations* 41 (1986): 295–323.

———. "Female Education and Spiritual Life: The Case of Ministers' Daughters." In *Current Issues in Women's History.* Ed. Arina Angerman, Geerte Binnema, Annemieke Keunen, Vefie Poels, Jacqueline Zirkzee, and Judy de Ville, 39–60. New York: Routledge, 1989.

Bishop, Selma L. *Isaac Watts's Hymns and Spiritual Songs (1707): A Publishing History and a Bibliography.* Ann Arbor, Mich.: Pierian Press, 1974.

Black, Frank Gees. "Edward Kimber: Anonymous Novelist of the Mid-Eighteenth Century." *Harvard Studies and Notes in Philology and Literature* 17 (1935): 27–42.

Bleecker, Ann Eliza. *The Posthumous Works of Ann Eliza Bleecker.* Ed. Margaretta V. Faugeres. New York: T. and J. Swords, 1793.

Bolton, Charles K. "Circulating Libraries in Boston, 1765–1865." *Publications of the Colonial Society of Massachusetts* 11 (1906–7): 196–207.

Bond, Donald F., ed. *The Spectator.* Oxford, England: Clarendon Press, 1965.

"Books in Colonial Virginia." *Virginia Magazine of History and Biography* 10 (1903): 389–405.

Sources

Bowes, Frederick P. *The Culture of Early Charleston*. Chapel Hill: Univ. of North Carolina Press, 1942.

Bradstreet, Anne. *The Complete Works of Anne Bradstreet*. Ed. Joseph R. McElrath, Jr., and Allan P. Robb. Boston: Twayne, 1981.

Bridenbaugh, Carl. *Peter Harrison: First American Architect*. Chapel Hill: Univ. of North Carolina Press, 1949.

Bristol, Roger P. *Supplement to Charles Evans' American Bibliography*. Charlottesville: Univ. Press of Virginia, 1970.

British Library General Catalogue of Printed Books to 1975. London: Clive Bingley, 1979.

Britten, James. "Jane Colden and the Flora of New York." *Journal of Botany, British and Foreign* 33 (1895): 12–15.

Brock, C. Helen. "The Influence of Europe on Colonial Massachusetts Medicine." In *Medicine in Colonial Massachusetts, 1620–1820*. Colonial Society of Massachusetts, *Publications*, no. 57 (1980): 101–16.

Brown, W. E. M. *The Polished Shaft: Studies in the Purpose and Influence of the Christian Writer in the Eighteenth Century*. London: Society for the Propagation of Christian Knowledge, 1950.

Bruce, Philip Alexander. *Institutional History of Virginia in the Seventeenth Century*. New York: G. P. Putnam's Sons, 1910.

Bullough, Vern L. "An Early American Sex Manual, Or, Aristotle Who?" *Early American Literature* 7 (1973): 236–46.

Bullough, Vern L.; Brenda Shelton; and Sarah Slavin. *The Subordinated Sex: A History of Attitudes toward Women*. Rev. ed. Athens: Univ. of Georgia Press, 1988.

Burr, Esther Edwards. *The Journal of Esther Edwards Burr, 1754–1757*. Ed. Carol F. Karlsen and Laurie Crumpacker. New Haven, Conn.: Yale Univ. Press, 1984.

Butler, Jon. "Magic, Astrology, and the Early American Religious Heritage, 1600–1760." *American Historical Review* 84 (1979): 317–46.

———. "Thomas Teackle's 333 Books: A Great Library on Virginia's Eastern Shore, 1697," *William and Mary Quarterly*, 3d. ser., 59 (1992): 449–91.

Byrd, William. *The London Diary (1717–1721) and Other Writings*. Ed. Louis B. Wright and Marion Tinling. New York: Oxford Univ. Press, 1958.

———. *The Secret Diary of William Byrd of Westover, 1709–1712*. Ed. Louis B. Wright and Marion Tinling. Richmond, Va.: Dietz Press, 1941.

Cadbury, Henry Joel. "Harvard College Library and the Libraries of the Mathers." *Proceedings of the American Antiquarian Society* 50 (1940): 20–48.

Carr, Lois Green, and Lorena S. Walsh. "The Planter's Wife: The Experience of White Women in Seventeenth-Century Maryland." *William and Mary Quarterly,* 3d ser., 34 (1977): 542–71.

———. "The Standard of Living in the Colonial Chesapeake." *William and Mary Quarterly,* 3d. ser., 45 (1988): 135–59.

Carter, Landon. *The Diary of Colonel Landon Carter of Sabine Hall, 1752–1778.* Ed. Jack P. Greene. Richmond: Virginia Historical Society, 1987.

"Catalogue of the Library of Daniel Parke Custis." *Virginia Magazine of History and Biography* 17 (1909): 404–12.

Chapman, Clayton Harding. "Benjamin Colman's Daughters." *New England Quarterly* 26 (1953): 169–92.

Childs, St. Julien R. "A Letter Written in 1711 by Mary Stafford to Her Kinswoman in England." *South Carolina Historical Magazine* 81 (1980): 1–7.

Cohen, Hennig. *The South Carolina Gazette, 1732–1775.* Columbia: Univ. of South Carolina Press, 1953.

Cohen, Patricia Cline. *A Calculating People: The Spread of Numeracy in Early America.* Chicago: Univ. of Chicago Press, 1982.

———. "Safety and Danger: Women on American Public Transport, 1750–1850." *Gendered Domains: Rethinking Public and Private in Women's History.* Ed. Dorothy O. Helly and Susan M. Reverby, 109–22. Ithaca, N.Y.: Cornell Univ. Press, 1992.

Cohen, Sol, ed. *Education in the United States: A Documentary History.* New York: Random House, 1973.

Colden, Cadwallader. *The Letters and Papers of Cadwallader Colden.* 9 vols. *Collections of the New-York Historical Society,* vols. 50–56 and 67–68. New York: New York Historical Society, 1918–37.

Colden, Jane. *Botanic Manuscript of Jane Colden.* Ed. H. W. Rickett and Elizabeth C. Hall. New York: Garden Club of Orange and Dutchess Counties, 1963.

Cometti, Elizabeth. "Some Early Best Sellers in Piedmont North Carolina." *Journal of Southern History* 16 (1950): 324–37.

Cone, Kate M. "Cotton Mather's Daughter," pt. 1, *Outlook* 81 (7 Oct. 1905): 324–29; and pt. 2, *Outlook* 81 (14 Oct. 1905): 372–75.

Cott, Nancy F. *The Bonds of Womanhood: "Woman's Sphere" in New England, 1780–1835.* New Haven, Conn.: Yale Univ. Press, 1977.

Cowell, Pattie. "Early New England Women Poets: Writing as Vocation." *Early American Literature* 29 (1994): 103–21.

———. Introduction to *Ornaments for the Daughters of Zion,* by Cotton Mather. Delmar, N.Y.: Scholar's Facsimiles and Reprints, 1978.

———. "Knowledge and Power: Cultural Scripts in Early America." Review of *Worlds of Wonder, Days of Judgment,* by David D. Hall; and *Knowledge Is Power,* by Richard D. Brown. *American Literary History* 4 (1992): 339–44.

———, ed. *Women Poets in Pre-Revolutionary America, 1650–1775: An Anthology.* Troy, N.Y.: Whitston, 1981.

Cowen, David L. "The Boston Editions of Nicholas Culpeper." *Journal of the History of Medicine and Allied Sciences* 11 (Apr. 1956): 156–65.

Cox, Edward, and Edward Berry. *A Catalogue of a Very Large Assortment of . . . Books . . . Which Are to Be Sold by Cox & Berry at Their Store in King-Street, Boston.* [Boston, 1772?].

Craven, Wayne. *Colonial American Portraiture: The Economic, Religious, Social, Cultural, Philosophical, Scientific, and Aesthetic Foundations.* New York: Cambridge Univ. Press, 1986.

Crawford, Mary Caroline. *Social Life in Old New England.* Boston: Little, Brown, 1914.

Cressy, David. "Books as Totems in Seventeenth-Century England and New England." *Journal of Library History* 21 (1986): 92–106.

Cummings, Hubertis M. "An Account of Goods at Pennsbury Manor, 1687." *Pennsylvania Magazine of History and Biography* 86 (1962): 397–416.

———. *Richard Peters: Provincial Secretary and Cleric, 1704–1776.* Philadelphia: Univ. of Pennsylvania Press, 1944.

Darton, F. J. Harvey. *Children's Books in England: Five Centuries of Social Life.* Cambridge, England: Cambridge Univ. Press, 1958.

Davidson, Cathy N., ed. *Reading in America: Literature and Social History.* Baltimore, Md.: Johns Hopkins Univ. Press, 1989.

———. *Revolution and the Word: The Rise of the Novel in America.* New York: Oxford Univ. Press, 1986.

Davis, Harold E. *The Fledgling Province: Social and Cultural Life in Colonial Georgia, 1733–1776.* Chapel Hill: Univ. of North Carolina Press, 1976.

Davis, Richard Beale. *A Colonial Southern Bookshelf: Reading in the Eighteenth Century.* Mercer University Lamar Memorial Lectures, no. 21. Athens: Univ. of Georgia Press, 1979.

———. *Intellectual Life in the Colonial South, 1585–1763.* 3 vols. Knoxville: Univ. of Tennessee Press, 1978.

DePauw, Linda Grant. *Founding Mothers: Women in America in the Revolutionary Era.* Boston: Houghton Mifflin, 1975.

DePauw, Linda Grant, and Conover Hunt. *Remember the Ladies: Women in America, 1750–1815.* New York: Viking, 1976.

Derounian-Stodola, Kathryn Zabelle. "The Indian Captivity Narratives of Mary Rowlandson and Olive Oatman: Case Studies in the Continuity, Evolution, and Exploration of Literary Discourse." *Studies in the Literary Imagination* 27 (1994): 33–46.

———. "The Publication, Promotion, and Distribution of Mary Rowlandson's Indian Captivity Narrative in the Seventeenth Century." *Early American Literature* 23 (1988): 239–61.

Drinker, Elizabeth. *The Diary of Elizabeth Drinker.* Ed. Elaine Forman Crane and others. Boston: Northeastern Univ. Press, 1991.

Dunlap, Jane. *Poems Upon Several Sermons, Preached by . . . George Whitefield, While in Boston.* Boston, 1771.

Eames, Wilberforce. *Early New England Catechisms.* 1898. Rpt. New York: Burt Franklin, n.d.

Eaves, T. C. Duncan, and Ben D. Kimpel. *Samuel Richardson: A Biography.* Oxford, England: Clarendon Press, 1971.

Edgar, Walter B. "Some Popular Books in Colonial South Carolina." *South Carolina Historical Magazine* 72 (July 1971): 174–78.

Ellis, John Harvard. Introduction to *The Works of Anne Bradstreet,* by Anne Bradstreet. 1867. Rpt. New York: Peter Smith, 1932.

Elmen, Paul. "Richard Allestree and *The Whole Duty of Man." The Library,* 5th ser., 6 (1951): 19–27.

Escott, Harry. *Isaac Watts: Hymnographer.* London: Independent Press, 1962.

Evans, Charles. *American Bibliography.* 12 vols. Chicago: for the author, 1903–34.

Fairchild, Hoxie Neale. *Religious Trends in English Poetry.* New York: Columbia Univ. Press, 1939.

Fénelon, François de Salignac de la Mothe. *Instructions for the Education of a Daughter [Traité de l'education des filles],* translated by George Hickes. London: For Jonah Bowyer, 1707.

Fernow, B., ed. *Documents Relating to the History of the Early Colonial Settlements Principally on Long Island.* Albany: Weed, Parsons, 1883.

Fiering, Norman. "The First American Enlightenment: Tillotson, Leverett, and Philosophical Anglicanism." *New England Quarterly* 54 (Sept. 1981): 307–44.

Fithian, Philip Vickers. *Journal and Letters of Philip Vickers Fithian, 1773–1774: A Plantation Tutor of the Old Dominion.* New edition. Ed. Hunter Dickinson Farish. Williamsburg, Va.: Colonial Williamsburg, 1965.

Foote, Henry Wilder. *Robert Feke: Colonial Portrait Painter.* Cambridge, Mass.: Harvard Univ. Press, 1930.

Sources

Ford, Paul Leicester, ed. *The Journals of Hugh Gaine, Printer*. 2 vols. New York: Dodd, Mead, 1902.

Ford, Worthington Chauncey. *The Boston Book Market, 1679–1700*. Boston: Club of Odd Volumes, 1917.

Foxcroft, Thomas. *A Sermon Preach'd at Cambridge, After the Funeral of Mrs. Elizabeth Foxcroft*. Boston: B. Green, for Samuel Gerrish, 1721.

Franklin, Benjamin. *Benjamin Franklin: Writings*. Ed. J. A. Leo Lemay. New York: Library of America, 1987.

————. *Benjamin Franklin's Autobiography: A Norton Critical Edition*. Ed. J. A. Leo Lemay and P. M. Zall. New York: Norton, 1986.

————. *The Papers of Benjamin Franklin*. Ed. Leonard W. Labaree and others. 31 vols. to date. New Haven, Conn.: Yale Univ. Press, 1959–.

Frost, J. William. *The Quaker Family in Colonial America: A Portrait of the Society of Friends*. New York: St. Martin's Press, 1973.

Furlong, E. J., and D. Berman. "George Berkeley and *The Ladies Library*." *Berkeley Newsletter* 4 (1980): 4–7.

Gardiner, R. H., ed. *Mrs. Gardiner's Receipts from 1763*. Hallowell, Me.: Ruth Richards, R. H. Gardiner, and W. T. Gardiner, 1938.

Gathorne-Hardy, Robert, and William Proctor Williams. *A Bibliography of the Writings of Jeremy Taylor to 1700*. DeKalb: Northern Illinois Univ. Press, 1971.

Gifford, George E., Jr. "Botanic Remedies in Colonial Massachusetts, 1620–1820." In *Medicine in Colonial Massachusetts, 1620–1820*. Colonial Society of Massachusetts Publications 57 (1980): 263–88.

Goldberg, Rita. *Sex and Enlightenment: Women in Richardson and Diderot*. Cambridge, England: Cambridge Univ. Press, 1984.

Goodfriend, Joyce D. *The Published Diaries and Letters of American Women: An Annotated Bibliography*. Boston: G. K. Hall, 1987.

Grant, Anne. *Memoirs of an American Lady, with Sketches of Manners and Scenes in America as They Existed Previous to the Revolution*. Ed. James Grant Wilson. New York: Dodd, Mead, 1903.

Gratz, Simon, ed. "Some Material for a Biography of Mrs. Elizabeth Fergussin, née Graeme." *Pennsylvania Magazine of History and Biography* 39 (1915): 257 ff.

Grimes, J. Bryan, ed. *North Carolina Wills and Inventories*. 1912. Rpt. Baltimore, Md.: Genealogical Publishing Co., 1967.

Guerra, Francisco. *American Medical Bibliography, 1639–1783*. New York: Lathrop C. Harper, 1962.

Halifax, George Savile, Marquis of. *The Complete Works of George Savile,*

First Marquess of Halifax. Ed. Walter Raleigh. Oxford, England: Clarendon Press, 1912.

[Hall, David]. *Imported in the Last Ships from London*. [1754?].

Hall, David D. "The Uses of Literacy in New England, 1600–1850." In *Printing and Society in Early America*. Ed. William L. Joyce, David D. Hall, Richard D. Brown, and John B. Hench, 1–47. Worcester, Mass.: American Antiquarian Society, 1983.

———. *Worlds of Wonder, Days of Judgment: Popular Religious Belief in Early New England*. Cambridge, Mass.: Harvard Univ. Press, 1990.

Hallenback, Chester T. "A Colonial Reading List." *Pennsylvania Magazine of History and Biography* 56 (1932): 289–340.

Hambrick-Stowe, Charles E. *The Practice of Piety: Puritan Devotional Disciplines in Seventeenth-Century New England*. Chapel Hill: Univ. of North Carolina Press, 1982.

Hamilton, Dr. Alexander. *Gentleman's Progress: The Itinerarium of Dr. Alexander Hamilton, 1744*. Ed. Carl Bridenbaugh. Chapel Hill: Univ. of North Carolina Press, 1948.

———. *The History of the Ancient and Honorable Tuesday Club*. Ed. Robert Micklus. 3 vols. Chapel Hill: Univ. of North Carolina Press, 1990.

Hammond, Lansing Van Der Heyden. *Laurence Sterne's Sermons of Mr. Yorick*. 1948. Rpt. Hamden, Conn.: Archon Books, 1970.

Harris, James Rendel, and Stephen K. Jones. *The Pilgrim Press*. Cambridge, England: W. Heffer and Sons, 1922.

Harris, Sharon M. "Early American Women's Self-Creating Acts." *Resources for American Literary Study* 19 (1993): 223–45.

Harth, Erica. *Cartesian Women: Versions and Subversions of Rational Discourse in the Old Regime*. Ithaca, N.Y.: Cornell Univ. Press, 1992.

Hartley, Lodwick. "The Dying Soldier and the Lovelorn Virgin: Notes on Sterne's Early Reception in America." In *The Winged Skull: Papers from the Laurence Sterne Bicentenary Conference*. Ed. Arthur H. Cash and John M. Stedmond, 159–169. Kent, Ohio: Kent State Univ. Press, 1971.

Hayes, Kevin J. "Libraries and Learned Societies." In *Encyclopedia of the North American Colonies*. Ed. Jacob Ernest Cooke, 3:123–32. New York: Charles Scribner's Sons, 1993.

———. *The Library of William Byrd of Westover*. Madison, Wisc.: Madison House; Philadelphia: Library Company of Philadelphia, 1996.

Haywood, Eliza. *The Female Spectator: Being Selections from Mrs. Eliza Haywood's Periodical*. Ed. Mary Priestley. London: John Lane, The Bodley Head, 1929.

Hess, Karen. *Martha Washington's Booke of Cookery.* New York: Columbia Univ. Press, 1981.

Hill, Hannah. *A Legacy for Children.* Philadelphia: Andrew Bradford, 1717.

Hindle, Brooke. "A Colonial Governor's Family: The Coldens of Coldengham." *New York Historical Society Quarterly* 45 (1961): 233–50.

Hobby, Elaine. *Virtue of Necessity: English Women's Writing, 1649–88.* Ann Arbor: Univ. of Michigan Press, 1989.

Hoffman, Paul P., ed. *Virginia Gazette Daybooks, 1750–1752 and 1764–1766.* Charlottesville: Univ. of Virginia Library, Microfilm Publications, 1967. Microfilm.

Holmes, Thomas James. *Cotton Mather: A Bibliography of His Works.* 3 vols. Cambridge, Mass.: Harvard Univ. Press, 1940.

Hooker, Richard J., ed. *A Colonial Plantation Cookbook: The Receipt Book of Harriot Pinckney Horry, 1770.* Columbia: Univ. of South Carolina Press, 1984.

Hornberger, Theodore. "Benjamin Colman and the Enlightenment." *New England Quarterly* 12 (1939): 227–40.

Horowitz, Maryanne Cline. "The 'Science' of Embryology before the Discovery of the Ovum." In *Connecting Spheres: Women in the Western World, 1500 to the Present.* Ed. Marilyn J. Boxer and Jean H. Quataert, 86–94. New York: Oxford Univ. Press, 1987.

Howard, Leon. "Early American Copies of Milton." *Huntington Library Bulletin,* no. 7 (Apr. 1935): 169–79.

Hudak, Leona M. *Early American Women Printers and Publishers, 1639–1820.* Metuchen, N.J.: Scarecrow, 1978.

Hull, Suzanne W. *Chaste Silent and Obedient: English Books for Women, 1475–1640.* San Marino, Calif.: Huntington Library, 1982.

Hunter, J. Paul. *Before Novels: The Cultural Contexts of Eighteenth-Century English Fiction.* New York: Norton, 1990.

Iredell, James. *The Papers of James Iredell.* Ed. Don Higginbotham. Raleigh, N.C.: Division of Archives and History Department of Cultural Resources, 1976.

James, Edward T.; Janet Wilson James; and Paul S. Boyer, eds. *Notable American Women, 1607–1950.* 3 vols. Cambridge, Mass.: Harvard Univ. Press, Belknap Press, 1971.

Jefferson, Thomas. *Thomas Jefferson: Writings.* Ed. Merrill D. Peterson. New York: Library of America, 1984.

Johnson, Herbert A. *Imported Eighteenth-Century Law Treatises in American Libraries, 1700–1799.* Knoxville: Univ. of Tennessee Press, 1978.

Johnson, Thomas H. "Jonathan Edwards and the 'Young Folks' Bible.'" *New England Quarterly* 5 (1932): 37–54.

———. "Jonathan Edwards's Background of Reading." *Transactions of the Colonial Society of Massachusetts, 1930–1933* 28 (1935): 193–222.

Johnston, Carolyn. *Sexual Power: Feminism and the Family in America.* Tuscaloosa: Univ. of Alabama Press, 1992.

Jones, Eva Eve. "Extracts from the Journal of Miss Sarah Eve." *Pennsylvania Magazine of History and Biography* 5 (1881): 19–36.

Jones, Howard Mumford. "The Importation of French Books in Philadelphia, 1750–1800." *Modern Philology* 32 (1934): 157–77.

———. "The Importation of French Literature in New York City, 1750–1800." *Studies in Philology* 28 (1931): 767–83.

Karpinski, Louis C. *Bibliography of Mathematical Works Printed in America Through 1850.* Ann Arbor: Univ. of Michigan Press, 1940.

Kaser, David. *A Book for a Sixpence: The Circulating Library in America.* Pittsburgh, Pa.: Beta Phi Mu, 1980.

Kearney, Flora McLaughlin. *James Hervey and Eighteenth-Century Taste.* Muncie, Ind.: Ball State Univ., 1969.

Keeble, N. H. *The Literary Culture of Nonconformity in Later Seventeenth-Century England.* Athens: Univ. of Georgia Press, 1987.

Keep, Austin Baxter. *History of the New York Society Library.* 1908. Rpt. Boston: Gregg, 1972.

Kennedy, James; W. A. Smith; and A. F. Johnson. *Dictionary of Anonymous and Pseudonymous English Literature (Samuel Halkett and John Laing).* Edinburgh: Oliver and Boyd, 1926–34.

Kerber, Linda K. *Women of the Republic: Intellect and Ideology in Revolutionary America.* Chapel Hill: Univ. of North Carolina Press, 1980.

Keymer, Tom. *Richardson's Clarissa and the Eighteenth-Century Reader.* New York: Cambridge Univ. Press, 1992.

Kierner, Cynthia A. *Traders and Gentlefolk: The Livingstons of New York, 1675–1790.* Ithaca, N.Y.: Cornell Univ. Press, 1992.

[Kimber, Edward]. *The Ladies Complete Letter-Writer.* London: Published for the editor and sold by T. Lownds, 1763.

Kimber, Sidney A. "The 'Relation of a Late Expedition to St. Augustine,' with Biographical and Bibliographical Notes on Isaac and Edward Kimber." *Papers of the Bibliographical Society of America* 28 (1934): 81–96.

Koon, Helene. "Eliza Haywood and the *Female Spectator.*" *Huntington Library Quarterly* 42 (1978): 43–55.

Laurens, Henry. *The Papers of Henry Laurens.* Ed. Philip M. Hamer and others. 13 vols. to date. Columbia: Univ. of South Carolina Press, 1968—.

Law, William. *A Serious Call to a Devout and Holy Life.* Ed. Paul G. Stanwood. New York: Paulist Press, 1978.

LeFanu, William R. *Notable Medical Books from the Lilly Library, Indiana University.* Ed. S. O. Waife, Elizabeth McCain, Ruth Weber, and Charles E. Hammond. Indianapolis, Ind.: Lilly Research Laboratories, 1976.

Lemay, J. A. Leo. *A Calendar of American Poetry in the Colonial Newspapers and Magazines and in the Major English Magazines, through 1765.* Worcester, Mass.: American Antiquarian Society, 1972.

———. "The Origins of the Humor of the Old South." *Southern Literary Journal* 23 (1991): 3–13.

———, ed. *An Early American Reader.* Washington, D.C.: United States Information Agency, 1988.

———, ed. *Robert Bolling Woos Anne Miller: Love and Courtship in Colonial Virginia, 1760.* Charlottesville: Univ. of Virginia Press, 1990.

Letzring, Monica. "Sarah Prince Gill and the John Adams–Catharine Macaulay Correspondence." *Proceedings of the Massachusetts Historical Society* 88 (1976): 107–11.

Levenduski, Cristine Marie. "Elizabeth Ashbridge's 'Remarkable Experiences': Creating the Self in a Quaker Personal Narrative." Ph.D. dissertation. Univ. of Minnesota, 1989.

"Libraries in Colonial Virginia." *William and Mary College Quarterly* 11 (1894): 169–75.

Library Company of Philadelphia. *A Catalogue of Books Belonging to the Library Company of Philadelphia: A Facsimile of the Edition of 1741 Printed by Benjamin Franklin.* Ed. Edwin Wolf 2d. Philadelphia: Library Company of Philadelphia, 1956.

———. *The Charter, Laws, and Catalogue of Books, of the Library Company of Philadelphia.* Philadelphia: Joseph Crukshank, 1770.

"The Library of John Parke Custis, Esq., of Fairfax County, Virginia." *Tyler's Quarterly Historical and Genealogical Magazine* 9 (1927): 97–103.

Lloyd, Mary. *Meditations on Divine Subjects . . . To Which Is Prefixed, An Account of Her Life and Character, by E. Pemberton.* New York: J. Parker, 1750.

Lockridge, Kenneth A. *On the Sources of Patriarchal Rage: The Commonplace Books of William Byrd and Thomas Jefferson and the Gendering of Power in the Eighteenth Century.* New York: New York Univ. Press, 1992.

Lougee, Carolyn C. "*Noblesse,* Domesticity, and Social Reform: The Education of Girls by Fénelon and Saint-Cyr." *History of Education Quarterly* 14 (1974): 87–111.

Lowenstein, Eleanor. *Bibliography of American Cookery Books, 1742–1860.* Worcester, Mass.: American Antiquarian Society, 1972.

Main, Gloria L. "The Standard of Living in Southern New England, 1640–1773." *William and Mary Quarterly,* 3d ser., 45 (1988): 124–34.

Malloy, Jeanne M. "American Secular Prose Dialogues Before 1790." Ph.D. dissertation. Univ. of Delaware, 1991.

Margolis, Maxine L. *Mothers and Such: Views of American Women and Why They Changed.* Berkeley: Univ. of California Press, 1984.

Markham, Gervase. *The English Housewife.* Ed. Michael R. Best. Montreal: McGill–Queen's Univ. Press, 1986.

Mason, John E. *Gentlefolk in the Making: Studies in the History of English Courtesy Literature and Related Topics, from 1531 to 1774.* 1935. Rpt. New York: Octagon Books, 1971.

Mather, Cotton. *The Angel of Bethesda.* Ed. Gordon W. Jones. Barre, Mass.: American Antiquarian Society and Barre Publishers, 1972.

———. *Diary of Cotton Mather.* Ed. Worthington Chauncey Ford. 1911. Rpt. New York: Frederick Ungar, n.d.

McCorison, Marcus A. *The 1764 Catalogue of the Redwood Library Company at Newport, Rhode Island.* New Haven, Conn.: Yale Univ. Press, 1965.

McKay, George L. *American Book Auction Catalogues, 1713–1934: A Union List.* New York: New York Public Library, 1937.

McLaughlin, Eleanor Commo. "Equality of Souls, Inequality of Sexes: Woman in Medieval Theology." In *Religion and Sexism: Images of Woman in the Jewish and Christian Traditions.* Ed. Rosemary Radford Ruether, 213–66. New York: Simon and Schuster, 1974.

Mein, John. *A Catalogue of Mein's Circulating Library.* Boston: [McAlpine and Fleeming], 1765.

Merchant, Carolyn. *The Death of Nature: Women, Ecology, and the Scientific Revolution.* San Francisco: Harper and Row, 1980.

Messenger, Ann. *His and Hers: Essays in Restoration and Eighteenth-Century Literature.* Lexington: Univ. Press of Kentucky, 1986.

Middlekauff, Robert. *Ancients and Axioms: Secondary Education in Eighteenth-Century New England.* New Haven, Conn.: Yale Univ. Press, 1963.

Millburn, John R. *Benjamin Martin: Author, Instrument-Maker, and "Country Showman."* Leiden, Netherlands: Noordhoff, 1976.

Sources

———. *Benjamin Martin: Author, Instrument-Maker and "Country Showman: Supplement.* London: Vade-Mecum Press, 1986.

———. *Retailer of the Sciences: Benjamin Martin's Scientific Instrument Catalogues, 1756–1782.* London: Vade-Mecum Press, 1986.

Miller, C. William. *Benjamin Franklin's Philadelphia Printing, 1728–1766: A Descriptive Bibliography.* Philadelphia: American Philosophical Society, 1974.

Miller, Perry. *The New England Mind: From Colony to Province.* 1953. Rpt. Boston: Beacon Press, 1966.

Monaghan, E. Jennifer. "Literacy Instruction and Gender in Colonial New England." In *Reading in America: Literature and Social History.* Ed. Cathy N. Davidson. 53–80. Baltimore, Md.: Johns Hopkins Univ. Press, 1989.

Morgan, Edmund S. *The Puritan Family: Religion and Domestic Relations in Seventeenth-Century New England.* New York: Harper and Row, 1966.

Morison, Samuel Eliot. "Old School and College Books in the Prince Library." *More Books: Bulletin of the Boston Public Library* 11 (1936): 77–93.

Morris, David B. *The Religious Sublime: Christian Poetry and Critical Tradition in Eighteenth-Century England.* Lexington: Univ. Press of Kentucky, 1972.

Mott, Frank Luther. *Golden Multitudes: The Story of Best Sellers in the United States.* New York: Macmillan, 1947.

National Union Catalog: Pre-1956 Imprints. 754 vols. London: Mansell, 1968–81.

Nelson, William, ed. *Calendar of New Jersey Wills, Vol. 1: 1670–1730.* Vol. 23 of *Documents Relating to the Colonial History of the State of New Jersey.* Paterson: New Jersey Historical Society, 1901.

New-York Society Library. *The Charter, and Bye-Laws, of the New-York Society Library; With a Catalogue of the Books Belonging to the Said Library.* New York: H. Gaine, 1773.

Newton, Sarah Emily. "An Ornament to Her Sex: Rhetorics of Persuasion in Early American Conduct Literature for Women and the Eighteenth-Century American Seduction Novel." Ph.D. dissertation. Univ. of California, Davis, 1976.

Norton, Mary Beth. "The Evolution of White Women's Experience in Early America." *American Historical Review* 89 (1984): 593–619.

———. *Liberty's Daughters: The Revolutionary Experience of American Women, 1750–1800.* Boston: Little, Brown, 1980.

Oberholtzer, Ellis Paxson. *The Literary History of Philadelphia.* 1906. Rpt. Detroit, Mich.: Gale, 1969.

"Old Letters." *Virginia Historical Register and Literary Notebook* 4 (1851): 83–86.

Oxford, Arnold Whitaker. *English Cookery Books to the Year 1850*. London: Oxford Univ. Press, 1913.

Papenfuse, Edward C.; Alan F. Day; David W. Jordan; and Gregory A. Stiverson. *A Biographical Dictionary of the Maryland Legislature, 1635–1789*. 2 vols. Baltimore, Md.: Johns Hopkins Univ. Press, 1979.

Parkman, Ebenezer. *The Diary of Ebenezer Parkman, 1703–1782*. Ed. Francis G. Walett. Worcester, Mass.: American Antiquarian Society, 1974.

Parks, Stephen. "George Berkeley, Sir Richard Steele, and *The Ladies Library*." *Scriblerian* 8 (Autumn 1980): 1–2.

Pelletreau, William S., ed. *Abstracts of Wills on File in the Surrogate's Office, City of New York . . . 1730–1744*. Vol. 27 of *Collections of the New-York Historical Society*. New York, 1895.

———, ed. *Abstracts of Wills on File in the Surrogate's Office, City of New York . . . 1744–1753*. Vol. 28 of *Collections of the New-York Historical Society*. New York, 1896.

———, ed. *Abstracts of Wills on File in the Surrogate's Office, City of New York . . . 1754–1760*. Vol. 29 of *Collections of the New-York Historical Society*. New York, 1897.

Perlmann, Joel, and Dennis Shirley. "When Did New England Women Acquire Literacy?" *William and Mary Quarterly*, 3d ser., 48 (1991): 50–67.

Phillips, Patricia. *The Scientific Lady: A Social History of Women's Scientific Interests, 1520–1918*. London: Weidenfeld and Nicolson, 1990.

Pinckney, Eliza Lucas. *The Letterbook of Eliza Lucas Pinckney, 1739–1762*. Ed. Elise Pinckney. Chapel Hill: Univ. of North Carolina Press, 1972.

Pope, Alexander. *Poetry and Prose of Alexander Pope*. Ed. Aubrey Williams. Boston: Houghton Mifflin, 1969.

Porterfield, Amanda. *Female Piety in Puritan New England: The Emergence of Religious Humanism*. New York: Oxford Univ. Press, 1992.

Potts, William John. "Bathsheba Bowers." *Pennsylvania Magazine of History and Biography* 3 (1879): 110–12.

Powell, William S. "Books in the Virginia Colony Before 1624." *William and Mary Quarterly*, 3d ser., 5 (1948): 177–84.

Poynter, F. N. L. *A Bibliography of Gervase Markham, 1568?–1637*. Oxford, England: Oxford Bibliographical Society, 1962.

Prince, Thomas. *The Sovereign God Acknowledged and Blessed, Both in Giving and Taking Away: A Sermon Occasioned by the Decease of Mrs. Deborah Prince*. Boston: Rogers and Fowle, for T. Rand, 1744.

Sources

Prior, Mary Barbot. "Letters of Martha Logan to John Bartram, 1760–1763." *South Carolina Historical Magazine* 59 (1958): 38–46.

Rabisha, William. *The Whole Body of Cookery Dissected.* London: R. W. for Giles Calvert, 1661.

Raesly, Ellis Lawrence. *Portrait of New Netherland.* New York: Columbia Univ. Press, 1945.

Ramsay, Martha Laurens. *Memoirs of the Life of Martha Laurens Ramsay.* Ed. David Ramsay. Philadelphia: James Maxwell, 1811.

Ravenel, Harriot Horry. *Eliza Pinckney.* New York: Charles Scribner's Sons, 1896.

Reilly, Elizabeth Carroll. "The Wages of Piety: The Boston Book Trade of Jeremy Condy." In *Printing and Society in Early America.* Ed. William L. Joyce, David D. Hall, Richard D. Brown, and John B. Hench, 83–131. Worcester, Mass.: American Antiquarian Society, 1983.

Reliquiae Turellae, et Lachrymae Paternae: The Father's Tears over his Daughter's Remains. Boston: S. Kneeland and T. Green, for J. Edwards and H. Foster, 1735.

Reynolds, Myra. *The Learned Lady in England, 1650–1760.* Boston: Houghton Mifflin, 1920.

Rivington, James, and Samuel Brown. *A Catalogue of Books, Sold by Rivington and Brown.* [Philadelphia?], 1762.

Roscoe, S. John. *Newbery and His Successors, 1740–1814: A Bibliography.* Wormley, England: Five Owls Press, 1973.

Rosenbach, A. S. W. *Early American Children's Books.* 1933. Rpt. New York: Kraus, 1966.

Ross, Ruth Robinson. *Union Library Company of Hatborough: An Account of the First Two Hundred Years, Done Out of the Original Records.* Hatboro, Pa.: Union Library Company, 1955.

Ryan, Mary P. *Womanhood in America from Colonial Times to the Present.* 2d ed. New York: New Viewpoints, 1979.

Sabin, Joseph; Wilberforce Eames; and R. W. G. Vail. *Bibliotheca Americana.* 29 vols. New York: Bibliographical Society of America, 1868–1936.

Salmon, Marylynn. *Women and the Law of Property in Early America.* Chapel Hill: Univ. of North Carolina Press, 1986.

Saunders, Richard H., and Ellen G. Miles. *American Colonial Portraits: 1700–1776.* Washington, D.C.: Smithsonian Institution Press, 1987.

Schiebinger, Londa. *The Mind Has No Sex?: Women in the Origins of Modern Science.* Cambridge, Mass.: Harvard Univ. Press, 1989.

Scholten, Catherine M. "'On the Importance of the Obstetrick Art': Changing Customs of Childbirth in America, 1760–1825." *William and Mary Quarterly,* 3d ser., 34 (1977): 426–45.

Senex [pseud.]. "Female Education in the Last Century." *American Annals of Education* 1 (1831): 522–26.

Sewall, Joseph, and Thomas Prince. Preface to *The Compleat Body of Divinity,* by Samuel Willard. Boston, 1726.

Sewall, Samuel. *The Diary of Samuel Sewall, 1674–1729.* Ed. M. Halsey Thomas. New York: Farrar, Straus, 1973.

———. "Letter-Book of Samuel Sewall." *Massachusetts Historical Society Collections,* ser. 6, vols. 1–2 (1886).

Shea, Daniel B., Jr. *Spiritual Autobiography in Early America.* Princeton, N.J.: Princeton Univ. Press, 1968.

Shera, Jesse H. *Foundations of the Public Library: The Origins of the Public Library Movement in New England, 1629–1855.* Chicago: Univ. of Chicago Press, 1949.

Shevelow, Kathryn. "Fathers and Daughters: Women as Readers of the *Tatler.*" In *Gender and Reading: Essays on Readers, Texts, and Contexts.* Ed. Elizabeth A. Flynn and Patrocinio P. Schweickart. 107–23. Baltimore, Md.: Johns Hopkins Univ. Press, 1986.

Shields, David S. "The Manuscript in the British American World of Print." *Proceedings of the American Antiquarian Society* 102 (1992): 403–16.

———. *Oracles of Empire: Poetry, Politics, and Commerce in British America, 1690–1750.* Chicago: Univ. of Chicago Press, 1990.

———. "The Religious Sublime and New England Poets of the 1720s." *Early American Literature* 19 (1984–85): 231–48.

Shipton, Clifford K. "Literary Leaven in Provincial New England." *New England Quarterly* 9 (1936): 203–17.

———. *New England Life in the Eighteenth Century: Representative Biographies from Sibley's Harvard Graduates.* Cambridge, Mass.: Harvard Univ. Press, Belknap Press, 1963.

Shipton, Clifford K., and James E. Mooney. *National Index of American Imprints through 1800: The Short-Title Evans.* Worcester, Mass.: American Antiquarian Society and Barre Publishers, 1969.

Singleton, Esther. *Social New York under the Georges, 1714–1776.* 1902. Rpt. New York: Benjamin Blom, 1968.

Slotten, Martha C. "Elizabeth Graeme Ferguson: A Poet in 'The Athens of North America.'" *Pennsylvania Magazine of History and Biography* 108 (July 1984): 259–88.

Sources

Smith, Daniel Blake. *Inside the Great House: Planter Family Life in Eighteenth-Century Chesapeake Society.* Ithaca, N.Y.: Cornell Univ. Press, 1980.

Smith, Hilda. "Gynecology and Ideology in Seventeenth-Century England." In *Liberating Women's History: Theoretical and Critical Essays.* Ed. Berenice A. Carroll. 97–114. Urbana: Univ. of Illinois Press, 1976.

Smith, Captain John. *The Complete Works of Captain John Smith (1580–1631).* Ed. Philip L. Barbour. Chapel Hill: Univ. of North Carolina Press, 1986.

Sommerville, C. John. *The Discovery of Childhood in Puritan England.* Athens: Univ. of Georgia Press, 1992.

———. *Popular Religion in Restoration England.* Gainesville: Univ. Presses of Florida, 1977.

Spruill, Julia Cherry. *Women's Life and Work in the Southern Colonies.* Chapel Hill: Univ. of North Carolina Press, 1938.

Stanwood, P. G. General introduction to *Holy Living and Holy Dying,* by Jeremy Taylor. Oxford, England: Clarendon Press, 1989.

Stearns, Raymond Phineas. *Science in the British Colonies of America.* Urbana: Univ. of Illinois Press, 1970.

Sterne, Laurence. *Letters of Laurence Sterne.* Ed. Lewis Perry Curtis. Oxford, England: Clarendon Press, 1935.

Stiles, Ezra. *The Literary Diary of Ezra Stiles.* Ed. Franklin Bowditch Dexter. 3 vols. New York: Charles Scribner's Sons, 1901.

Stiverson, Cynthia Z., and Gregory A. Stiverson. "Books Both Useful and Entertaining: A Study of Book Purchasing by Virginians in the Mid-Eighteenth Century." Unpublished research report, Colonial Williamsburg, Williamsburg, Va., 1976.

———. "The Colonial Retail Book Trade: Availability of Reading Material in Mid-Eighteenth-Century Virginia." In *Printing and Society in Early America.* Ed. William L. Joyce, David D. Hall, Richard D. Brown, and John B. Hench, 132–73. Worcester, Mass.: American Antiquarian Society, 1983.

Straus, Ralph. *The Unspeakable Curll: Being Some Account of Edmund Curll, Bookseller; to Which Is Added a Full List of His Books.* London: Chapman and Hall, 1928.

Thomas, Isaiah. *The History of Printing in America.* Ed. Marcus A. McCorison. New York: Weathervane Books, 1970.

Thompson, Roger. *Sex in Middlesex: Popular Mores in a Massachusetts County, 1649–1699.* Amherst: Univ. of Massachusetts Press, 1986.

———. *Unfit for Modest Ears: A Study of Pornographic, Obscene and Bawdy*

Sources

Works Written or Published in England in the Second Half of the Seventeenth Century. Totowa, N.J.: Rowman and Littlefield, 1979.

———. *Women in Stuart England and America: A Comparative Study.* London: Routledge and Kegan Paul, 1974.

———. "Worthington Chauncey Ford's *Boston Book Market, 1679–1700:* Some Corrections and Additions." *Proceedings of the Massachusetts Historical Society* 86 (1974): 67–78.

Tinling, Marion, ed. *The Correspondence of the Three William Byrds of Westover, Virginia, 1684–1776.* 2 vols. Charlottesville: Univ. Press of Virginia, 1977.

Tolles, Frederick B. *James Logan and the Culture of Provincial America.* Boston: Little, Brown, 1957.

———. *Meeting House and Counting House: The Quaker Merchants of Colonial Philadelphia, 1682–1763.* 1948. Rpt. New York: Norton, 1963.

Toulouse, Teresa. "'Syllabical Idolatry': Benjamin Colman and the Rhetoric of Balance." *Early American Literature* 18 (1983–84): 257–74.

Turell, Ebenezer. *The Life and Character of the Reverend Benjamin Colman.* Boston: Rogers and Fowle, 1749.

Tuttle, Julius Herbert. "The Libraries of the Mathers." *Proceedings of the American Antiquarian Society* 20 (1910): 269–356.

Tyler, Moses Coit. *A History of American Literature.* 2 vols. New York: G. P. Putnam's, 1878.

Ulrich, Laurel Thatcher. "'A Friendly Neighbor': Social Dimensions of Daily Work in Northern New England." *Feminist Studies* 6 (1980): 392–405.

———. *Good Wives: Image and Reality in the Lives of Women in Northern New England, 1650–1750.* 1982. Rpt. New York: Vintage Books, 1991.

———. *A Midwife's Tale: The Life of Martha Ballard, Based on Her Diary, 1785–1812.* New York: Vintage Books, 1991.

———. "Vertuous Women Found: New England Ministerial Literature, 1668–1735." *American Quarterly* 28 (1976): 20–40.

Upshur, Anne Floyd, and Ralph T. Whitelaw. "Library of the Rev. Thomas Teackle," *William and Mary Quarterly,* 2d ser., 23 (1943): 298–308.

Vail, Anna Murray. "Jane Colden, an Early New York Botanist." *Contributions from the New York Botanical Garden* 4 (1966–67): 21–34.

Vail, R. G. W. "What a Young Puritan Ought to Know." *Proceedings of the American Antiquarian Society* 49 (1939): 259–66.

Van Horne, John C. "Report of the Librarian." In *Annual Report of the Library Company of Philadelphia for the Year 1985.* Philadelphia: LCP, 1986.

————. "Report of the Librarian." In *Annual Report of the Library Company of Philadelphia for the Year 1986*. Philadelphia: LCP, 1987.

Wall, A. J. "Samuel Loudon (1727–1813) (Merchant, Printer and Patriot)." *New York Historical Society Quarterly Bulletin* 6 (1922): 75–92.

Walsh, Lorena S. "The Experiences and Status of Women in the Chesapeake, 1750–1775." In *The Web of Southern Social Relations: Women, Family, and Education*. Ed. Walter J. Fraser, Jr.; R. Frank Sanders, Jr.; and Jon L. Wakelyn, 1–18. Athens: Univ. of Georgia Press, 1985.

————. "'Till Death Us Do Part': Marriage and Family in Seventeenth-Century Maryland." In *The Chesapeake in the Seventeenth Century: Essays on Anglo-American Society*. Ed. Thad W. Tate and David L. Ammerman, 126–52. Chapel Hill: Univ. of North Carolina Press, 1979.

[Walter, Thomas.] "An Account of Mrs. Katharin Mather by Another Hand." In *Victorina: A Sermon Preached on the Decease and at the Desire of Mrs. Katharin Mather*, by Cotton Mather. Boston: B. Green for Daniel Henchman, 1717.

Warner, Michael. *The Letters of the Republic: Publication and the Public Sphere in Eighteenth-Century America*. Cambridge, Mass.: Harvard Univ. Press, 1990.

Watkins, C. Malcolm. *The Cultural History of Marlborough, Virginia*. Washington, D.C.: Smithsonian Institution Press, 1968.

Watson, Alan D. "Women in Colonial North Carolina: Overlooked and Underestimated." *North Carolina Historical Review* 58 (1981): 1–22.

Watson, Patricia A. *The Angelical Conjunction: The Preacher-Physicians of Colonial New England*. Knoxville: Univ. of Tennessee Press, 1991.

Watt, Ian. *The Rise of the Novel*. Berkeley: Univ. of California Press, 1957.

Watters, Reginald Eyre. "The Vogue and Influence of Samuel Richardson in America: A Study of Cultural Conventions, 1742–1825." Ph.D. dissertation. Univ. of Wisconsin, 1941.

Watts, Isaac. *Psalms of David*. Philadelphia: B. F[ranklin] and H. M[eredith], for Thomas Godfrey, 1729.

Weeks, Stephen B. "Libraries and Literature in North Carolina in the Eighteenth Century." *Annual Report of the American Historical Association for the Year 1895*. Washington, D.C., 1896.

Wertz, Richard W., and Dorothy C. Wertz. *Lying-In: A History of Childbirth in America*. Expanded ed. New Haven, Conn.: Yale Univ. Press, 1989.

Wheatley, Phillis. *The Poems of Phillis Wheatley: Revised and Enlarged Edition*. Ed. Julian D. Mason, Jr. Chapel Hill: Univ. of North Carolina Press, 1989.

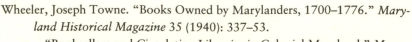

Sources

Wheeler, Joseph Towne. "Books Owned by Marylanders, 1700–1776." *Maryland Historical Magazine* 35 (1940): 337–53.

———. "Booksellers and Circulating Libraries in Colonial Maryland." *Maryland Historical Magazine* 34 (1939): 111–37.

———. "The Laymen's Libraries and the Provincial Library." *Maryland Historical Magazine* 35 (1940): 60–73.

———. "Reading and Other Recreations of Marylanders, 1700–1776." *Maryland Historical Magazine* 38 (1943): 37–55, 167–80.

———. "Reading Interests of Maryland Planters and Merchants, 1700–1776." *Maryland Historical Magazine* 37 (1942): 26–41, 291–310.

———. "Reading Interests of the Professional Classes in Colonial Maryland, 1700–1776." *Maryland Historical Magazine* 36 (1941): 184–201, 281–301.

Wigglesworth, William C. "Surgery in Massachusetts, 1620–1820." In *Medicine in Colonial Massachusetts, 1620–1820.* Colonial Society of Massachusetts *Publications* 57 (1980): 215–26.

Wilson, James Southall. "Best-Sellers in Jefferson's Day." *Virginia Quarterly Review* 36 (1960): 222–37.

Wilson, Joan Hoff. "Dancing Dogs of the Colonial Period: Women Scientists." *Early American Literature* 7 (Winter 1973): 225–35.

Winans, Robert B. "Bibliography and the Cultural Historian: Notes on the Eighteenth-Century Novel." In *Printing and Society in Early America.* Ed. William L. Joyce, David D. Hall, Richard D. Brown, and John B. Hench, 174–85. Worcester, Mass.: American Antiquarian Society, 1983.

———. *A Descriptive Checklist of Book Catalogues Separately Printed in America, 1693–1800.* Worcester, Mass.: American Antiquarian Society, 1981.

———. "The Growth of a Novel-Reading Public in Late-Eighteenth-Century America." *Early American Literature* 9 (1975): 267–75.

Winship, Michael P. "Behold the Bridegroom Cometh! Marital Imagery in Massachusetts Preaching, 1630–1730." *Early American Literature* 27 (1992): 170–84.

Winterich, John T. *Early American Books and Printing.* Boston: Houghton Mifflin, 1935.

Wolf, Edwin, 2d. *The Book Culture of a Colonial American City: Philadelphia Books, Bookmen, and Booksellers.* Oxford, England: Clarendon Press, 1988.

———. "The Dispersal of the Library of William Byrd of Westover." *Proceedings of the American Antiquarian Society* 68 (1958): 19–106.

————. "Great American Book Collectors to 1800." *Gazette of the Grolier Club,* new ser., no. 16 (June 1971): 3–70.

————. *The Library of James Logan of Philadelphia, 1674–1751.* Philadelphia: Library Company of Philadelphia, 1974.

————. "More Books from the Library of the Byrds of Westover." *Proceedings of the American Antiquarian Society* 88 (1978): 51–82.

————. "A Parcel of Books for the Province in 1700." *Pennsylvania Magazine of History and Biography* 89: (1965): 428–46.

————. "Report of the Librarian." In *Annual Report of the Library Company of Philadelphia.* Philadelphia: Library Company of Philadelphia, 1963–85.

————. Review of *A Book for a Sixpence: The Circulating Library in America,* by David Kaser. *Pennsylvania Magazine of History and Biography* 104 (1980): 383–85.

Woloch, Nancy. *Women and the American Experience.* New York: Alfred A. Knopf, 1984.

Woodfin, Maude H., and Marion Tinling, eds. *Another Secret Diary of William Byrd of Westover.* Richmond, Va.: Dietz Press, 1942.

Wright, Louis B. *The First Gentlemen of Virginia: Intellectual Qualities of the Early Colonial Ruling Class.* San Marino, Calif.: Huntington Library, 1940.

————. "The 'Gentleman's Library' in Early Virginia: The Literary Interests of the First Carters." *Huntington Library Quarterly* 1 (1937–38): 3–61.

————. "The Purposeful Reading of Our Colonial Ancestors." *ELH* 4 (1937): 85–111.

Wright, Louis B., and Marion Tinling, eds. *The Secret Diary of William Byrd of Westover, 1709–1712.* Richmond, Va.: Dietz Press, 1941.

Wroth, Lawrence C. *An American Bookshelf, 1755.* Philadelphia: Univ. of Pennsylvania Press, 1934.

[————.] "The Colonial Scene—1602–1800." *Proceedings of the American Antiquarian Society* 60 (1950): 53–160.

Index